DOING THE
BIBLE
BETTER

The Bible Challenge and the Transformation of the Episcopal Church

Marek P. Zabriskie

D0862502

Morehouse Publishing
NEW YORK

Morehouse Publishing, 4785 Linglestown Road, Suite 101, Harrisburg, PA 17112

Morehouse Publishing, 19 East 34th Street, New York, NY 10016

Morehouse Publishing is an imprint of Church Publishing Incorporated.
www.churchpublishing.org

Cover design by Laurie Klein Westhafer
Typeset by Rose Design

Library of Congress Cataloging-in-Publication Data

Zabriskie, Marek P.
 Doing the Bible better : the Bible challenge and the transformation of the Episcopal Church /
Marek P. Zabriskie.
    pages cm
Includes bibliographical references.
 ISBN 978-0-8192-2932-8 (pbk.)—ISBN 978-0-8192-2933-5 (ebook) 1. Bible—Criticism,
interpretation, etc. 2. Bible—Devotional use. 3. Episcopal Church. 4. Anglican Communion.
I. Title.
 BS511.3.Z33 2014
 220.088'28373—dc23
                        2014014958

Printed in the United States of America

Contents

Acknowledgments

I have been blessed from the moment that I sat by the fireside on Christmas Day 2010 and pondered my personal need to re-engage Scripture in a more significant and regular way. My own decision to re-read the entire Bible in a year started that day, and it led to the beginning of The Bible Challenge, which grew providentially from my own personal joy and transformation through engaging God's Word. Along the way, friends and colleagues suggested ideas that helped this ministry which started in my living room spread to more than 2,500 churches and over a quarter of a million people in over 40 countries.

I am most grateful to the Rev. Frank Allen, a colleague and friend, who has done an astonishing job as Rector of St. David's Episcopal Church in Radnor, Pennsylvania. It was from reading St. David's newsletter on Christmas Day in 2010 that I saw Frank's invitation to members of his church to read the Bible with him. While Frank uses a one-year Bible, I chose to read the entire Bible. My main contribution was to find a way to disseminate this challenge to as many people as possible in my congregation and beyond, to offer a regular reading plan and tips on how to read the Bible prayerfully each day. Over time, as members of our church and friends beyond asked questions or asked for additional resources or support, I put things in place to assist them.

Members of the national church staff, especially Anne Rudig, Director of Communications, were extremely helpful in offering ideas as I launched the website for The Bible Challenge. They communicated effectively about The Bible Challenge to the Episcopal Church and the Anglican Communion. Chuck Robertson, Canon to the Presiding Bishop, wisely advised me to focus first on the 80 million Anglicans around the world before reaching out to denominations beyond. I am also thankful for the support and creative wisdom of the Rev. Scott Gunn, Executive Director of Forward Movement, who was an early believer and helped to publish *The Bible Challenge.*

I will always be grateful that Archbishop Rowan Williams, who was serving as the Archbishop of Canterbury at the time, Bishop Frank Griswold, an old friend and the former Presiding Bishop of the Episcopal Church, and Professor Walter Brueggemann, another old friend and one of the world's great Bible scholars, agreed to serve on our advisory board of the Center for Biblical Studies, which I created to share The Bible Challenge. Their initial support engendered great trust in this initiative. Since then over 60 bishops from around the Anglican Communion have lent their support to The Bible Challenge along with archbishops, seminary and cathedral deans, biblical scholars, theologians, priests and lay leaders, and authors throughout the Church.

Although it must have been extremely hard to drag my brothers and me to church each Sunday, I am most grateful to my parents for raising us in the church. Something stuck that gave me a foundation to return to later in my spiritual journey. Along the way, Fr. Tom Flynn, professor of philosophy at Emory University and one of the great scholars of modern French thought, played a pivotal role in helping me return to the Christian roots. I will be forever grateful to him. I am extremely grateful to Mims, my wife, and our daughters Emily, Marguerite and Isabelle, who have often had to share me more with the church than they might have liked. Along with my relationship with God, they give my life its deepest meaning and joy.

Finally, I am very grateful to Davis Perkins and Church Publishing for allowing me to tell the story about the growth of The Bible Challenge and what I have learned and to the members of St. Thomas' Episcopal Church, where I have been privileged to serve as Rector since 1995. We have worked together to help our church grow stronger with each year and form faithful Christian disciples. It was through working, leading, serving, ministering, and learning in this environment that many of the seeds of The Bible Challenge were sown and first came to fruition. Due to the success of what we encountered together, I was able to hear God quietly whisper in my ear that this ministry was meant to be shared with others throughout the Episcopal Church and the Anglican Communion. Long ago it grew beyond my wildest expectation. It is clearly God's will for each of us to engage the Word more regularly and in a prayerful manner.

With love and prayers,
Marek

Introduction

"Heaven and earth will pass away, but my words will not pass away."
—MATTHEW 24:35

"Your words were found, and I ate them, and your words became to me a joy and the delight of my heart; for I am called by your name, O Lord of hosts."—JEREMIAH 15:16

"The Bible as a book stands alone. There never was, nor ever will be, another like it. As there is but one sun to enlighten the world naturally, so there is but one Book to enlighten the world spiritually. May that Book become to each of us the man of our counsel, the guide of our journey, and our support and comfort in life and in death."—A. GALLOWAY

• ◆ •

The Bible Challenge has been a gift to me from the first day that I stumbled upon it. Friends and colleagues furnished virtually every helpful idea along the way. God worked through the network of clergy and scholars that I had developed over the years. All along the way, God whispered thoughts into my head and heart that allowed this ministry to be born and to grow rapidly.

The ministry was born of my own spiritual longing to draw closer to God through reconnecting with all of God's Word found in the Bible. Like a good Anglican, I was well-acquainted with the Daily Lectionary. I was so well acquainted that at times it seemed as if I had forgotten that we have a Bible full of many lessons that are never read in church and never read by many clergy or lay persons.

What captured me was not how reading all of the Bible could transform others' lives, but how it quickly transformed my own. For years, I focused my spiritual journey on reading the mystics and the great spiritual writers across the centuries. I was well-versed in Franciscan, Benedictine, Celtic, and Anglican spirituality. I sometimes found the Bible boring. When I read it in Hebrew, Greek, and Latin I discovered a powerfully heady adventure, but one that did little to touch my heart or change my life, ministry, preaching, or behavior.

Then through an episode that I recount in this book, God brought me back to the Bible—the foundational book of our faith—in a new way. I found it incredibly stimulating and refreshing. It was like switching from watered down coffee to drinking espresso. I had been reading the words of people who were inspired by the Bible, but less and less of the Bible itself. It was as though I was living through others, who wrote about what it was like to go fishing, raise a family, play sports, read interesting books, and take vacations without ever doing any of these things on my own. Suddenly, I was back re-engaging Scripture in a disciplined daily practice. It felt great. Just as suddenly, people started to notice a difference in my sermons and in my behavior, attitudes, communications, and demeanor. I was more joyful, upbeat, content, and appreciative of others. I felt far more connected to God, grateful for life, patient, kind, and able to exercise more self-control. My life and my ministry still held much room for improvement, but there was an excitement and passion present that had been missing, as well as much less restlessness in my life.

As I started to invite others to walk alongside me on this journey of reading the Bible in a year, I was astonished at how many were interested in doing so. It was something that they had on their bucket lists, but almost none of them was going to do unless someone nudged them, showed them a simple way to do it over the course of a year, gave them some support, and helped to hold them accountable. Within a few weeks, over one hundred-eighty members of my church and more than ninety friends from outside our membership had accepted the challenge to read the entire Bible in a year. Our church is three hundred and sixteen years old. We had never before had ninety people from outside of our church agree to do something with us for a year in the three centuries that we have been together. We probably have never had one hundred-eighty people in our parish agree to do something for a full year either, other than worship. We live in an age where people are searching for challenges and measureable achievements that they can strive toward. And this was a challenge.

One by one, we started to hear positive reports from people who were participating in what I dubbed The Bible Challenge. People started to come alive spiritually. Many said that it was the most significant spiritual experience that they had ever had in their life. Friends spoke to friends and family about it. Entire book clubs decided to do it. Word of mouth spread. Participants found that the time they spent each day quietly reading the Bible became their sanctuary. It was like a mini-Sabbath that centered them and prepared them for the rest of the day. Instead of waiting for Sunday to have a spiritual moment, they were starting to have these moments every day. This alone was transformative. Participants began coming to church spiritually alive instead of expecting a one hour worship service to make up for having done nothing all week, or in many cases over two or three weeks, to grow closer to God.

As we saw our church being transformed spiritually, God whispered in my ear to share The Bible Challenge with others. I mentioned it to a few colleagues and shared handouts that I had created to help members of my church get started. I designed additional materials to help clergy lead their parishes in participating in The Bible Challenge. I then spoke to a few bishops, who courageously encouraged their whole dioceses to join them in reading the entire Bible or the New Testament, Psalms and Proverbs in a year, or one of the gospels during Lent. Every individual, church, school, and diocese was free to tailor The Bible Challenge to suit their life or community. Soon, these churches, bishops, and dioceses were telling others.

Within three years, over twenty-five hundred churches and more than two hundred and fifty thousand people in over forty countries were participating in The Bible Challenge. Those were just the faith communities that we were fairly certain were participating. Rarely a week passes when we do not hear about another church or diocese that has been taking part. Today, more than forty-five bishops are leading their entire dioceses in The Bible Challenge.

What is at stake? Episcopalians are the best educated among the twenty-two thousand Christian groups and denominations in the United States, but when you ask about biblical literacy we drop to almost dead last. For years, we have joked about being the Christians who do not know our Bible. Yet it is no joke. During the past few years, I have been astonished by one story after another illustrating the lack of biblical knowledge in the Episcopal Church. We pride ourselves on reading a lot of Scripture in church each Sunday, but 90 percent of what we hear is forgotten within seventy-two hours. Less than 5 percent of Episcopalians attend a regular Bible study. The rest merely hear the Bible read in church, or in some cases read it on their own. Anglicanism today, however, does not have a strong tradition of private devotional reading of the Bible. While we are extremely well-educated on the whole, there is an enormous gap between our knowledge about science, math, history, literature, economics, politics, and culture and our understanding of the Bible.

I recently attended a conference of Episcopal leaders from across the country. One of my colleagues shared a shocking but true story. He had been recruited from one of the denomination's largest churches to lead a vital Midwestern parish. They chose well. He is a dynamic young priest who is passionate about serving God and building a strong Episcopal church. Early into his first year of ministry, several men in the church asked him to start a men's Bible study. "You get 12 men together and I'll be there," he told them. They recruited other men, and he joined them. At the start of the first meeting, the head of the search committee, who had spent over a year working together to identify their new Rector and offer his name to the Vestry for consideration as their next spiritual leader, raised his hand. "Before we get started, I have a question," he said, holding out his Bible. "Where in this book do I find the New Testament?" His new rector was speechless. The question was serious. Here was a very committed Episcopalian who had been identified by his parish as an outstanding leader with excellent judgment and a great commitment to his church, who had been charged with overseeing the search process to identify their new rector, and he was biblically illiterate.

At one of the most prestigious Episcopal churches on the East Coast, the head of the Altar Guild went to the lectern to mark the Bible for the morning's worship service. She turned to a fellow member of the Altar Guild and asked, "Fran, where do I find Paul's Letter to the Romans? I need to mark the Bible for the service this morning." Her Altar Guild colleague responded, "You must be the only person in our church who is not doing The Bible Challenge." Indeed, over two hundred and fifty members of their church had committed to reading the entire Bible in a year. It was transforming the parish, yet this very significant leader of the church was biblically illiterate.

After hearing one story after another like these, I have been stunned by how biblically illiterate we Episcopalians are and how our clergy, myself included, have spent much of our ministries answering questions that people are not asking. In our sermons, lectures, and classes, we are often building a theological and biblical skyscraper that soars towards heaven. The only problem is that the first ten floors are missing. Well-known church leaders and those sitting in our pews, along with others who do not come to church, do not know where to find the New Testament in the Bible. We need to reclaim our own story and the book that is at the center of our common life. We need to rediscover a simple and prayerful way of reading the Bible and helping our members and those who come to us to develop a daily spiritual practice. The Reveal Study by the Willow Creek Community Association notes that the Bible is the single best spiritual tool for developing strong Christian lives, but it is the very thing that we neglect to use effectively to help our members and those who are seekers around us connect more closely with God. In fact, many priests and bishops have succumbed to a false belief that our people could not and should not read the Bible on their own without a priest being in the room to guide them and explain what the Bible is saying.

In my church we now carry out more than sixty-five different ministries. Other churches may offer more or far less, but in most Episcopal churches it is very hard to tell what is most important to the parish. All things seem equal. Worship; walking the labyrinth; taking a study course; serving as an usher, acolyte, receptionist or chalice bearer; sorting clothes at a rummage sale; serving food at a homeless shelter; and teaching Sunday school are all viewed as equally important. In most of our churches, the strongest emphasis is put on worship. We say that worship is at the heart of all that we do, which is theologically correct, but it leaves us with significant problems. First, the average Episcopalian now worships only once a month. You cannot achieve success in anything if you do it just once a month. Dieting, studying a foreign language, learning to play an instrument, or trying to give up smoking will never work if you do it one day a month. Second, studies used by the American Bible Society reveal that even if we get large numbers of people to worship with us, there is no measureable moral difference in their behavior from the lives of those who never worship in church. What a shocking revelation.

The American Bible Society notes that people who engage Scripture four times or more a week, however, have measurably higher moral behavior. There is something about engaging God's Word regularly that creates a spiritual athlete who is much closer to God and more effective at living a godly life and sharing Christ with others. Since around 1950 the average Sunday attendance in Episcopal churches has been dropping. I am not sure that this will turn around anytime soon.

On the other hand, many of our churches are seeing more of our people throughout the week and over the weekend taking part in a myriad of different activities and ministries. Hence, while we may have fewer Sunday worshipers, many churches are connecting with more people and having them benefit from their participation in programs as they serve others through a wide array of opportunities.

The downside is that we appear to be producing a highly biblically illiterate Christian, whose faith is inarticulate and whose commitment to a daily spiritual practice is almost nil. This will eventually undermine our denomination and close many churches. It is hard after all to build a strong church with biblically illiterate Christians. What we have seen is that The Bible Challenge changes lives. Studies by the American Bible Society note that if a person reads Scripture each day for twenty-one days, there is an 80 percent chance that they will read the Bible regularly for the rest of their lives. They will glean far more from our Sunday worship, follow the sermon more closely, be looking to have the preacher preach rather than merely explain the passage that was read, and become a more committed, articulate, and contagious Christian. They become more generous, loving, patient, kind, joyful, and forgiving.

We urge everyone to think of The Bible Challenge as a five year ministry. You cannot change the spiritual DNA of a faith community in a year. You may make great strides, but one year is almost never sufficient time to transform an organization or community. In every case, you will have early adopters who will jump aboard and try something new. But there will be lots who think, "This is the Rector's new pet project. I'm not going to do this." After hearing others speak about their positive experiences, however, many of these people can be won over and encouraged to join The Bible Challenge.

People who are not strong readers or who have very limited time to read can participate by reading just the New Testament, Psalms, and Proverbs in a year or take on one of the Fifty Day Bible Challenges which we offer. There is room for everyone to participate in one way or another. If a rector of a parish or a bishop of a diocese or a head of a school decides to dedicate five years of continuous focus to offering The Bible Challenge, then he or she can play an instrumental role in transforming the spiritual DNA of their faith community from a very low to a very high level of biblical literacy. The church will come alive in the process, lives will be transformed and countless beautiful loving actions will take place.

Lastly, there is a global component to this endeavor. Anglicans have experienced extreme conflict over the past decade or longer regarding issues that the Bible addresses and our cultures cause us to view quite differently. Good people on both sides of controversial issues have cited compelling biblical reasons for their strongly held views. In many cases, people who have not read the entire Bible in their lifetime or who rarely read it at all are speaking on behalf of God and God's will without having much acquaintanceship with the Scriptures. We will never read the Bible in one uniform way. One of the beauties of Christianity is that each reader brings a different lens, history, set of experiences, and personality type to reading God's Word. We therefore discover different things and have much to teach and learn from one another. But if we all agreed on something, it might hold us together and give us a common bond to share.

What if we all could agree that prayerful reading of the Bible, as if it were a love letter written from God to each one of us, was vital to our spiritual lives? What if we could all agree not to use the Bible as ammunition for controversial debates, but as a guide for holy living? What if we could all commit to put a regular engagement with the Bible at the heart of our common life? What if each time we gathered, we read a portion of Scripture and offered prayers for one another?

Perhaps it is a fantasy, but I think not. I believe that there is an incredible spiritual hunger in the world today, perhaps as much as the world has ever known. The longing to know God and to experience God's love has never been stronger. We Anglicans have a glorious form of worship. We are held together by The Book of Common Prayer, which is one of the great treasures of Christianity. We also have a very reasonable and wise way of engaging Scripture. Many of us nurture a daily spiritual conversation with God that has its roots sunk deeply in Benedictine spirituality. I am more bullish than ever on the future of Anglicanism, especially if we reconnect as a faith tradition in a profound way with the book that is the spiritual foundation of all that we do.

In his book *Opening the Bible*, Roger Ferlo tells the story about how a generous parishioner at his church in Greenwich Village in New York City offered to purchase Bibles for the entire church and place them in the church pews. It was a very well-meaning idea. Ferlo notes that many people liked the idea of having Bibles handy: some, he suspects, never noticed their presence, but a number of people felt quite uneasy about having them in the pews because it reminded them of raucous tent revivals and evangelical preachers whooping up the crowd—not that any of them had ever attended a tent revival; they had an image in their minds, and it was not the image that they wanted to see their Episcopal church imitate. The truth is that most Episcopalians and many mainline Christians are afraid of the Bible. It is a great book to have a well-dressed lay person or a clergyman read aloud from a distance to us at worship, but God forbid that we be asked to pick it up and read it for ourselves or discuss it with others

Yet, as Ferlo notes, that English Reformation began with a clarion call and ringing endorsement of every believer's right to read the Bible freely and openly. The church struggled for over two centuries to allow the Bible to be translated into English and then to make this translation available to Christians in every church. Before his death, Henry VIII ordered a copy of the Bible to be placed in every church throughout England. It was chained to a post inside the church, where it could not be removed and where people in the village or surrounding community or city could come and read through it in English at their leisure. It was a pioneering move.

Henry VIII's Archbishop of Canterbury, Thomas Cranmer, led a spiritual revolution following Henry's death. Cranmer substantially increased the amount of Scripture to be read aloud during public worship. Churchgoers went from hearing snippets of the Bible to hearing almost the entire Bible read aloud in church over the course of a year. No passages or verses were omitted. The entire New Testament and most of the Old Testament were read in a year, far different from today's Daily Lectionary or the Revised Common Lectionary. Cranmer wrote magnificent homilies, including one on the Bible, to be read in every church across England. The Book of Common Prayer, which he authored, is saturated with Scripture. Some 70 percent of the book came directly from the Bible.

While most mainline Christians stand at some distance from the Bible, the majority of them truly want to know and learn from their Bible. The key is that clergy must help the laity to read it for themselves and stop standing as intermediaries between the Bible and the people. People in our church pews need help, advice, and guidance in reading the Bible. If we can provide that effectively, we will always have a job and play an important role in developing a thriving faith community. If we try to monopolize the Bible as the Church's book, of which the clergy are the indispensable experts needed to help others comprehend it, then we will silently and slowly kill our churches and leave our people stunted like small children in their spiritual growth.

Reading Scripture on our own can be challenging, confusing, disappointing, and sometimes a downright alienating experience when we arrive at bewildering passages without the guidance of a trained reader of the Bible to assist us. Together, however, we can learn how to read it prayerfully and find enormous joy and spiritual benefits from doing so each day. That is what The Bible Challenge and this book attempt to do. I close this introduction with some thoughts shared by a few of the participants in The Bible Challenge:

My own Bible reading has been nothing short of profound. I am humbled and amazed at just how much this is speaking to me. Each day if I accomplish nothing else, I manage to get my reading done. It has become as vital to me as drinking water. And I am continually amazed at the grace that intercedes each and every time. Alright, I confess that parts of the Old Testament have been wrought with sacrifice that does not resonate with me! But still the word speaks to my living day and the glory is everywhere! If my enthusiasm continues (which I hope and pray it will) I cannot wait to get to the end and do it again. Why oh why did I not do this earlier!—JAN

While I spent eight months to finish reading the Bible from creation to Revelation. It is only a start! It was a difficult, enjoyable and challenging experience. . . . I

*did most of my reading and listening in the still of the night and often wondered at the genius of the authors of the King James Version and how they were inspired. While I had frequent contact with the Bible in the past, particularly during the time of my service as Rector's Warden at St. Thomas and as a lay reader of the Episcopal Church in Haiti, my absorption was in fits and starts. Now, in a sense, I have put it all together. Yet there is no such thing as finishing with the Bible. It is a trip through eternity. Is it also a reminder of ourselves.—*HENRY

*I am moving along, slightly ahead of plan. . . . This is one of the most reward-ing experiences of my life. I have let go of trying to remember and understand all the different facts and thoughts. There is no final exam upon completion. Rather, I try to be in the moment and appreciate the words as I move forward. It may sound trite, but I am feeling like a much more complete human being, I truly appreciate the fulfilling feeling that reading the Bible is providing me. My favorite time is getting up first on Saturday and Sunday and sitting with my cup of coffee and Bible. I almost get disappointed when my family starts to stir and it is time to put my reading down and begin the day's activities. This is a summer I will always cherish, for many reasons.—*TRICIA

*This year I tried for the second time to participate in the Bible challenge. I have succeeded without missing a day since January first—a discipline I am thrilled to have accomplished. I am leaving for Istanbul and the Greek isles and my Bible was the first thing I packed. Currently, I am reading Corinthians and it is hard to believe I will be where Paul wrote his famous letters.—*PAM

*Each morning I begin with some quiet time reading God's Word, and it has made a great deal of difference in my life. It provides a strong spiritual start to each day and keeps me centered throughout the day. I had to get up at 6:00 a.m. yesterday to get my Bible reading in, and it kept me centered through a long day of confer-ences until about 14 hours later.—*CHIP

*I have been reading it on my Nook, the NIV Study Bible version. That makes it easier to travel with and find myself able to read it on the train and even the sub-way up in NYC. . . . It also forces me to read it more like a story—and while you can skim paragraphs when it was getting a bit tedious with the "rules" and family lineages, you can't skim whole pages at a time and you really can't "look ahead." I have found reading the Bible interesting and clearly I had never seen many of the passages in the normal Sunday readings, so I have found it worth-while. I appreciate your support.—*STEVE

*I love reading the Bible. It is moving. I always say "No!!" when we have to go to bed (when the Bible story is over). We do gratitude journals after we read the Bible. I like writing about what I am grateful for.—*TEDDY, AGE 7

Reading the 'entire Bible' has always been on my 'bucket list'. As a life-long, Canadian Anglican, I have been somewhat ashamed that I've never taken the time to read the cornerstone of our faith. So far, I'm a third of the way through. The plan established by the Bible Challenge is a smart one in that every day, a section of the Old Testament, Psalms, and New Testament are read vs. a 'cover-to-cover' approach. I choose to read before going to bed and it's become a little habit now for months. Thank you Bible Challenge for getting me started on a long, anticipated goal!—DEBBIE

CHAPTER 1

How the Church Has Inadvertently Kept the Bible in Captivity

"The word is near to you, on your lips and in your heart."—Romans 10:8

"Blessed Lord, who hast caused all holy Scriptures to be written for our learning: Grant that we may in such wise hear them, read, mark, learn and inwardly digest them; that, by patience and comfort of thy holy Word, we may embrace and ever hold fast the blessed hope of everlasting life, which thou has given us in our Savior Jesus Christ; who liveth and reigneth with thee and the Holy Ghost, one God, for ever and ever, Amen."—The Book of Common Prayer

"I have myself for many years made it a practice to read through the Bible once every year. I have always endeavored to read it with the same spirit and temper of mind which I now recommend to you; that is, with the intention and desire that it contribute to my advancement in wisdom and virtue . . . My custom is, to read four or five chapters every morning, imme- diately after rising from my bed. It employs about an hour of my time, and seems to me the most suitable manner of beginning the day."—President John Adams in a letter to his son

· ◆ ·

By 2010, the parish that I served had grown from roughly twenty-five to sixty-five ministries. When I first arrived, it seemed at times like nothing moved in the parish unless I pushed it. I was reminded of the story of a pastor in a small town who went down to the train station every night. Word spread through the town that he sat by the railway each night until almost midnight. Members of his church members were perplexed by his behavior. Finally, one of his church wardens approached him and said, "People in the parish are concerned about you, Tom. They want to know why you come down to the railroad and sit there so late every night." He responded, "The reason I visit the railroad station every night is that when the 11:35 express rolls through town, it's the only thing that moves around here that I don't have to push."

By 2011, our church was just the opposite. We had added as many as forty new ministries, and leading our church was like riding a wild bronco. It was all that I could do to hold the reins. I had learned how to delegate effectively, how to select great lay leaders, and how to surround myself with very gifted staff members, each of whom excelled at things at which I was not nearly as skilled. I had long ago learned to lead our church without knowing many of the details about each of our ministries. I served as an orchestra conductor striving to make the ministries produce a harmonic sound and keep all of us together and focused on what was most important.

By Christmas Day 2010, I was delighted, but exhausted. The evening before, we had hosted close to twelve hundred members and visitors for worship at four Christmas Eve services, along with one Christmas Day service. As she was leaving the church, a woman said to me, "I've just hosted twenty-five people at my home for dinner!" She looked happy, but tired. I thought to myself, we just hosted over a thousand people. I was thrilled we had done that, but I, too, was tired. Leading our church is like coaching a football team. By the end of December, I am usually worn down and ready for a rest. I also reach a point where I am spiritually exhausted. That particular Christmas Day, I remember feeling as though I had used up all of my spiritual reserves.

After our teenage girls and my wife and I had exchanged gifts and enjoyed a nice Christmas dinner, I sat down by the fire with my Welsh Pembroke Corgi, Winston, whom I call the son that we never had. I was reading through a stack of newsletters, and I read in a friend's newsletter that he was inviting his parish to read the Bible with him in a year. What a fabulous idea, I thought to myself.

A Novel Idea: Read The Entire Bible With My Church

The idea of inviting my church to read the entire Bible had never crossed my mind. Over the years I had started all sorts of classes and Bible studies, but we always read one book of the Bible at a time or studied some aspect of Christianity or Christian spirituality. When we studied the Bible, sometimes it felt like we were dissecting something that was dead rather than engaging something alive and transformative.

I studied to prepare for the ministry at the Yale Divinity School and its Episcopal counterpart the Berkeley Divinity School. It was heady stuff, and I loved it. I had great professors. Many were nationally or internationally known in their respective fields. They were so brilliant that I developed a great fear that I could never say anything in a sermon or in a class or in the churches that I would serve in the years to come that wouldn't be slightly, if not sometimes significantly, inaccurate. I feared having one of my professors point out corrections about details from church history or quotations from Scripture that I had used. Their knowledge was so vast. Their minds were warehouses of information. Yet, for all of my learning at their feet, it felt as though the Bible had become an ancient document of incredible complexity that we dusted off or like a cadaver picked apart, muscle by muscle, bone by bone.

Dissecting The Word of God: The Bible As Cadaver

The approach to studying the Bible that I was trained to follow and share with others makes me think of that great American painting by Thomas Eakins, who was one of Philadelphia's pre-eminent painters in the late nineteenth century. In 1875, Eakins produced *The Gross Clinic*, perhaps his greatest masterpiece. In his painting, Eakins captures renowned Philadelphia surgeon Dr. Samuel D. Gross presiding over an operation to remove part of a diseased bone from a patient's thigh. Gross lectures in an amphitheater crowded with students eager to learn from his vast reservoir of knowledge. Measuring ninety-six by seventy-eight inches, *The Gross Clinic* is one of the artist's largest works. Eakins was elated by the project and stated, "it is very far better than anything I have ever done." Public reaction to the painting, however, was less enthusiastic. The painting was finally purchased by a medical college for the unimpressive sum of two hundred dollars. Today the once maligned picture is celebrated as perhaps the greatest nineteenth-century medical history painting and one of the most important portraits in American art.

The body in Easkin's painting is stiff. It lies inert. Its skin is pale. Its lifeblood and energy appear drained. Its days of transforming the lives of others appear to be over. Still, it continues to be a fine teaching tool for students. At times, it feels as though the Church has transformed the life-transforming and awe-inspiring Word of God into a cadaver—a dead object—worthy of study by academics and students. This is not what the Bible was intended to be.

Thomas Cranmer Called For Reading The Entire Bible

As I sat by the fireside, I pondered my own relationship with the Bible. I had read the Daily Lectionary for over twenty years, but at times it had grown tiring. The lectionary had evolved over the centuries. Back in 1549, when Archbishop Thomas Cranmer, the first Archbishop of Canterbury selected by King Henry VIII, created the first Book of Common Prayer in English history, Cranmer arranged a reading plan that clergy and lay persons could use to engage the Bible each day. It called for considerable reading on a daily basis.

People who followed Cranmer's reading plan read through the entire New Testament three times each year and almost the entire Old Testament. Nothing was omitted: every violent or gruesome story, scenes depicting God acting badly, portraits of Jesus' disciples bungling along or simply not comprehending his message, redundant passages, unflattering portraits of kings and religious leaders, stories of debauchery and strange behavior, hard-to-decipher passages were read by lay persons and clergy alike. Nothing was deemed too difficult or too unsavory.

Over time, however, the lectionary has become something much different. Today, the Church's lectionary has become a sort of sanitized Bible, where most of the unpleasant stories that would not make for good bedtime reading have been removed. Many lessons that portray God as violent, unfair, cold, angry, or vengeful have been omitted. Baffling passages whose meaning cannot be easily determined have been expunged. Many things that have been deemed to be too unattractive to read aloud in front of children have been cut. The result is something akin to the Bible produced by Thomas Jefferson.

The Temptation To Create A Smaller Bible

The Life and Morals of Jesus of Nazareth or what is more commonly known as the *Jefferson Bible* was a book constructed by our third president in the latter years of his life by literally cutting and pasting sections of the New Testament to create the Bible he thought was more reasonable. In many ways, Jefferson was ahead of his time. In the centuries that followed, scholars figuratively created their own Bibles, suggesting that various parts did not belong in the original text, were later additions, or could never have been said by Jesus or other figures of the Bible. Some, like Jefferson, omitted any miracles and boiled the Bible down to a series of aphorisms or stories that were insightful and believable, while omitting anything that seemed to defy logic, reason, and the laws of science.

Jefferson's Bible omits most mentions of the supernatural, all sections of the gospels that speak about the Resurrection and Jesus' miracles, as well as any passage that refers to Jesus being divine. In an 1803 letter to Joseph Priestley, an eighteenth century English theologian who was a philosopher, chemist, educator, and political theorist, Jefferson stated that he conceived the idea of writing his view of the "Christian System" in a conversation with Dr. Benjamin Rush, a prominent Philadelphia physician who became the Surgeon General in the Continental Army and was a writer, educator, humanitarian, and the founder of Dickinson College.

In his letter to Priestly, Jefferson proposed beginning with a review of the morals of the ancient philosophers, moving on to the "deism and ethics of the Jews," and concluding with the "principles of a pure deism" taught by Jesus, "omitting the question of his deity." Jefferson explained he did not have the time, and urged the task on Priestley as the person best equipped to handle it. Jefferson accomplished a more limited goal in 1804 when he wrote "The Philosophy of Jesus of Nazareth," a predecessor to *The Life and Morals of Jesus of Nazareth*. He described it in a letter in 1813 to his predecessor as President, John Adams:

> In extracting the pure principles which he taught, we should have to strip off the artificial vestments in which they have been muffled by priests, who have travestied them into various forms, as instruments of riches and power to themselves . . . We must reduce our volume to the simple evangelists, select, even from them, the very words only of Jesus. . . . There will be found remaining the

most sublime and benevolent code of morals which has ever been offered to man. I have performed this operation for my own use, by cutting verse by verse out of the printed book, and arranging the matter which is evidently his, and which is as easily distinguishable as diamonds in a dunghill. The result is an octavo of forty-six pages, of pure and unsophisticated doctrines.

Jefferson never referred to his work as a "bible." Indeed, the full title of his 1804 version was *The Philosophy of Jesus of Nazareth, being Extracted from the Account of His Life and Doctrines Given by Matthew, Mark, Luke and John; Being an Abridgement of the New Testament for the Use of the Indians, Unembarrassed [uncomplicated] with Matters of Fact or Faith beyond the Level of their Comprehensions.* Literally using a razor, Jefferson cut and pasted verses from the gospels of Matthew, Mark, Luke, and John in chronological order. He mingled the thoughts and accounts of each evangelist to create a single flowing narrative. Thus, he began with the second and third chapters of the Gospel of Luke and followed them with the first chapter of Mark and the third chapter of Matthew. Consistent with his naturalist outlook, most supernatural events were omitted.

Therefore *The Life and Morals of Jesus of Nazareth* begins with an account of Jesus' birth but it omits all references to angels, Jesus' genealogy, prophecy, miracles, the virgin birth, the divinity of Jesus, and, of course, Jesus' Resurrection.

Jefferson's razor also removed all supernatural acts of Christ, any mention of receiving the Holy Spirit, any discussion of angels, Noah's Ark, the Great Flood, times of tribulation, and the Second Coming of Jesus. All focus on Jesus' Resurrection and any talk of a future kingdom, eternal life, Heaven and Hell, the Devil, and a Day of Judgment was omitted as well. Rejecting the Resurrection of Jesus, the work ends with the words: "Now, in the place where He was crucified, there was a garden; and in the garden a new sepulcher, wherein was never man yet laid. There laid they Jesus. And rolled a great stone to the door of the sepulcher, and departed." These words correspond to the ending of John 19 in the Bible.

Despite the stated intent of the 1804 version being "for the Use of the Indians," there is no record of this or the work which Jefferson composed after it being used for that purpose. Indeed, Jefferson did not make his biblical and ethics works public. Instead, he acknowledged the existence of his work to only to a few friends, saying that he read it before retiring at night, as he found this project intensely personal and private. Historians believe that Jefferson created the book for his own satisfaction, supporting the Christian faith as he saw it.

The Lectionary: A Somewhat Shallow Theological Pool

Just as Jefferson created the Bible he found edifying to his own life and acceptable to his own belief system, so the Church has come to use the Lectionary as its Bible within the Bible to the point that some clergy and most mainline Christians have never read it in its entirety. Hence, many of us who studied in mainline church seminaries were raised to read only the Lectionary or selections from the Bible on a daily basis. For the first decade or more after being ordained, I was diligent about doing so. If I missed a day or two, I always caught up. Sometimes I would read three or four days of lessons in a row to catch up. After a decade, I gave myself a break and just read the readings for the day even if I had missed several days before. I never felt like I was going deeper or learning anything new. I finally hired a classicist to come to my office each day one summer, and we read the Bible together in Hebrew, Greek, and Latin. It was an incredibly stimulating experience. For two hours we sat and studied the Bible in ancient languages, guessing at what various words meant, how they should be translated, and how they fit together in a sentence. Sometimes the Greek was unclear and the Latin was easier to follow. At other times it was just the opposite. Reading through Genesis in Hebrew was very challenging, but it got easier as we read further and I increased my knowledge of Hebrew vocabulary. Every time he left my office I felt as though my brain was on steroids.

As exciting as this practice was, however, it did nothing to change my preaching or my ministry. Members of my church did not indicate they found my sermons more inspiring or illuminating. My ministry did not become more energized. My wife and family never commented on any change in my behavior. I did not feel or appear to be more patient, gentle, kind, or forgiving. I did not exercise more generosity or self-control. It was a great intellectual experience, but it did not change me. Sitting by the fireside reading my friend's invitation to his entire parish to read the Bible with him in a year seemed novel and exciting. I ripped out the page and put it in a pile of things to take back to my office as a great idea to do someday with my church. It was too late, however, to implement it in my parish for 2011.

What did dawn on me was it would be a great way for me to get back into reading the Bible; if I missed a day, I would just pick up where I left off. I recognized how lax I had become in reading Scripture. I had been spending all of my energy researching and preparing sermons and occasionally writing about passages of Scripture for the sake of influencing others, but I was not feeding or challenging myself.

The Bible as Transformational Reading

I decided to take my friend's invitation personally and read the entire Bible. It would be the first time in more than twenty years. Instead of reading snippets of Scripture, skipping significant sections along the way, and occasionally jumping around, I would read each book in its entirety and in order until I had finished the entire Bible. I sat by the fireside and began with Genesis, a book I have always loved. As I read through the ancient stories of Adam and Eve, Cain and Abel, Jacob and Esau, Abraham and Sarah, Isaac and Rebekah, I felt myself reconnecting with Scripture.

I realized that my education and training had turned the Bible into a complicated text of truths and half-truths, stories that had been edited and redacted, a long history of oral tradition that was eventually set down on papyrus, and then copied and recopied over the centuries by scribes who sometimes made significant errors. Occasionally, these errors changed the meaning of a story or a teaching. Like many mainline clergy, I received little or no training in seminary as to how to help church members and spiritually-inclined seekers read the Bible on their own. I had almost no training on how to lead Bible studies or how to equip ordinary people successfully to read through the entire Bible. I guess my professors thought that this was too basic to teach, or that we could figure this out on our own. Leading a Bible study and helping lay people prayerfully engage the Bible was something that we would learn by trial and error after graduating from seminary and being unleashed on a parish.

Holding the Bible Hostage

By the time I left seminary, I knew more about the theories of how the Old Testament was constructed than I knew about the most life-giving passages that would speak to someone seeking solace and spiritual sustenance. I was part of a long line of clergy who had managed unknowingly to take the Bible away from the people and make it "the Church's book." The Church had inadvertently begun to hold the Bible hostage from the very people it served. As I read, I realized that if I was going to help others enjoy and glean spiritual fruit from reading the Bible each day, then I had to read it on a regular basis for my own spiritual growth and renewal and not solely as a means for study and sermon preparation.

There are over six billion Bibles in circulation today. It has been translated into over two thousand languages. Eighty-eight percent of Americans own a Bible, on average 3.4 Bibles per household. Most of these Bibles are on shelves or in attics or basements gathering dust. According to Mark Forshaw, the Executive Director for Global Scripture Impact at the American Bible Society, 88 percent of Americans believe the Bible contains everything a person needs to know to live a meaningful life; 79 percent believe that God regularly speaks to us through the Bible; and 74 percent report that they use the Bible to guide them in major decisions. On the other hand, 32 percent report that the Bible is hard to understand, and 30 percent claim that the Bible teaches intolerance.

We live in a time when the Bible is being discovered online. Similar to the invention of the printing press, the technology is fostering a new Reformation. Yet, only one in five Americans reads the Bible four times or more a week. We know that reflection on Scripture is the number-one catalyst for spiritual growth. Regular engagement with the Bible is head and shoulders above all other spiritual instruments and practices. We do not need to print and sell more Bibles. What we need is to read the ones that we have. We need to find exciting and stimulating ways to engage God's Word so our lives can be transformed in ways that lead us to find greater meaning and to serve God more faithfully.

CHAPTER 2

Reclaiming the Bible as Our Book, not just the Church's Book

"Your Word is a lamp to my feet and a light to my path."—PSALM 119:105

"I came that they may have life, and have it abundantly."—JOHN 10:10

"The Word of God well understood and religiously obeyed is the shortest route to spiritual perfection. And we must not select just a few favorite passages to the exclusion of others. Nothing less than the whole Bible can make a whole Christian."—A.W. TOZIER

"I saw that the most important thing I had to do was to give myself to the reading of the Word of God, and to meditation on it. . . . What is the food of the inner man? Not prayer, but the Word of God; and . . . not the simple reading of the Word of God, so that it only passes through our minds, just as water runs through a pipe, but considering what we read, pondering over it, and applying it to our hearts."—GEORGE MÜLLER

•◆•

Christmas Day 2011 was the beginning of a new chapter of my spiritual journey in committing to read a portion of the Bible every day. I was hardly a pious saint. I read that first evening with a glass of single malt scotch by the fireside and started to make my way through Genesis. I read each day in the morning and I read again in the evening. After five days, I felt so spiritually renewed that I sent out a few invitations to members of my congregation who had participated in a group called Beer, Burgers, and the Bible, or simply B.B.B, which was a four-week program. Each gathering involved a cookout at a different person's home that included a wonderful selection of beer and a basic teaching on how the Bible was put together and how to get the most out of reading it. I offered what I called "a ten thousand foot view of how the Bible was constructed" and what the various sections—the Torah, the wisdom writings, the historical books, and the prophets—had to teach us, as well as an overview of the gospels, Paul's major writings and the shorter epistles.

I began by holding out a copy of the Koran and stating that the 1970s rock star Cat Stevens had given it to me, which quickly caught their attention. I explained that I had been a newspaper reporter before entering seminary. After deciding to leave reporting, which I greatly enjoyed, I spent a summer working for St. James's Church, Piccadilly, a sort of hip, somewhat radical Church of England parish. It had once been one of London's most fashionable churches and a popular wedding venue. Archbishop William Temple had served as Rector there during the First World War. The Vicar during my time was Donald Reeves, who was an incredibly imaginative church leader and one of the most interesting people I have ever met. He was a sort of religious genius who pushed against boundaries and reached out to anyone in need, collecting a hodgepodge of crazy and yet saintly figures whom he built into a loving congregation of spiritual castaways. Donald made it easy for anyone with any ache and hurt in life to come and find a spiritual home. One of the people whom Donald gathered around him was Bishop Trevor Huddleston, who had been a missionary in South Africa and served as Archbishop Desmond Tutu's first spiritual guide and mentor. Bishop Trevor lived in the church rectory.

In my first week of working for Donald, I learned that Cat Stevens, now a Muslim convert who had changed his name to Yusuf Islam, had recently been a speaker at the church. The reporter in me was disappointed not to have had the chance to hear him speak and interview him. When someone suggested that it would be easy to visit the former singer at his mosque in Green Park, I jumped at the chance. I made my way to the mosque and asked for him. After I removed my shoes, we were introduced. I was struck by his incredible and almost unnerving zeal. We conversed for a short while, but he was not prepared to grant a full interview; I would have to wait until September. By then, I would be off at Yale, so I had to decline. Instead, he summoned a fellow Muslim and asked him to bring me a copy of the Koran. It was quickly fetched, and Yusuf Islam presented me with the book and tried to convert me on the spot. He urged me to read it and to accept Allah as my personal savior. Being bound for seminary, I was not converted by his hard sell. Instead, I took the Koran with me and tried over the next twenty years to read it on numerous occasions. I never got very far. I would start with the best of intentions, quickly get bogged down and eventually lose interest. I never found any parts that seemed to flow and make me want to continue reading. It felt like a collection of sayings that had no overall coherence. Some of it made no sense at all. Unlike the Bible, there was no narrative, and there were no easy to follow stories that could capture a novice reader's attention. Hence for twenty years the Koran was moved, unread, from place to place in my office and home. It collected dust and from time to time was re-opened, read briefly, and then placed back on a shelf. I was never quite sure where it was to be found between my reading sessions.

Sitting in front of twenty church members at BBB, I explained that my relationship to the Koran was similar to how I suspected most mainline Christians related to the Bible. They own a copy. They have tried to read it, but they have failed to make much progress. I offered to provide them with a ten thousand-foot view of the Bible, which would allow them to see how it was put together and where to turn for the books, passages, and sayings that have the most life-transforming impact. I wanted them to fall in love with the Bible and find in it some of the spiritual wealth that I and so many others had discovered.

Within a few years' time, over one hundred and twenty-five members of our parish and their friends participated in this program. I felt proud to have created and led it, but I realized after several years that very few of those who participated in Beer, Burgers, and the Bible had developed a regular daily practice of reading Scripture. Instead, they enjoyed my brief teachings along with the food and fellowship, but they were no more spiritually nourished on a regular basis in God's Word after the program had concluded than they were before it had begun.

A Personal Transformation

As I pondered my friend's invitation to read the Bible in a year, I sensed my own spiritual poverty and need to reconnect profoundly with Scripture. I liked the idea of reading the entire Bible, omitting nothing and picking up each day where I had stopped the day before. It had been over twenty years since I had read the entire Bible. In fact, I had only done it once in my life. It was time to do it again. I picked up my New Oxford Annotated Translation and began reading Genesis. I read with delight and wasn't anxious to stop. There was no test. There was no sermon to prepare, no class notes to create, and no discussion group to facilitate. It was just the Word of God and me.

The following morning, I got up, fixed a pot of tea and continued in Genesis. The chapters flew by. The narrative reads like a novel at times. As I read that night, I decided to throw in a psalm and a chapter of the Gospel of Matthew. I wanted to read a portion of the Christian story alongside the ancient Jewish Scriptures. As an Episcopalian accustomed to the patterns of the Lectionary, I was doing what came naturally. The difference was that I was starting from the beginning of both the Old and New Testaments and reading each book in succession, and limiting my reading of the Psalms to one or two a day. More significantly, I was omitting nothing. When I was done, I would be able to say I had read the entire Bible and feel the accomplishment and sense the connectedness of the Scripture.

In five days I felt more spiritually alive than I had in years. The combination of reading God's Word, not as a means to an end, but to allow it to speak to me and bring about transformation and healing was invigorating. The time of sitting in silence and solitude and knowing that I was doing something that God honored brought me a sense of peace and centeredness and an indescribable sense of blessing. My mind tends to race like a machine, yet in this quiet of each morning and evening I felt spiritually collected, centered, and renewed. It was as if a spiritual well within me was being refilled each time I sat down to read. I sensed God was nudging me to share this experience with others.

Sharing the Joy with Others

I decided to put together an email based on a book that I had been trying to write on ethics. The message I sent was upbeat and easy to understand:

Dear _____.

John Adams, our second President of the United States, used to read the entire Bible each year from cover to cover. He studied the Scriptures every Thursday, Friday, Saturday and Sunday mornings.

Andrew Jackson, our seventh President, referred to the Bible as "the rock on which our Republic rests." He read three to five chapters of the Bible each day.

Abraham Lincoln, our sixteenth President, called the Bible "the best gift God has ever given to man . . . But for it we could not know right from wrong."

Woodrow Wilson, our twenty-eighth President, once noted, "The Bible is the Word of life. I beg that you will read it and find this out for yourself. When you have read the Bible you will know it is the Word of God, because you will have found in it the key to your own heart, your own happiness, and your own duty."

Dwight D. Eisenhower, our thirty-fourth President, and his family used the Bible each day during family devotions with each family member taking his or her turn in reading a passage.

Jimmy Carter, our thirty-ninth President, reads the Bible daily and has taught a Sunday school class for over three decades.

Ronald Reagan, the fortieth President, wrote, "Inside the Bible's pages lie all the answers to all the problems man has ever known. I hope Americans will read and study the Bible. . . . It is my firm belief that the enduring values presented in its pages have a great meaning for each of us and for our nation. The Bible can touch our hearts, order our minds, and refresh our souls."

This year I have decided to read the entire Bible. It's been a long time since I have done it, and it is something that everyone should do at least once. My plan is to read three chapters of the Old Testament, a psalm and a chapter of the New Testament each day.

I have been reading the Book of Genesis with a cup of tea in the morning or seated by the fire at night. It is so enjoyable that I want to encourage you to do this as well. I would like to invite you to accept the challenge of reading the entire Bible this year. I suggest reading the New Oxford Annotated Bible printed by Oxford University Press. It's an excellent translation with fine footnotes that prove most helpful.

If you do not have a Bible and would like to accept this challenge, I will gladly provide you with a copy at no cost to you. Just let me know if you need one. Either way, let me know if you will join me in reading the entire Bible this year.

I want to keep track of how many invitees will accept this wonderful challenge. I believe that taking time to read the Bible for 15 or 30 minutes each day will transform our lives, our marriages and our families. It will help us to be better parents, spouses, neighbors, Christians, workers and citizens.

It will help keep our head and our heart in the right place and prepare us for eternity with God. I hope that you will accept the Bible challenge as together we seek to lead more ethical lives.

> With warmest regards,
> *Marek*

For whatever reason, I did not quote what a bunch of saints, bishops, or theologians had to say about reading the Bible. Instead, I quoted several United States presidents. The quotes seemed to have more impact on those who read my invitation than quotes from a number of great theologians. Here were people we had read about in history classes and heard about all of our lives. They shaped our country and helped to lead our nation. Here was their testimony about the power of the Bible to transform our lives for the better.

I personalized each message by using the name of the person to whom I was writing and sent one email at a time. As I sent the messages to former participants in BBB, I felt as if I were fishing in a stocked pond. I started receiving positive responses, most of which read, "Thanks for the invitation. I have always wanted to do this. Count me in." I expected five or six persons might want to join me, but I was astonished when the number very quickly grew beyond that.

A Surprising Catch

One of my hobbies is fly fishing. I have a number of friends who are excellent fly-fishermen, and whenever I receive an invitation to go fishing, I clear my schedule so I can spend the day standing in a mountain stream. Most of my friends are better at fly fishing than I am. They use a greater assortment of flies; some tie their own. They also cast better and fish more often. The one thing that I like to do is to fish in the same hole until I catch every fish I possibly can. Sending out the email invitation was like fishing in the single hole where all the trout were hiding. I received one positive response after another. After writing to all the BBB participants, I decided to start inviting others in the parish whom I knew took their spiritual life seriously. I began receiving similar replies: "Thanks for the invitation. I have always wanted to do this. Count me in." The fisherman in me was taking over.

I then sent the same personalized invitation to members of our church about whose interest in the Bible and spirituality I was uncertain. I was once again amazed to receive similar positive responses. This emboldened me to write to persons on the fringe of the church or those whom I thought would not be interested in reading the Bible. They, too, welcomed the opportunity to do something measureable and concrete to strengthen their spiritual lives. Their average response to my invitation was almost identical.

We began announcing in church each Sunday how many people had signed up for what I began to call The Bible Challenge. The first Sunday there were twenty-seven, then fifty-four, then seventy-nine. Soon we were over one hundred. The Bible Challenge began taking off because both the idea and the method for doing it were simple, and there was a great interest in reading the world's all-time best-selling book.

We began praying each Sunday for those who were participating in The Bible Challenge. I believe strongly in the power of prayer. We offer prayers every Sunday in church, but we do not pray Sunday after Sunday specifically for any of our sixty-five different ministries. We began praying each week for The Bible Challenge participants and those who were contemplating joining. The prayer enforced our priority that reading the Bible was not just one among our different ministries, it was *our main focus*. Engaging God's Word was the best way that we knew to form Christians, and we did not want that getting lost among everything from polishing the church silver to serving as an usher to raking leaves on the church property. Each of our ministries is important, but the Bible is what fuels us spiritually more than anything else that we have to offer. Reading God's Word each day helps to bring forth the spiritual fruit that St. Paul speaks about in his Letter to the Galatians: love, joy, peace, patience, kindness, generosity, faithfulness, gentleness, and self-control. (Gal. 5:22–23)

Spreading the Word Widely

I preached a sermon on the importance of reading the Bible each day and the impact it was making on my own life. My personal witness captured people's attention. People could sense my passion and my spiritual vitality. As people left worship, I stood at the church door with a pad of paper and took down the names of those who said they wanted to join the program. Within a day another fifty people agreed to accept the challenge.

A few years ago, a member of my church told me something simple and profound, which I did not learn in seminary, but which is vital to parish ministry: "People want to be part of something successful." He is absolutely right. When my friend issued the invitation to his church to join him in reading the Bible, he put a paragraph in his church newsletter. That was all. There was nothing personal about it. To the best of my knowledge, it was not communicated in any other way. As a result, only seven of the three thousand church members accepted his invitation. When only seven do something, it seems unusual. The vast majority of people in the church think, "God bless those spiritual Green Berets. They are doing something that I could never do." But when a large number of people commit to doing something, then others begin to think, "This must be really good, if so many people are doing it." That's how The Bible Challenge began to work in our church, and it unleashed a great power.

In fairness to my friend's church, he has offered a similar challenge every year of his ordained ministry, and this, along with his extremely strong sense of faith and devotion to God, has helped him to build one of the strongest and most vital Episcopal churches in the United States. His devotion to the Word of God has had a great impact on his life that overflows into the life of his church. He has touched the lives of countless other people, including me.

Inspired by the positive response that we received from members of our church, I began contacting friends outside the church. I sent the invitation to people with whom I play tennis regularly and to friends my wife and I see socially. Most rarely attend church and do little to nurture their spiritual lives. I sent invitations to friends across the country and even some overseas, friends from all different stages of my life. I began to fear that they might think that I had become excessively religious or born again or wildly evangelical. Nevertheless, I continued to send invitations. I should never have worried, as soon I was receiving the same kind of responses from these non-church-going friends saying, "Thanks for the invitation. I have always wanted to do this. Count me in." It was startling how similar their responses were to those of the members of my own church who attended worship Sunday after Sunday.

I started to realize that reading the entire Bible was on a lot of people's bucket lists. A huge number of people, churchgoers or not, want to read the Bible through at least once in their lifetimes. I also realized that most of these people, however, will never read the entire Bible or succeed in it unless they are given a nudge or an invitation. Almost all of them need some support and a little coaching. We work to provide that support through The Bible Challenge, and we urge every clergy person to do the same when he or she leads a parish to participate. The support is a great gift that we can give our church members as well as members of the wider community. We have found it attracts people to church and transforms the nature of our congregational community in positive ways.

I sent an invitation out to the Dean of the Yale Divinity School. The Dean, a friend of mine, responded, "Count me in. I will begin reading it on my iPhone each day." My head began to spin. I was weak at using technology and learning how to integrate it into my life. I was well behind others on the learning curve. I never made use of an iPod or downloaded much music. I was slower than most to use email, Facebook, and other technological innovations. I realized, however, a lot of people were more technologically advanced than I was, and they would want to read the Bible on their smart phones and tablets. When I mentioned to a few people that the Dean of the Yale Divinity School was participating in The Bible Challenge by reading the Bible on his iPhone, others asked if they could participate in this way as well. Soon scores of people began downloading the Bible for free and participating digitally. I realized there was an enormous spiritual hunger throughout our world, and yet we in the Church were, at times, inadvertently hiding the Bible from the very people whom we are trying to serve. Instead of using the technology to offer them the whole thing, we edited it down to bite-sized pieces and omitted anything that we thought would be too challenging or upsetting.

Creating a Critical Mass

We live in an age of challenges. People want to run marathons or compete in triathlons. Some enter multi-day-long bicycle races. Others travel around the world to chart the number of species of birds they have seen. Some keep track of where they have played golf across the country and even overseas, saving a golf ball from each course. We like to measure what we do. We note how much weight we have lost or how many miles we have run or walked. We count how many errands we have completed. Our spiritual life feels like the only area where we do not take measurements. Hence, it does not pique our interest in the same way. We cannot chart our progress or see the difference that it is making as easily as following mile markers.

Spiritual challenges often seem reserved for monks and nuns or for the saints and martyrs about whom we read but never imagine emulating. With The Bible Challenge we had discovered something that was manageable and measurable, but not overwhelming in scope. It could be done at any time and in any place by any person who desired to participate. You did not have to be a saint, a seminarian, a church-goer, or even a believer in God to join in. You could have more questions than answers about faith and God and the Bible, and you were welcome. No class attendance was required, no specific hour had to jive with participants' schedules. No one had to go to church or meet in a certain location; no one asked for money; there was no chance of being embarrassed about being biblically illiterate. The Bible Challenge was simple, and it broke down many of the barriers that many people who have spiritual needs and desires feel when they think about church.

Instead, there was an opportunity to take on a great spiritual challenge, to move at one's own pace, to be given a guided way of working through the entire Bible in a year, and to have a chance to overcome biblical illiteracy. There was also no punishment or embarrassment for falling behind. When anyone said to me, "I'm reading the Bible a bit each day, but I won't be able to finish it in a year," I responded, "That's terrific. Don't worry about finishing in a year. The key is that you read a little bit each day, and let what you read transform your life. If it takes you two or three years to read through the entire Bible, you will get more out of it than someone reading it rapidly."

A critical mass of participants began to develop. As more people signed up to participate, we could see a large percentage of our membership were accepting the challenge. Others began to think, "I don't want to be the only person not doing this," or "If so many are participating, this must be something really good. I will do it, too." I sent out over six hundred personalized invitations and preached about it. For several Sundays, we announced how many had signed up. We mentioned The Bible Challenge in our written Sunday announcements and on our weekly email message that goes out to the parish. Within six weeks, we had over one hundred and eighty church members and more than ninety friends from beyond our church who agreed to participate.

I began to see that engaging the Bible on a daily basis could not only transform and inspire individuals, it could also transform an entire spiritual community. If five people out of two thousand do something, it is not likely to change that community dramatically. But if one hundred and eighty out of fourteen hundred people in a community and ninety more in the surrounding community do something together, it has the power to transform the entire community. We began to see that occurring.

As I engaged God's Word twice a day, reading considerable amounts of Scripture and letting nothing get between me and my daily Bible reading, people began to notice a difference in me. My family noted that I seemed more peaceful, patient, and happy. Colleagues at work found me more spiritually alive, easier to work with, and less business-like. My emails softened, and a more generous spirit seemed to flow through my communications and interactions with others. Parishioners started to comment about my sermons, noting that there was something different about them. "Whatever you are doing, keep it up," said one church member. "It's been wonderful to hear your messages." I started quoting Scripture more in sermons and in articles that I wrote for our church newsletter and other communications to the parish. Our members were appreciative. It was as if they had been surviving on heavily processed food as I quoted spiritual writers and shared stories and vignettes from life, but did not quote the Bible. With my new use of the Bible they were being given farm fresh produce.

Reclaiming the Good Book

The Bible Challenge helped us realize how the Church had inadvertently turned the Bible into "the Church's book" instead of making it available to the congregation. It was as though we had kept the Bible locked away in a vault. Everyone knew it was there, but few took the opportunity to read it. For many of our members, the Bible was as odd as the Koran. They had never read it for themselves. Some had never even opened it. They could not find a book in either testament, tell you where the story of David and Goliath was found, or tell you more about David than that he slew a giant named Goliath. I found leaders of our church—members of our Vestry and Sunday school teachers—who had never so much as read through one complete book of the Bible. What were we doing all these years?

I recently returned from a sabbatical spent in Spain, where I walked the Camino to Santiago de Compostela. I spent four months traveling and studying Spanish intensively. I worshipped in over fifty Spanish churches and was shocked to see how little the Bible was used. The church in Spain focuses almost exclusively on the Mass, the saints, the feast days, Holy Week, the rosary, private devotions, pilgrimage, and confession. Only once did I hear or read about a priest encouraging his people to read the Bible. In Salamanca, I met a priest who had over three hundred members of his church joining him each week for a wide variety of Bible studies. It was fabulous to witness his work, but elsewhere there seemed to be a biblical famine. As a result, the Church seemed moribund. Young people had no interest whatsoever in the Church, and the focus appeared to be completely inward instead of outward as a truly alive church will always be.

I found a connection between the struggling church in Spain and the continuing decline of mainline Christianity in the United States. People have become disconnected from the Good Book, which is the foundation of the Church. As a result, churches are producing anemic Christians whose faith is so weak that even their own children are barely affected. Parents are throwing off such dim spiritual wattage that it rarely if ever engages their children. Yet, as person after person began to engage the Bible regularly and began to develop a daily spiritual discipline, we were seeing lives changed and transformed in beautiful spiritual ways.

Through time in prayer, I sensed God nudging us to share The Bible Challenge with others. We were witnessing such a positive response and impact that I knew that this wasn't meant to be kept to ourselves. It was meant to be shared. In 2012 I created the Center for Biblical Studies to share and promote The Bible Challenge with others. Soon another church agreed to participate, then another, and another. Kirk Smith, the Episcopal Bishop of Arizona, agreed to lead his entire diocese in The Bible Challenge; Bishop Greg Rickels of the Episcopal Diocese of Olympia agreed as well. Bishops from Tanzania and Kenya soon followed. In less than two years we had over forty bishops leading their entire dioceses: more than twenty-five hundred churches in over forty countries participating in The Bible Challenge. A spiritual revolution was beginning.

Two Great Role Models

I based The Bible Challenge on two people, neither of whom was a theologian or a clergyman. Neither attended seminary. The first was John Adams, our second president. He read through the entire Bible every year of his adult life. It shaped his character and the decisions he made, which in turn shaped our nation. Adams offered a profound model for us to follow. His practice was regular. He did it first thing in the morning. Both his life and our country were shaped by his faithful, prayerful daily reading of Scripture.

The second person was Greg, one of several care-givers who tended to my father-in-law as he was dying of Parkinson's Disease. Greg never went to college. He didn't read many books I was aware of, but he did read the Bible. Greg would sit for hours with my father-in-law quietly reading. He did not need a master's degree in divinity to figure out its message. Greg did not need to attend seminary or read Bible commentaries or have a clergy person looking over his shoulder to teach him that when the Bible said that God commanded Moses, Joshua, or David to enter a village and kill all the Edomites, including the women and children, and they did so, that was not how God really worked. When my father-in-law or mother-in-law became anxious about a matter, Greg would simply say, "Everything is going to be alright. God is watching over you. Jesus is with you." I will always remember that. Most ministry is that simple. It involves being with people, listening attentively, expressing compassion, and encouraging trust in God so that the Almighty can be the rock and hope of those who are going through difficult times. I am convinced when we spend considerable time each day prayerfully reading God's Word, God shapes our souls and begins to work in powerful ways through us. We may not even aware of the ways in which God is touching others through us. I am equally convinced that if we do not give ourselves to this prayerful reading each day, many occasions for caring for others and serving God pass us by and our lives are greatly diminished as are the lives of those around us.

The Testimony of Others

Here is what some of the spiritual leaders in various churches and dioceses have had to say about The Bible Challenge:

> *The Cathedral set about the Bible Challenge in early fall with over 140 parishioners committed to be a part of this new, exciting and promising journey. Many voiced their enthusiasm in taking on such an arduous task while others spoke honestly of their hesitancy in the midst of their desire and longing to be a part of this spiritual practice. The Bible Challenge is a blessing and a gift for our parish as so many have been drawn into God's Word and into the intimacy of the transforming truth of God's love for humanity. It is more than a program or a Bible study. It truly has become a profound and defining part of our life together as a community of faith. Our weekly conversation groups produce honest discussions as we seek to ask the difficult questions and to struggle with the text. Community is formed simply through the knowledge that fellow parishioners are engaged together in reading the Bible. Many hallway conversations on Sunday mornings revolve around the prior week's readings and the challenges they produced. These*

conversations are not confined within the church walls but occur in the community as well—the grocery store, the coffee shop, the local YMCA. One parishioner said, "I travel a great deal for work and this keeps me tied to my church and to my faith. I know I am not alone in this discipline. It is empowering to be connected to fellow Christians through the Scripture." It is amazing to witness God speaking to us, individually and collectively, through this daily practice and thrilling to ponder where the Spirit is taking us. No doubt the Bible Challenge is prompting the people of Christ Church Cathedral into deeper engagement with Holy Scripture. Thanks be to God for drawing us back to that which contains all things necessary for salvation.—THE REV. CANON GENE B. MANNING, SUB DEAN, CHRIST CHURCH CATHEDRAL IN NASHVILLE, TENNESSEE

The Bible Challenge is enriching every aspect of our parish's life, from worship to fellowship to formation to mission. Those who are participating are discovering new aspects of Scripture by reading "the whole," so that when a text comes up in the Lectionary, there is a deepened sense of connection and context. We're talking about this experience in every corner of the parish, making associations with the biblical stories and our daily lives. A wonderful sense of community has developed among those who are engaging The Bible Challenge, a community full of spirit and joy. Most of all, the daily reading of scripture is undergirding all that we do, deepening our sense of God's presence, our gratitude for God's love for us, and our part in Jesus' life, death and resurrection, and ergo, God's mission.—THE REV. PAIGE BLAIR, RECTOR OF ST. PETER'S CHURCH, DEL MAR, CALIFORNIA

We are excited to say that in the Diocese of Upper South Carolina 52 percent of our congregations have accepted Bishop Andrew Waldo's challenge to read the Bible in one year. To support our participants, we have created a closed Facebook group which has activity on it every day. We also send out any posts by the Bishop to our email list of participants. Everywhere that I go in our Diocese, someone talks to me about The Bible Challenge. We have youth, children and adults participating. It has been exciting to read the posts on Facebook and to hear our members engaging Scripture at a deep level.—THE REV. KELLIE WILSON, CANON FOR CHRISTIAN FORMATION IN THE EPISCOPAL DIOCESE OF UPPER SOUTH CAROLINA

The Bible Challenge is going incredibly well. We have at last count 255 people signed on—and more that are sort of reading along with their spouse but haven't exactly signed up. It's been pretty remarkable to hear people that have been going to church for 50 or 60 years and never read Genesis. I just did the Bible Book Club this morning (we do this informal discussion on the readings each week on Tuesday night and again Wed morning with childcare, so different demographics can make the discussion groups), and I continue to have a wonderful time engaging people in the Scriptures.—THE REV. DAVID ANDERSON, RECTOR OF ST. LUKE'S EPISCOPAL CHURCH IN DARIEN, CONNECTICUT

Holy Trinity in West Palm has approximately 80 people who have started the Bible challenge. We are offering two opportunities a week to discuss anything that might have come up for anyone. I have been pretty astounded by the enthusiasm down to several even thanking me for inviting them to do this. Go figure. Anyway we are having fun with this.—THE REV. DAVID WILT, RECTOR OF HOLY TRINITY EPISCOPAL CHURCH IN WEST PALM BEACH, FLORIDA

The Bible Challenge has continued to grow. At this point perhaps more than 90 people are reading along, and some are friends and co-workers recruited by our members to join in. What I've found noteworthy is that many people don't feel they can read the Bible on their own, and have been frustrated or intimidated by past attempts. Knowing that others are doing this is encouraging to them. Also, I send by email simple daily notes with a few remarks about each chapter (we read one chapter each day) and this has helped readers navigate the peculiarities of the first century Christian setting encountered in the Gospels we've read so far. Now, many have asked, "What will we read next year?" Thanks be to God—THE REV. DAVE ROBINSON, RECTOR OF ST. MATTHEW'S CHURCH IN MAPLE GLEN, PENNSYLVANIA

We have 86 members of our Bible Challenge Email group. There may be others who have joined in but are not in the email group. We will have our first "gathering" tonight to talk about the readings. We will have a second meeting on Thursdays at Noon. Thanks for conceiving and leading this for all of us, Marek!— THE REV. MERRILL WADE, RECTOR OF ST. MATTHEW'S EPISCOPAL CHURCH, AUSTIN, TEXAS

St. John's Church began its second year of The Bible Challenge in January. In terms of numbers participating the first year was what might be termed a mild success, as a little more than twenty parishioners took up the challenge. The insights and stories that have arisen from those twenty individuals, however, have been greatly encouraging. It was a pleasant surprise to discover several young people among those taking up the challenge. One family instituted a nightly reading of Scripture, followed by their children writing reflections in what they called "gratitude journals." One high schooler discovered the Bible was not the book of rules she had thought it was. And one recent college graduate found The Bible Challenge a helpful way to help sort through vocational questions.

Among adults following The Bible Challenge, one woman said she had a sense that it "all did hang together in a funny sort of way." When she completed The Bible Challenge, she went back to reread the Minor Prophets, which had captured her imagination. A few sought out commentaries for insight into confusing or troubling passages. A few pulled me aside to ask questions, which I enjoyed. And, there were, of course, those who said they were confused or intimidated by what they read and had trouble making sense of it all, but persevered anyway. Overall, there has been a sense of discovery and wonder among parishioners who participated in The Bible Challenge, some of whom have enthusiastically started The Bible Challenge anew this year. For this, I am deeply grateful. The Bible is the foundation of Christian life and spirituality. If one does not know the stories of our faith, spiritual life itself is lacking. The biblical stories are, as anyone is quick to discover, deeply moving, thrilling, sometimes profoundly disturbing and frequently puzzling. In short, they are a reflection of life itself. Engaging these stories as God's living Word, can enrich life, provide insights into some of life's enigmas and, most important, connect us to one another and God in new ways.

One thing we discovered to be essential, however, is a regular meeting time to come together, ask questions and share insights. This discovery is itself perhaps the greatest gift of The Bible Challenge: learning that scripture is not just the stories of our faith, but the stories that pull us together and hold us together in God. We are looking forward to a second year of The Bible Challenge and the ways in which it will enrich our common life.—JOSEPH L. PACE IS RECTOR OF ST. JOHN'S EPISCOPAL CHURCH, WEST HARTFORD, CONNECTICUT

We are going gangbusters! Wonderful conversations and people are choosing a variety of ways to commit to reading the Bible—and, they are doing it and getting a lot out of it. We are checking in quarterly and will hold a reader's celebration at the end of the year. I'm most excited about their reflections and questions. Our parish Bible study is hard to stop now on Sundays—I have to remind them that it's time to worship! Thanks for a terrific idea! I think we will probably have even a better challenge next year.—REV. BETSY SEEGER, RECTOR OF ST. ELIZABETH'S CHURCH IN BURIEN, WASHINGTON

I had decided in October–November to invite my congregation to join me in reading/rereading the Bible in 2012 and looking for options for daily readings I found your web-site. I am using your reading schedule, and 67 participants have accepted my invitation. Not all of them are reading the entire Bible, but many are, and the responses have been wonderful. Thank you for sharing your plan and your resources.—THE REV. LINDA GOSNELL—ASSISTANT RECTOR, HOLY CROSS EPISCOPAL CHURCH, SIMPSONVILLE, SOUTH CAROLINA

Our parishioners are giving us very positive feedback about The Bible Challenge. They are enjoying reading the Bible as well as the accompanying commentary. The demographic of Saint Michael's is on the upper end range—parishioners in their 60, 70, 80s and 90s! So The Bible Challenge is adding another new lifeline to our aging church. Everyone is catching the vision.—SUSAN CALDWELL, DIRECTOR OF CHRISTIAN EDUCATION, SAINT MICHAEL AND ALL ANGELS, CORONA DEL MAR, CALIFORNIA

Thirty-three individuals have accepted the Challenge for 2013, and we have commenced. One participant is in his early teens, reading with a parent, while another is at university.—THE REV'D CANON JAMES M. CLEMENT, CANON ASSISTANT TO THE DEAN, THE CATHEDRAL CHURCH OF ST. PAUL, PEORIA, ILLINOIS

The Bible Challenge is going quite well so far, our average Sunday attendance is around 275 and we have 69 people participating in the Bible Challenge, so about 25 percent. Many people have remarked what a good experience it has been for them, though of course some lament over making it through some of the Old Testament passages. We've done a few open forums for folks to come and ask questions and reflect on what they've been reading, and I'm planning our Fall forums to focus on issues of the Bible (text criticism; how we got the Bible; cultural context of the Bible; etc.). I'm also planning to create a reading plan for the Apocrypha to offer to people when we conclude this year. I've also sent our participants links to Bible Briefs (from VTS) so that they can have a short summary/overview of the books that they're reading.—THE REV. ROBERT BLACK, ASSISTANT RECTOR, ST. FRANCIS EPISCOPAL CHURCH, GREENSBORO, NORTH CAROLINA

Thank you so much for sending the information on The Bible Challenge. I especially like your call for us to think of this as a three- to five-year ministry, rather than a "once and done" affair. Holy Covenant is stepping onto new ground with The Bible Challenge. One of my parishioners joined the effort because her daughter, who is Muslim, told her she had already read the Bible and is now reading the Koran. My parishioner decided it was about time to read her own sacred text. Many of those involved are already seeing themes, encountering stories and making new connections with scripture.—FR. DION THOMPSON, RECTOR OF HOLY COVENANT EPISCOPAL CHURCH IN BALTIMORE, MARYLAND

CHAPTER 3

Losing Our Focus on the Bible

"I will meditate on your precepts, and fix my eyes on your ways. I will delight in your statutes; I will not forget your Word."—PSALM 119:15–16

"In the beginning was the Word, and the Word was with God, and the Word was God. He was in the beginning with God. All things came into being through him, and without him not one thing came into being."—JOHN 1:1–3

"Having knowledge of the Bible is essential to a rich and meaningful life."—Billy Graham

"The Bible is the greatest benefit which the human race has ever experienced. A single line in the Bible has consoled me more than all the books I ever read besides."—Immanuel Kant

• ◆ •

When I arrived at the church where I currently serve as rector, they did not have even one single Bible study. The interim rector had tried to start a Bible study that some members of the church attended, but it stopped as soon as she left. Many ministries and activities in mainline churches are rector-centric. They operate well under the leadership of a good rector or pastor, but soon after the clergy person departs, they lose their energy, focus, and leadership and soon cease to function. A new spiritual leader is eventually called and much of her or his time is spent on starting these ministries back up and re-energizing the church. Often, many good programs simply die during the transition time. It's a questionable model to follow.

St. Thomas' Church had about twenty-five ministries when I arrived and they were the usual ministries found in most mainline churches: ushers, lay readers, altar guild members, acolytes, choir members, and Sunday school teachers; there were no trained Bible study leaders. We had a number of outreach ministries that helped church members use their time, talents, and energy to improve the condition of others, especially those who were poor and suffering. These ministries were a great strength of our church, as it is for many mainline churches. We are often weak in teaching God's Word, but we are strong when it comes to serving those in need.

The efforts of many of our churches can be best summarized when Jesus speaks of judging the nations and explains that when he returns in his glory surrounded by angels:

All nations will be gathered before him, and he will separate people from one another as a shepherd separates the sheep from the goats, and he will put the sheep at his right hand and the goats to the left. Then the king will say to those at his right hand, "Come, you that are blessed by my Father, inherit the kingdom prepared for you from the foundation of the world; for I was hungry and you gave me food, I was thirsty and you gave me something to drink, I was a stranger and you welcomed me, I was naked and you gave me clothing, I was sick and you took care of me, I was in prison and you visited me." Then the righteous will answer him, "Lord, when was it that we saw you hungry and gave you food, or thirsty and gave you something to drink? And when was it that we saw you sick or in prison and visited you?" And the king will answer them, "Truly I tell you, just as you did it to one of the least of these who are members of my family, you did it to me." Then he will say to those at his left hand, "You that are accursed, depart from me into the eternal fire prepared for the devil and his angels; for I was hungry and you gave me no food, I was thirsty and you gave me nothing to drink, I was a stranger and you did not welcome me, naked and you did not give me clothing, sick and in prison and you did not visit me." Then they also will answer, "Lord, when was it that we saw you hungry or thirsty or a stranger or naked or sick or in prison, and did not take care of you?" Then he will answer them, "Truly I tell you, just as you did not do it to one of the least of these, you did not do it to me." And these will go away into eternal punishment, but the righteous into eternal life. (Matthew 25:32–46)

We in the mainline church understand Jesus' call to service. We often excel at outreach and caring for the poor and needy. What we do not get and what we rarely excel at is helping our members to engage the Bible regularly. Today, after almost two decades of ministry in my current parish, we have expanded our number of ministries to over sixty-five. We send mission teams to Honduras to serve in a girls' home and school located in a secure compound inside a city that has become known as "the murder capital of the world," due to drug trafficking and gang violence. We send another mission team to the Copan region of Honduras to install gravity-fed water systems that provide fresh water to remote villages. Each year, another village has its life completely changed as women and girls of the village no longer have to trudge several times each day up and down the mountain to bring fresh water to their homes. After our team leaves they can turn on a tap and enjoy fresh water for cooking, drinking, and other purposes. We host inner-city children for a summer camp and a harvest-festival on our forty-three-acre campus. We also house homeless families and prepare meals for them. Our leaders and volunteers offer an array of classes, social activities, prayer groups, Bible studies, labyrinth walks, and choirs. It is an amazing congregation.

The downside is that there is so much to choose from that it is hard to identify our focus. The Bible is lost in a sea of opportunities and choices. What is the main thing in our parish? Three years ago, it would have been hard to say. No two parishioners would have given the same answer before we started a major focus on encouraging and helping our members to read the Bible daily. I believe Episcopal and mainline churches suffer from a similar lack of focus, especially a lack of focus on the Bible. We need to ask ourselves, "What is front and center in our churches?" Our answers vary from congregation to congregation and decade to decade, and that is a problem about which we should all be concerned.

Without a Strong Focus Our Churches Are in Peril

To examine the problem from a larger perspective, we might look at the Episcopal Diocese of Pennsylvania. When I joined the diocese in 1995, it was one of the five largest in the Episcopal Church. We had one hundred and sixty-seven churches in a five county area. In the eighteen years that followed, our diocese has closed twenty-seven churches. The dramatic shrinkage within our diocese has been incredible. Demographics have had much to do with it: our diocese was geographically one of the smallest in the Episcopal Church and also one of the most densely populated with Episcopal churches. In some areas, there were several Episcopal churches within walking distance of each other. Neighborhoods changed. Episcopalians died or moved out and were replaced by people who did not worship in our tradition or did not worship at all. We no longer needed two or three Episcopal churches within a short walking distance. When approached by diocesan leaders about merging the parishes to form one more robust congregation, most church members did not want to merge. They loved their own buildings, the sense of community with familiar faces, even as their congregations decreased in number. They did not want to close their buildings where they cherished memories of baptisms and confirmations, weddings and funerals, to attend another church of even the same denomination if it meant closing their own building. Eventually, many of these churches could no longer afford a priest. Their annual giving stagnated or decreased. They had no choice but to eliminate ministries, cut staff, or spend down their endowment, if they were fortunate enough to have one. They began a slow death spiral until they no longer had the energy and membership needed to sustain a congregation, operate a building, and carry out their mission.

I would argue, however, that they closed for another reason as well. Most churches closed because they lost their spiritual focus. For decades we, as Episcopalians, based our ministry on a particular style of worship that is extraordinarily beautiful, but somewhat of an acquired taste. The Episcopal Church was somewhat of a club that people joined and enjoyed and where they discovered values and shared them with their families. They made good friends, said their prayers, and gave financial support not only to operate their church but also to care for people who were less fortunate. As cultural shifts occurred, however, our numbers shrank. Episcopalians had a low birth rate. We failed to be strong evangelists and share our faith with those outside our churches. As a result, we slowly dwindled.

Furthermore, we were weak at teaching our own members how to read the Bible. Only a small percentage of our members read the Bible on a regular basis. We rested our hopes on offering lovely Sunday worship, where the Bible was read aloud while worshippers passively listened. A sermon was delivered, and the preacher usually explained how a particular passage from the Bible was relevant to the lives of those in the congregation. As the world became busier and Blue Laws were abolished, shopping malls and other stores stayed open on Sundays and soccer leagues and other sports and events encroached on Sunday schedules, worshipping at church began to be viewed as one option among many. People attended with less frequency, and when they came the lessons seemed less comprehensible because they had not heard what had been read over the previous weeks. In addition, since they came with less frequency and usually had no daily spiritual discipline of their own, they came with greater spiritual hunger and neediness and left with less spiritual satisfaction and nourishment. They were depending completely on the church—its worship, hymn-singing, and preaching—to make up for what they were not doing on their own.

Culture Changes and the Church

The Church was shifting its focus with each passing decade. In the Sixties, the Episcopal Church moved to the forefront of social change and championed the cause of integration, joining with leaders of the civil rights movement. It is an area of ministry on which our Church can look back with pride. Episcopal clergy and lay people marched alongside Dr. Martin Luther King, Jr. and other civil rights leaders. Southern clergy and lay leaders and others took great risks to champion this cause. Some conservative congregations, however, forced their clergy to leave, making it clear that they did not want to embrace change. Other church leaders spoke out against the Vietnam War, even attacking the president of the United States, the government, and the military. In one congregation outside of Washington, D.C. that had a large number of military personnel, service men began wearing their uniforms to church each Sunday as a form of silent protest while their rector frequently spoke out against the Vietnam War.

Around the same time a growing awareness of the severe limitations placed upon women in our culture was sweeping across our consciousness. Many vestries did not allow women to serve on the church's governance board and girls were not allowed to serve as acolytes. Breaking through such barriers took time, energy, and often resulted in some members of the church departing unhappily. Studies reveal that the number-one thing that drives people away from church is *conflict*. As the

Episcopal Church and other mainline churches championed important causes the ensuing conflict led many to leave their congregations and the church as a whole.

Sentiment against the Vietnam War and the Sixties counter-cultural movement of hippies and drugs led to a growing anti-establishment movement. College students thumbed their noses at established institutions ranging from government and the military to universities, schools, and the Church. Few things were viewed as more establishment than the Episcopal Church. Demographic studies indicate that the Episcopal Church and other mainline churches were home to large numbers of World War II veterans and other members of the Greatest Generation and their young children. A large percentage of those who were of college age in the Sixties, however, left the Church.

The Church Embraced Psychological Models

Following the focus on social justice, the Episcopal Church embraced a more psychological model. Priests began studying to become therapists and offer counseling. Jungian psychology, dream analysis, and getting in touch with one's inner self and inner child became the rage. Episcopalians embraced the writings of American psychiatrist and best-selling author Scott Peck, who made the speaking circuit in many Episcopal churches where parishioners eagerly read *The Road Less Traveled*. The focus eventually shifted from Scott Peck and a therapeutic model of understanding ministry to family systems theory as applied to the church. The church was seen as a dysfunctional family. The role of the church leader was to self-differentiate and help improve the health and functioning of the parish. Proponents included Rabbi Edwin Friedman, author of *Generation to Generation*, and Murray Bowen.

Finally, this focus shifted as the twenty-first century began and clergy started to see themselves as entrepreneurial leaders. Religious leaders took cues and gleaned insights from leaders in business and other professions. Soon congregations were drafting strategic plans, identifying core capacities and values, measuring outcomes, designing organizational charts, and making financial predictions to determine the future of their church. Vestries conducted three hundred and sixty degree interviews and assessments of their clergy and demanded that their leaders carry out semi-annual reviews of all personnel. Churches began to function like small to mid-sized businesses.

All of this provided benefits. The Church spoke out against legitimate concerns in the culture, which history has validated as being important to have opposed. Clergy became better at counseling and creating healthier congregations that were run more efficiently and had clear plans and direction. Nevertheless, there was enormous change, and many people resisted the change and found it to be disruptive.

Changes Unsettled the Church

A major move took place to create gender equality in the Episcopal Church on July 29, 1974. After a battle of over a century to allow women to have a greater role in the Church and experience equality with men, eleven women were ordained as Episcopal priests at the Church of the Advocate in Philadelphia by several bishops who broke ranks with their colleagues. Two years later, on September 16, 1976, women's ordination was approved by the Episcopal Church at its General Convention held in Minneapolis, Minnesota. Girls were also allowed to serve as acolytes. The foundations of an all-male Church were shaken.

At the same time, the one thing that bound Episcopalians together—our understanding of common prayer—was also changing. The Book of Common Prayer was revised in 1979, after several years of piloting temporary liturgies using things such as the so-called Zebra Book, a liturgy that was bound in a black and white striped cover. The new Book of Common Prayer led to an outcry by traditionalists within the Church who longed for the beautiful Elizabethan-age wording of their favorite prayers. The Prayer Book Society was formed to champion the 1928 Prayer Book, and there were more dissension and more departures from the denomination.

Finally, there were two decades of sexuality wars that focused primarily on the place of homosexuals in the Church. Once again, Episcopalians were at the forefront and can take pride for their achievements. Episcopal clergy were in many cases the first to speak out and call for equal rights for gays and lesbians and to demand a safe environment where homosexuals could be open about their sexual orientation and not viewed as strange, perverse and sinful, or third class citizens. This social concern created more tension than any other issue addressed by the Episcopal Church in the last century. Perhaps because it followed so much other significant social change, including speaking out against the government and the military, championing civil rights, allowing women to serve at all levels, and a new Prayer Book, the focus on human sexuality has seemed overwhelming to many Episcopalians. Many thought that it openly violated both the Church's teaching and biblical statements about homosexuality.

The expanding role of women in the Episcopal Church and the open inclusion of gays and lesbians led to an international conflict within the Anglican Communion. Anglicans in some countries in Africa, where female genital mutilation is practiced, where women have little or no say in leadership, and homosexuality is forbidden within the culture, felt as though Episcopalians were betraying the Bible. Serious examination of the Scriptures, however, discovered good arguments on both sides of the issues. Now, after decades of strife, a clearer understanding of these issues seems to be emerging within many parts of the Episcopal Church.

The Bible Was Lost amid the Changes

In all the changes and challenges, there has been much diversion from worship and the Bible. Individual concerns of just war theory, nuclear disarmament, women's rights, civil rights, and human sexuality have at times consumed our leadership and taken away from a focus on the Bible and creating strong disciples for Christ. At the same time, it may be argued that these are the very things that force us to examine the Bible more closely and take it more seriously. These vital issues have made us question our assumptions about what the Bible has to say regarding issues of major significance in our daily lives and in our global world. Just as the Bible was used to justify slavery during the Civil War and more recently Apartheid in South Africa, the Bible has been used to oppress women, homosexuals, prop up elitist institutions and behavior, separate classes, and support warfare and violence. By examining the Bible carefully, debating about what it says and why, we have made significant progress in our Church, in our society, and in our lives. The question, however, is how can we insure that the Bible is front and center in our churches and in our lives rather than something that is merely brought out from time to time to settle societal disputes? Can we allow it to be the inspiration for our daily living?

My Own Experience

Let me say a word about myself. I am a life-long Episcopalian. I must confess that attending church bored me to death when I was growing up. I was confirmed at thirteen and then tested my parents' patience severely for the next five or more years. I had stretches during high school and college where I tested every boundary possible. I enjoyed playing soccer, attending parties and having fun, and seemed to manage my studies and everything else on the side. I worked hard in college and received an excellent liberal arts education, but I was hardly a saint.

Nevertheless, I was surprised while attending my tenth college reunion at Emory University to be called to the front of the gathering and given a beach sandal. I asked what it was for. They explained that it was the "Flip Flop Award," for the member of our college class who had made the biggest turn-around after college. After graduating from Emory, I lived in Paris on three dollars a day, struggling to study French and trying to determine whether I would go into journalism, get a Ph.D. in philosophy, or study to become a priest. I returned to the United States and worked for almost four years as a newspaper reporter in Atlanta and later in Nashville, and served as a stringer for *Time* magazine, writing a few articles and helping to research other pieces. Throughout that time, I volunteered in the Episcopal Church, serving at St. Philip's Cathedral in Atlanta and later at St. Anne's

Church in Nashville. I became involved in youth ministry, lay reading, and visiting prisons and jails. I also helped with a soup kitchen, served regularly at a night shelter, was a big brother to a juvenile delinquent through the court system, and served as the sponsor for a convict recently released from prison.

I loved outreach and caring for others. I took the first two years of a course called Education for Ministry (EfM), and throughout it all I sensed a constant nagging that was calling me to give my entire life over to Christ and to serve God. I loved being a journalist, but I did not sense that it was my life's vocation. Serving God through the Church became something that I felt called to do with every waking hour of each day. I had gotten to know a Roman Catholic priest named Tom Flynn at Emory University, who is one of the leading scholars in the world on the French philosophers Jean Paul Sartre and Michel Foucault. Becoming friends with Fr. Flynn transformed my life. I spent so much time conversing with him about important issues in life and my own personal concerns, that I felt as though a mantle had been passed, obligating me to do for others what he had done for me. He had demonstrated a profound ability to listen attentively and allow me to share my story. He guided discussions with open questions and listened to me and to countless students share quandaries. He always asked, "So, what do you think your choices are?" rather than trying to guide me or others to what he perceived to be the best choice. I owe an amazing amount to him for altering the course of my life.

After fighting the call to the priesthood for over four years, I finally gave in. I started praying for the gifts needed to be a good priest. I literally said to God, "If this is what you want me to do with my life, then please give me the gifts needed to do it well." I took a voice and articulation class in an acting school and joined Toastmasters to help me get over my fear of speaking in public. I volunteered at the newspaper to go out on speaking engagements and was sent to talk about journalism in college seminars and before full auditoriums of elementary school students. I left journalism to attend the Yale Divinity School and its counterpart the Berkeley Divinity School at Yale, enjoying three of the best years of my life. It was a time of rich learning with great professors. My brain pulsed with knowledge and stimulation. I attended chapel faithfully, even racing with sweat from a game of ultimate Frisbee on the quadrangle to attend Evening Prayer, and made my prayer life a high priority.

I was ordained as a deacon in 1989 and to the priesthood in 1990 at St. George's Episcopal Church in Nashville, an extremely special moment in my life. I focused on working with youth and helping a church with great resources but virtually no hands-on outreach to become active in rolling up their sleeves and actually working with people in poverty and need. The church has gone on to do amazing things around the world and across the country as a result of some of the efforts that we began to make together in the two years that I served there.

I developed a passion for spirituality before I attended seminary and it strengthened while I was at Yale, I studied Benedictine, Franciscan, and Celtic spirituality and read as many of the mystics as I could. I was not focused strongly on the Bible, but spiritual growth was very important for me. For the first twenty-two years of my ordained ministry I taught some of this tradition and some of that. I was like a fountain that poured forth information and learning and perhaps a little wisdom. I was assembling truths from across the centuries of Christian learning and putting them together for myself and sharing them with others. The Bible had a place in all of it, but it was not front and center in my ministry or in the churches where I served. I wanted people to learn from me and attend my courses and be altered by what I said and taught. I had little concept of moving them to Scripture itself, making myself dispensable and Christ and God's Word indispensable in their lives.

For the first few years of my ministry, I read the Daily Lectionary every day, usually saying both Morning and Evening Prayer. Then I married and became a step-father overnight. My sleep patterns were disrupted. I found myself waking up tired and no longer free to get up at my own pace, put on a pot of coffee, and read Scripture in a silent spot. Soon I was only saying one of the Daily Offices each day. It was usually Morning Prayer, and I read all of the lessons from Scripture assigned for the day. After about fifteen years of this, the Bible could bore me at times. I was not going deeper; I was stagnating in my understanding. I began reading commentaries and working through one book at a time. My greatest joy, however, came from reading books on spirituality. I was reading books about the Bible, or about people shaped by the Bible, or books on spirituality written by people who were steeped in prayer and Scripture, but I was not drinking directly from the fountain of life and source of all wisdom itself. Something crucial was missing. It was not until Christmas Day 2010 when I accepted my friend's invitation to read the entire Bible in a year that I began to fall in love all over again with Scripture. That experience changed my life, and it led me to create The Bible Challenge, which in turn has transformed over a quarter of a million people's lives so far.

CHAPTER 4

Why the Bible Should Be *The* Spiritual Tool, not One among Many

"So faith comes from what is heard, and what is heard comes through the word of Christ."—ROMANS 10:17

"The Holy Scriptures are our letters from home."—AUGUSTINE OF HIPPO

"The deceit, the lie of the devil consists of this, that he wishes to make man believe that he can live without God's Word. Thus he dangles before man's fantasy a kingdom of faith, of power, and of peace, into which only he can enter who consents to the temptations; and conceals from men that he, as the devil, is the most unfortunate and unhappy of beings, since he is finally and eternally rejected by God."—DIETRICH BONHOEFFER

•◆•

If what I have said in our previous chapter is accurate, we in the mainline church excel at reaching out and helping others with significant needs in our society. We have also been courageous and at the forefront of many important social changes, which in turn has influenced other nations and is bringing about important changes throughout the world to improve the lives of men, women, and children and creating more equality and freedom. Where we in the mainline church do not excel, however, is helping our members to engage the Bible regularly. Why should that matter? The answer to that question is the focus of this chapter and the heart of this book. I have come to believe that the ability of mainline churches to help their members regularly engage Scripture will determine whether our churches grow over the next few decades or whether congregations continue to shrink and eventually die.

One of the saddest sights is seeing a church that was sold and converted into an architectural office or a restaurant. While demographics change around most every church over time, many of these churches would still be functioning and thriving today if they had not lost a clear sense of their focus and mission to help members and others engage Scripture and guide them on their journey with God. The need for hope; for God; for discovering purpose in our lives; for learning how to pray, love, forgive, be generous, patient, and kind; and to experience profound peace will never go away. The only question is whether or not churches will continue to find effective ways to help people address these concerns that are at the very heart of the human experience.

The Earthquake That Shifted My Viewpoint on Ministry

On August 23, 2011, I drove to Valley Forge, Pennsylvania to meet with the Rev. Simon Barnes, who was one of the senior members of the American Bible Society. Simon was part of a group of leaders who helped to transform the ABS from a well-endowed institution that spent its time and money encouraging Americans to purchase Bibles to a more strategic organization focused on helping people to read the Bible and endeavor to measure the impact it was having on their lives. After touring their office, Simon and I headed out to lunch. He is a sophisticated priest and savvy leader. Over lunch he opened my eyes to the impact that regular Scripture reading makes in the lives of individuals. Simon shared information from the Center for Biblical Engagement (CBE) at Back to the Bible, an organization based in Lincoln, Nebraska which has spent a lot of time researching why so many Americans *own* Bibles but *never read* them. Their main focus is to do something to help more Americans read the Bibles that they currently own. Their early research discovered that there exists no measurable differences in the behavior of those who attend church once a week versus those who never attend. That fact rocked my world.

For over twenty years of ordained ministry, I had worked hard to fill a church on Sunday morning with the expectation that those who attended would experience comfort, hope, healing, and forgiveness; receive strength; and become more generous, compassionate, patient, loving, and kind. Now, I was being informed that this is not the case. Had all of this effort, time, and ministry been wasted? Surely there was some significant impact to the ministry that I had performed over the years. Indeed, hundreds of people had thanked me for assisting them during a family member's illness or death, preparing them for marriage, visiting them in the hospital, baptizing their children, or visiting them at home. People had generally appreciated my sermons and the Sunday liturgies, which we took great effort to plan and craft.

All of this energy and activity helped to *maintain* a church. It kept parishioners satisfied and happy. I know that many experienced their faith becoming stronger as they listened to sermons and attended the classes we offered. But if people who came Sunday after Sunday demonstrated little or no difference in moral behavior as compared to those who never attended, then something was seriously wrong with the model of ministry that I and countless others were carrying out. I had the feeling that we in the mainline churches were somewhat akin to door-to-door encyclopedia sales people. Everything that we were promoting would eventually disappear if we did not adapt to a rapidly changing world and make significant changes. We had to find a way to share our vital contribution in a way that others could appreciate and utilize. The Sunday morning only model was a dinosaur on the verge of extinction.

Upon returning to the ABS, everyone in the large office looked shaken. "Did you feel it?" they asked us. "Feel what?" we replied. "The earthquake and the aftershock," they responded. "It struck in Virginia, and we could feel it all the way here." Simon and I were perplexed and shocked to hear the news. It was hard to fathom if you had not experienced it. Indeed, a 5.8 magnitude earthquake had rippled across Virginia, significantly damaging the Washington National Cathedral, sending hand-carved stones tumbling down from the stunning thirty-story tower, which is the highest point in our nation's capital.

The earthquake for me that day, however, was not the physical one that occurred in Virginia, but rather what I learned from Simon. If what he said was true, then I had to rethink putting all of my effort into making Sunday morning the mainstay of spiritual transformation. Such an approach to ministry was questionable at best. If the church was truly in existence to change lives and to measure the impact of these changes, then churches across the country and around the world had to refocus their mission strategies. If not, all of our time and effort and investment in beautiful churches with stunning spaces for worship, fellowship, prayer, and learning could soon crumble into a pile of rubble as our society becomes increasingly secular and full of other options for how we spend our time.

They Never Taught Me This in Seminary

CBE's study revealed some positive things as well: Christians who read or listen to the Bible at least four days a week exhibit very strong positive behavioral differences from those who engage Scripture less often. Controlling for other factors—age, gender, church attendance, and prayer—Christians who are engaged in Scripture most days of the week have lower odds of participating in the following behaviors:

- They are 36 percent less likely to smoke
- 57 percent less likely to get drunk
- 68 percent less likely to have sex outside of marriage
- 61 percent less likely to view pornography
- 74 percent less likely to gamble

The CBE discovered no statistical difference between Christians who read or listen to the Bible two or three days a week and those who do not engage Scripture at all or only once a week. Somehow, engaging Scripture "four times or more" a week makes all the difference.

In addition, more Scripture engagement also produces a Christian who is more involved in spreading the Good News. Controlling other factors, those who read or listen to the Bible at least four days a week demonstrate these behaviors:

- 228 percent greater chance of sharing their faith with others
- 231 percent greater chance of discipling others
- 407 percent greater chance of memorizing Scripture

While these figures are startling and impressive, the CBE notes that they are based on research with a select sample of the population, namely 8,665 self-identified Christian adults who were willing to participate in an on-line survey about Bible engagement.

Regularly Engaging the Bible Significantly Impacts Teenagers

In a follow up survey with a random sampling of 2,967 teens and adults from across the United States, the CBE confirmed Scripture engagement predicts moral behavior better than traditional measures of spirituality, such as church attendance and prayer. It is interesting to note that among teens, the CBE could find no effects for church attendance and prayer in alleviating risky behaviors. Identifying as a "born-again" Christian was the only significant factor for lowering the odds of getting drunk among teens. Teens who read or listen to the Bible at least four days a week have significantly lower odds of smoking, getting drunk, or engaging in risky behaviors than their peers who do not read the Bible at all. Teens who read the Bible one to three times a week are slightly less likely to smoke, get drunk, or participate in risky behaviors than those who do not engage Scripture at all. The CBE's models show that Bible engagement is the best spiritually-based predictor among thirteen to seventeen-year-olds, significantly predicting three out of five risk behaviors examined.

The revelations that Simon Barnes shared with me about the impact that regular engagement with the Bible makes upon Christians only confirmed what I had begun witnessing in my recent endeavors to help members of my church read through the entire Bible in a year. I was at the epicenter of a spiritual earthquake, which was radically changing the way that I viewed my ministry after over two decades of leading churches.

A Conference That Changed My Outlook on Ministry

Soon after my lunch with Simon, a special invitation came my way from the American Bible Society inviting me to attend a conference called "Uncovering the Word" in Orlando, Florida. I immediately accepted. The conference was held at a nice hotel on the outskirts of the city. I spent forty-eight hours inside the hotel and only once walked outside for a brief time while speaking to my wife on the telephone and stretching my legs in the park next the building. Inside the hotel, my view of creating Christian disciples was transformed.

I must confess that I have never felt deeply at home with those who refer to themselves as "evangelicals." While serving a church in Richmond, Virginia I experienced "evangelical" members of my own denomination who seemed to use the Bible to separate themselves from the rest of the members of our diocese. Some seemed to possess a smug superiority, acting aloof before other members of our diocese and denomination as though they alone read the Bible and understood it. Their behavior was off-putting. While serving the churches in the South, I read about and encountered some evangelicals who seemed to use the Bible as a weapon to browbeat opponents and draw circles of acceptance where they were always in and others were out. They seemed to function best when there was an enemy or group to attack or oppose. I did not like some of the things that I saw evangelicals doing. If anything, I leaned toward the Catholic side of Anglicanism. I respected some aspects of the Anglo-Catholic and the Liberal Catholic tradition in England. I appreciated Christians who understood the mystical side of Christianity and who left plenty of room for mystery. I harbored deep suspicions of anyone who tried to be the spokesperson for God as if God had personally communicated uniquely with some individual who could then tell us about God and who was going to enter heaven and who was not.

At the same time, I was growing in my appreciation of the Bible as God's life-transforming Word and the need for the Church to produce more committed, contagious, and articulate believers who were knowledgeable about the Christian message and eager to share it with others. I was slowly coming to respect and gravitate closer to the very folks that had made me feel like an outsider and whose manifestation of Christianity I sometimes chided or disrespected. I entered a conference room full of evangelicals. It was sort of like attending a tribal gathering, and I felt as though I was perhaps the only one who did not belong to the tribe. I wore my Episcopal clergy collar and soon realized that there were only one or two others wearing clergy collars in the entire ballroom. One was a Roman Catholic bishop. I believe that the other was an Anglican priest from overseas.

Nevertheless, I was intrigued. The room was packed with displays about the Bible and biblical resources, disciple-making programs, and ministries from around the world. The speakers were excellent. They said things I had never heard before. It was like learning a new language or taking a class in college that completely changed one's point of view.

Can We Measure Spiritual Growth?

I sensed a common thread among the speakers that resonated with the talks I had been having with the American Bible Society: *measurement*. Was it possible to measure spiritual growth? The question might seem preposterous at first, but why not consider it? We measure everything in our society from shoe size to sales in industry, attendance at sporting events, stock prices, the cost of inflation, the national debt, the unemployment level, church attendance, financial giving to our churches, how many children attend Sunday school, and how many worship services are held each year. Why not measure spiritual growth?

The question would probably shock most of my colleagues. I have long suspected that most mainline clergy are reluctant to measure anything. Many of us fear being held accountable for growth. The Book of Acts tells us, "The churches were strengthened in the faith and increased in numbers daily." (Acts 16:5) Elsewhere in the Acts the numbers of conversions are staggering. When Peter and John spoke to the people, priests, and the captain of the temple, they annoyed many of their listeners by proclaiming Jesus' Resurrection. They were arrested and put in jail. Yet, "many of those who heard the word believed; and they numbered about five thousand." (Acts 4:4) Acts tells us that the Early Church "devoted themselves to the apostle's teaching and fellowship, to the breaking of the bread and the prayers" (Acts 2:42), which is the best short definition of the Church that I know. It consists of four activities or actions—learning and living according to the teachings of those who followed Jesus; experiencing the fellowship of other Christians like coals nestled together in a fire radiating heat; participating in the Eucharist, Communion or the Mass; and praying for those inside and outside of the Church. This powerful formula ignited spiritual growth that could be measured: "And day by day the Lord added to their number those who were being saved." (Acts 2:47) What I heard sounded like apostasy to my Episcopal ears, and I liked it. It resonated powerfully within me. Why not try to measure spiritual growth? I also sensed there was that some strong financial support backing these ministries. People with resources were *investing* their financial capital in ministries that they believed could transform lives, and they wanted measurable evidence that their investment was achieving the results for which it was intended.

More Tolerant but Still Shrinking

The conference was completely counter-cultural to everything I had ever witnessed in the Episcopal Church and other mainline churches, which I saw was also part of the reason our churches have been decreasing in membership for the last half century. No one in the mainline church or the Episcopal Church wants to be held accountable for growth. We talk up a storm and pass countless resolutions and have risked creating great divisions among ourselves in order to become more inclusive, which is noble. The problem, however, as the former Dean of the Washington National Cathedral Sam Lloyd once said to me, is "If we are becoming so inclusive, then why aren't we growing?" Where are all the people that we are opening our doors to include? Why are our numbers decreasing as we open our doors wider?

One cause is that evangelicals and conservatives now feel unwelcome in our increasingly progressive churches. Everyone can be tolerated except someone who represents a conservative or traditional voice. That voice is often made to feel unwelcome at God's table. In addition, there is a complete lack of accountability in our Church. No one dreams of measuring a bishop's ministry and holding him or her accountable for growing the Church. The titular heads of the Church in the United States and England travel widely, preach and take part in ceremonies to *maintain* the Church, and *affirm* what is occurring, but no one holds them *accountable* for growth. If growth were deemed important, then church budgets on local, national, and international levels would be examined to see what funds were spent that led to growth in numbers and what funds produced no growth whatsoever. Immediately, the thought comes to mind that there are many kinds of growth. Certainly, there is growth in depth, producing more knowledgeable and committed Christians. But this, too, could and should be measured. The lack of accountability and willingness to demand that our spiritual leaders are moving us in directions that lead to growth is a key reason why the mainline churches are shrinking.

If a leader were given five years and could not produce growth, it would be fair for a congregation, a diocese, or a national church to change leaders and find someone who could grow their parish or diocese. In the end, the single best gauge of future performance is past performance. If a leader has not grown his or her previous church, those who consider hiring such a leader must strongly consider whether or not it makes sense to call that leader to their parish, diocese, or national church. We need bishops who know how to grow churches.

On both our national and international levels within the Episcopal Church and Anglican Communion, we have engaged leaders who are articulate and bright, but some of them have never served as full-time rectors of parishes and have little experience in growing a church. To put such people at the top of an organizational structure is an outward and visible sign we do not give priority to growing the Church at large and those who are identifying and selecting our leaders fail to see growth as a criterion for leadership. Our leaders have bought into a model of serving as stewards of a dying institution. We need a new narrative. We need leaders with an entrepreneurial spirit, who can seed growth.

We Have Lost Our Focus on the Bible

The most important reason for our lack of growth, however, is not the fact that our leaders are not being held accountable, but rather our lack of focus on the Bible. We have failed to harness the most powerful tool that we have to accomplish our mission and transform lives in significant, measurable ways. Too many of us have bought into a highly bureaucratic model of maintaining a large, cumbersome Church with lots of hierarchy and procedures that suck up much of our top leadership's time and energy. It is the black hole that absorbs the attention, talent, and time of our best and brightest. One needs only to attend the General Convention of the Episcopal Church to see how little focus our national church places on numerical growth, accountability, and measurement, as well as on the Bible. Evenings spent apart from the meetings and discussions and debates are like a floating cocktail party of old friends reuniting from across the country. Most of the deputies are repeaters who eagerly look forward to returning again to the next convention to get reacquainted with old friends. Much of this is great but there is a real missed opportunity that takes place every three years. Instead of exposing our leaders to best practices and studying where the greatest growth is occurring, our focus seems to be mostly on affirming diversity. While it sounds good, it is not leading to growth. We are becoming an increasingly smaller but more diverse group of people who will soon lack the power and financial resources to carry out our mission and make a difference in the world.

A Different Kind of Convention

The "Uncovering the Word Conference" was a completely different experience from attending a General Convention of the Episcopal Church. Everything was geared towards growth, conversion, impact, spiritual transformation, and measurement. The most powerful presentations came from Cally Parkinson, who helped to co-write *Move: What 1,000 Churches Reveal about Spiritual Growth*, and from other members of the Willow Creek Community Association.

Willow Creek is the third largest church in the United States, but it had begun to plateau in its growth. Its leaders also wanted to spend money more judiciously and minister more effectively. They decided to spend money in areas of ministry that helped people to grow spiritually and cut their spending in areas that did not lead to numerical growth or deeper individual spiritual growth. Parkinson noted they were surprised to learn three shocking facts about their congregation:

1. "increased participation in church activities by themselves *barely moved* our people to love God and others more;
2. we had a lot of dissatisfied people;
3. we had a lot of people so dissatisfied that they were ready to leave."

Willow Creek began a survey to inform the future direction of their church, which slowly evolved into the REVEAL Spiritual Life Survey—a tool that has since been used to study over fifteen hundred diverse congregations across the United States. Well over three hundred and fifty thousand people who attend these churches have supplied information about their spiritual journeys and growth that has led to a new way of understanding what it takes to lead and create a spiritually vibrant church.

Their learnings included:

- Church activities do not predict or drive long-term spiritual growth. In other words, increasing church attendance or having more people participate in ministries does not equate with increased spiritual growth. Church activities have the greatest influence in the *early* stages of spiritual growth, but things like personal spiritual practices, including prayer and Bible reading, have far more influence later in the spiritual journey.

- Many apathetic nonbelievers who attend church are unlikely to ever accept Christ. In fact, the longer they have attended church, the more likely they are content with the pace of their spiritual growth, or to say they are "stalled."

- Nothing has greater impact on spiritual growth than reflection on Scripture. If churches could do only one thing to help people at all levels of spiritual maturity and growth in their relationship with Christ, their choice is clear. They would inspire, encourage, and equip their people to read the Bible—specifically, to reflect on Scripture for meaning in their lives. The numbers say most churches are missing the mark because only one out of five congregants reflects on Scripture every day.

- Spiritually stalled or dissatisfied people account for one out of four church congregants. On average, 13 percent of all congregants select the word *stalled* to describe their pace of spiritual growth; 18 percent of those surveyed described themselves as "dissatisfied"—in some churches the number was as high as 50 percent.

- There is no "killer app" for spiritual growth. While the REVEAL study identified a number of churches that were spiritual powerhouses, the study found no "save the day" program that guarantees discipleship success.

- Leadership matters. The leaders of the more highly successful churches who participated in the REVEAL survey have diverse personalities and styles. Some are quiet and reserved. Others are very self-assured and commanding. They all share one key attribute: they possess an unrelenting, uncompromising focus and drive to help grow people into disciples of Christ.

These findings continued the earthquake I began to experience after meeting Simon Barnes. I began to feel that these evangelical leaders gathered at the conference were light years ahead of Episcopal and mainline church leaders across the United States. We were using the Bible much as we had for over four hundred and fifty years, but now we were using only selections so as not to challenge our members with the more difficult passages. We were amateurs in a world where others had become serious professionals capable of sharing and teaching God's Word and helping others to learn to read the Word of God on their own in order to experience bold spiritual transformation.

Two Days Spent at Yale Is Very Revealing

The final part of this welcomed but disruptive spiritual earthquake in my life came from attending a two-day conference sponsored by the Berkeley Divinity School at Yale and the Yale Divinity School. During that conference, the Rev. Jay Sidebotham, former rector of the Church of the Holy Spirit in Lake Forest, Illinois and the founder of Renewal Works, spoke along with Eric Arnson, who is a brilliant business thinker and worked for many years for McKinsey & Company, consulting with Fortune 500 companies around the world. He retired early and had a buy-out clause, which prevented him from consulting with any competitors of his former firm for a period of time.

Somehow, he stumbled into the Willow Creek Community Church and was impressed by what they were doing. Arnson offered to give them one free day of consulting each month and played a pivotal role in shaping and developing the REVEAL study. Between Cally Parkinson's presentation in Orlando and Arnson's in New Haven, I learned that the REVEAL study discovered four groups of congregants in virtually every church they surveyed across the United States. They surveyed over fifteen hundred congregations of all sizes and many different denominations. The four groups consist of people who are:

- **Exploring Christ**—These are people who have often recently joined a congregation, know little about how it functions and are just learning the ropes. They self-describe as "I believe in God, but I am not sure about Christ. My faith is not a significant part of my life."

- **Growing in Christ**—These are people who have started to make their way into the life of the church and have learned a bit about how the congregation functions. They may now serve on the altar guild or be a lay reader or an usher. They know how to have flowers given as a memorial to a loved one who has died and understand similar functions of the church. They self-describe as "I believe in Jesus, and I am working on what it means to get to know him."

- **Close to Christ**—These are people who, as they drive off the church property following worship on Sunday, have Jesus riding in the passenger seat beside them. They are on a true spiritual journey, but they continue to be the pilot of their own plane. Jesus is in the navigator's seat, offering wisdom and direction, which they may freely accept or decline. They self-describe as "I feel really close to Christ and depend on him daily for guidance."

- **Christ-Centered**—These folks drive off the church property following Sunday worship, but Jesus is driving the car and they are riding in the passenger seat. It's a completely different experience. Jesus is helping to take charge of their lives. They have surrendered themselves to God, an anathema to most mainline Christians and Episcopalians, who are so well-educated and trained that the idea of surrendering to anyone or anything sounds abhorrent. These persons self-describe as "My relationship with Jesus is the most important relationship in my life. It guides everything that I do."

The crucial problem for mainline churches and Episcopalians is that we are producing very few people who would be classified as "Close to Christ" or "Christ-Centered." We excel at producing people who are "Growing in Christ," but we stall after getting them to this level of spiritual growth and development, which is a critical issue for our churches.

What fed my spiritual earthquake was to learn from Jay, Cally, and Eric that in each case the number-one way to help someone take the next step forward in their faith journey, regardless of where they were, was regular engagement with Scripture. It was not attending Sunday worship, serving on the altar guild, becoming an usher, teaching Sunday school, practicing Centering Prayer, working at a soup kitchen, participating in a mission trip, going on spiritual retreat, taking a pilgrimage, or walking a labyrinth. All of these are great ways to participate in the life of the church, but none of these is the number-one spiritual tool to help individuals grow in their knowledge and love of Jesus. The number-one spiritual tool is regular engagement with Scripture. The problem is this tool is our weakest suit in the Episcopal and mainline churches. This is where we often get a failing grade. Yet this alone is the number-one way to help people grow in their relationship with Christ. The time is ripe for Episcopalians and mainline church members to put the Bible back in the center of our ministry and lives.

CHAPTER 5

Why Sunday Cannot Be the Only Spiritual Day of the Week

". . . . my heart stands in awe of your words. I rejoice at your Word like one who finds a great spoil."—PSALM 119: 161–162

"Indeed, the word of God is alive and active, sharper than any two-edged sword, piercing until it divides soul from spirit, joints from marrow; it is able to judge the thoughts and intentions of the heart."—HEBREWS 4:12

"When you read God's Word, you must constantly be saying to yourself, 'It is talking to me and about me.'"—SOREN KIERKEGAARD

•◆•

Mainline Christian denominations have been steadily decreasing for the past fifty years. We have long prided ourselves on our focus on social justice, and we have been strong leaders in this important area of ministry. We have championed important causes. People once filled our churches to hear what our clergy had to say about the issues. That is no longer the case in most churches. People are less inclined to look to the clergy to make pronouncements on vital ethical issues, especially as they have increasingly come to divide our nation. People are bombarded by communications coming at them from all directions, and it is easy for them to access information and viewpoints of specialists and world-renowned thinkers about any topic that concerns them. There is less need to look to the parish priest to address social issues.

As the mainline church continues to focus on social causes, the populace in general has become more concerned about developing a close relationship with God, finding purpose in their daily lives, and nurturing their families and vital relationships. They are interested issues such as forgiveness, alleviating stress, and developing the moral and spiritual life of their children. Church conflicts and talk about taking sides on divisive issues are about the last things prospective or current church members want to hear about when they come to worship on Sundays.

Growing Churches Focus on the Bible

Across the United States the churches that are growing are strongly focused on the Bible. They do not use it to shine a light on divisive social issues such as stem cell cloning or abortion, but rather to focus on the daily needs and challenges facing their members and guests. The hunger for this type of study is universal. In addition, these churches build a strong foundation of small groups that meet during the week and encourage their members to develop a deeper knowledge of the Bible. The priority for many of these churches is in what they contribute to the lives of their members during the week as opposed to merely on Sunday. The entire week is seen as a time of teaching and growing in faith.

By contrast, Episcopalians are the best-educated Christians in the United States, according to church historian and author Diana Butler Bass. While not a numerically large denomination, Episcopalians have historically outpunched our weight in terms of holding political office or serving as heads of corporations and other institutions. Until twenty years ago, Episcopalians produced more senators and congressman and CEOs than any other denomination, including the Roman Catholic Church, which is over thirty times larger. To this day, Episcopalians have produced more United States presidents than any other religious group.

Eight Words That Changed the Church

Being an Episcopalian once carried a great deal of prestige. We were the church of the upper crust and high society, the pedigreed elite and ruling class of those who could afford country clubs, private schools, and Ivy League educations. In his book *Bobos in Paradise*, author, essayist, and social commentator David Brooks notes that "about half of the couples who were featured in the late fifties" in *The New York Times* "were married in an Episcopal ceremony. Today fewer than one in five of the marriages of the *Times* are Episcopalian, while around 40 percent are Jewish, and there are many more Asian names." I used to read through those pages to see the weddings that my friends had officiated at over the weekend. Now, it makes little sense. I suspect that Brooks' current numbers are overinflated and that today less than 5 percent of the weddings covered in the *Times* involve an Episcopal ceremony.

Today there are swarms of people featured who are being married by a justice of the peace, a rabbi, an imam, or, even more commonly, a universalist minister—a title that any American adult can receive after spending about ten minutes on the computer and filling out a form. Where have the prestige and the cachet of the Episcopal Church gone? They have clearly diminished. In many ways the Episcopal Church was a club. We thrived and reached our pinnacle in the late Fifties, when membership in a prestigious club was at its height.

One can just imagine a couple talking to friends and saying, "Our daughter is getting married to a young man who attended Deerfield and Yale and is now working at J.P. Morgan. She is active in the Junior League, and they are buying a house in Greenwich, Connecticut, where his family lives, and joining the Episcopal Church." To say this was to signify that they had all the right tickets—the right schools, the right job, the right community, the right volunteer organization and the right church. It was all upward, exhilarating, and elitist. The Episcopal Church was clearly part of the upper crust, which brought it into conflict when addressing biblical initiatives.

Then the Sixties happened. People protested against the Vietnam War. A drug culture broke out. Whether or not it was because of drugs, many young people lost interest in the upward path that led a person from high school to college to their first job, then to graduate school, marriage, starting a family, and settling in a nice neighborhood. All of a sudden that sounded boring. A generation was spawned that rebelled against institutions, thumbed its nose at major companies, conservative political parties, elitist schools and universities, establishment organizations, and mainline churches. The winds were starting to blow against mainline churches.

On September 19, 1985, Bishop Edmund Browning was elected to succeed the Most Reverend John Maury Allin as the XXIV Presiding Bishop of the Episcopal Church at the General Convention of the Episcopal Church held in Anaheim, California. He was elected to a twelve-year term, and in many ways he was a wonderful presiding bishop of the church.

Shortly after his election, Bishop Browning shared his vision for the Episcopal Church:

> There are tremendous global issues that face us all. My hope is that the Church can continue to hold these issues before the full membership, as well as society, to bring about some well-being for all. I think the Church has a role in being both prophetic in holding up issues, and using all its influences to try to bring about better conditions for the poor, the hungry, both in this country as well as in the global village.

Then he uttered eight words that began to change the very nature of the once staid and elite Episcopal Church: "There will be no outcasts in the Church."

The idea that there would be no outcasts in the Episcopal Church became a sort of clarion call throughout the denomination over the following two decades. Everyone was welcome in the Episcopal Church. The doors were flung wide open. It was no longer an institution for the well-educated, well-dressed, well-groomed, well-behaved, and socially-established members of America's tonier communities. The doors were now open to anyone.

On January 16, 1986, Bishop Browning was installed as the Presiding Bishop in the Washington National Cathedral. During his sermon, he addressed the deepening rift within the church over issues such as the ordination of women and homosexuality, by saying "[do not ask me] to honor one set of views and disregard the other. I may agree with one, but I will respect both . . . the unity of this church will be maintained not because we agree on everything but because—hopefully—we will leave judgment to God."

Browning's theologically liberal views earned him admiration from progressives and intense criticism from the conservative wing of the church. A rift developed during his tenure over whether openly homosexual clergy could be ordained and whether same sex unions could be blessed by the church. The tensions broke into a public exchange at the 1991 General Convention in Phoenix, Arizona during a session of the House of Bishops that prompted Browning to make the unusual move of calling for a closed session gathering. Like the car ad, "This is not your father's Oldsmobile," suddenly, it was no longer your mother's and father's Episcopal Church.

The Advent of the Baptismal Covenant

The once aristocratic spiritual home of captains of industry like J.P. Morgan was now filling with people of all races and socio-economic strata, widely-varying educational backgrounds, a broader spectrum of theological and political beliefs, and different sexual orientations The Episcopal Church stood at the forefront of social change. All sorts of causes were embraced. There were few liberal causes that the Church's hierarchy chose not to champion. The idea of the church being a "social club" was now over. The question is what concept or image of the church had replaced it? What was the substance upon which the Episcopal Church stood? What were its unifying values? The Church now focused on the Baptismal Covenant, which became a de-facto credo for the Church.

At every baptism in the Episcopal Church, each worshiper stands up and recites the Baptismal Covenant with the congregation. Each person states that he or she will "seek and serve Christ in all persons, loving their neighbor as themselves" and promising to "strive for justice and peace among all people, and respect the dignity of every human being." They pledge to "continue in the apostles' teaching and fellowship, in the breaking of bread, and in the prayers," and vow to "persevere in resisting evil" and whenever they sin, to "repent and return to the Lord." They also commit to "proclaim by word and example the Good News of God in Christ."

These are great ideals, but there is little direct biblical guidance offered. The Baptismal Creed is an amalgam of biblical themes that merge with the progressive ideals of extending tolerance to everyone and refraining from making anyone feel judged or excluded. The closest thing that mirrors Scripture is the vow to "continue in the apostles' teaching and fellowship, in the breaking of bread, and in the prayers," which comes directly from Acts 2:42. The Baptismal Covenant thus became the focal point for a generation of Episcopalians who repeat it like a mantra, but no longer read the Bible.

While we continued to outpunch our weight as a denomination, the media no longer turned to Episcopal bishops or to leaders in the Evangelical Lutheran Church in America or to the Moderator of the Presbyterian Church for sound-bites about major moral issues facing the nation. Newspapers eliminated their religion reporters, and the few articles about religion in the newspaper often portrayed the church in a negative light, especially with the focus in the last ten years on the child sexual abuse scandal of the Roman Catholic Church, which claims to have 68 million members. (This number is greatly inflated as Roman Catholics do not remove people from their church rolls unless specifically asked.) The clout of the mainline church had vanished. The number of worshipers in Episcopal, Presbyterian, Lutheran, Methodist and Congregational churches continued to drop steadily.

In the Episcopal Church, we have been operating for too long on an old bureaucratic model of ministry that was designed for a growing and thriving church, but which sucks up far too much energy maintaining a shrinking institution of highly educated people. Our best energies as a national church have been expended on debates over contentious ethical issues and operating a growing bureaucracy in a day and age when most church members no longer understand what a diocese is or what the National Church contributes to their own spiritual journey. The tides were changing, and churches and dioceses that did not shift with them began closing and shrinking. The Church was actually initiating more Christ-like initiatives, speaking prophetically and serving the poor in profound ways, but the focus on the Bible was becoming obscured at times.

Why Has the Bible Disappeared from Sight?

Speaking at a clergy conference in the Diocese of Pennsylvania, author Diana Butler Bass noted that Episcopalians have a higher percentage of members with advanced degrees than any of the 21,985 other Christian denominations and groups in the United States. Educating our children is among our highest priorities. Our members go on to receive more advanced degrees per capita than any other Christian group in the United States. Only Hindus and Jews rank ahead of us in terms of other religious groups' ability to produce members with advanced degrees. When the question is asked about biblical literacy, however, the tables are reversed. Episcopalians rank almost last among Christian groups when it comes to knowing our Bible.

Why does this matter? Our inability to draw wisdom and understanding readily from the Bible produces Christians with an anemic faith, like a low wattage light bulb that dimly glows. Not being steeped in our Bible matters greatly because almost all of the growing churches in the United States are biblically centered. For years Episcopalians have laughed that we are the denomination that knows little about the Bible, and for the past fifty years our denomination has steadily declined. There is a strong correlation between our decline and our inability to engage regularly with the Bible and draw from it daily spiritual wisdom and power. We can no longer pride ourselves on being the denomination that does not know the Bible unless we want our churches to vanish completely.

What are the obstacles that deter Episcopalians from regular Bible reading? For one, many Episcopalians associate the practice with evangelicals and fundamentalists. We have a quiet fear that if we read the Bible it might lead us in an undesirable direction or transform us into people we do not want to be. We have mental images of people who read the Bible and become overly vocal about their faith. Many of us find this offensive and fear that it could happen to us. Episcopalians as a rule, therefore, place little focus on regularly reading the Bible. An outward and visible sign is how hard it is to find a Bible in the pews of most Episcopal churches.

As our members are well educated, so are our clergy. Episcopal clergy are often second career persons. Many began as lawyers, doctors, teachers, business executives, administrators, or leaders in other fields who left to pursue a call and attend seminary. Hence, many have more than one master's degree. Our heightened focus on education means that we teach others to read and study Scripture. We sometimes place the Bible like a cadaver on an operating table before a group that gathers around a priest or teacher who helps them to examine each sinew or muscle, or, in the case of the Bible, questions dates, locations, and details relating to each text. As a result, mainline church members often believe that they need a priest or trained teacher in the room with them in order to comprehend what lies between the covers of the Bible. Most Episcopalians believe that they are not equipped to read it on their own—even if only to seek spiritual wisdom and strength.

The Lectionary Has Taken the Focus Away from the Bible

Many Episcopal clergy have been indoctrinated to believe the Lectionary rather than the entire Bible is what we are meant to read. Hence, they attempt to discourage church members from reading from the whole Bible, as if various passages of Scripture may be harmful to the spiritual health of one who is not ordained. Yet, as we have noted, when Archbishop Thomas Cranmer, who authored and edited the first Book of Common Prayer in 1549, created a reading plan, it called for reading the entire New Testament three times and almost the entire Old Testament in the course of each year. No verses were omitted. My church belongs to a group of endowed churches that represent many of the largest and best-run Episcopal churches in the country. From conversations with colleagues in this group over the past two decades, I suspect that in the average large Episcopal congregation fewer than 5 percent of the members regularly attend a Bible study. The remaining 95 percent only engage Scripture when they come to church for worship, where it is read aloud.

According to Kirk Hadaway, Officer for Congregational Research in the Episcopal Church, information on the activities of Episcopalians is rather difficult to come by, since surveying members is difficult and costly. However, 84 percent of Episcopal churches say they have regular Bible studies in addition to Sunday school, with 44 percent indicating that Bible studies are a key activity or major emphasis. The Episcopal Church does not know how many Bible studies are offered, which in itself is interesting. We measure membership, average Sunday attendance, baptisms, and confirmations, but we do not measure how many Bible studies are held or how many people attend them. If we were serious about the Bible, we would measure our study of it.

Clarifying what it means to be an Episcopalian is even more difficult, but among those who consider themselves Episcopalians and have responded to national surveys, merged data from 2006–2012 indicate that 30 percent of adult Episcopalians attend church nearly every week or more. When we look at the people in the pews, as did a major survey conducted by the Office of Congregational Research and the Church Pension Group, the Episcopalians who attend church regularly are much more active in ministries and study opportunities. This survey revealed that 74 percent of Episcopalians report attending worship nearly every week or more. I know of no rector of a large Episcopal church who sees this kind of attendance.

The survey reported that 26 percent of the active members surveyed said they attended a Bible study or prayer group. Of this group of active members, 41 percent reported that they were engaged in some form of devotional activity, which may or may not include personal Bible study every day, and another 21 percent did so a few times each week. Unfortunately, the Episcopal Church does not have any further information regarding the Bible reading practices and habits of its members or their practice of reading through the entire Bible.

Biblical literacy is a bit subjective unless we are talking about a Bible test of some sort. A few surveys have tried such a thing, but they are quite old. The Episcopal Church did ask if active members could recite the Apostles' Creed. A total of 55 percent could recite all of it and another 31 percent could recite some of it. The Creed is not directly about the Bible, but it gets at religious literacy. Where Episcopalians do excel is when it comes to reading the Bible in worship. Our worship is traditional and often lively and well-executed. We read as many or more passages from the Bible in worship than any denomination or group in the United States and beyond. The Gospel has a prominent and featured role in our worship. Why then are we so biblically ignorant?

Faith Does Not Necessarily Come from What Is Heard

St. Paul wrote that faith comes from hearing. He was writing about the power of preaching and communicating the faith of Jesus Christ through the spoken word. Hearing the Bible read aloud in church, however, is different. We assume that our listeners are learning the Bible stories and the teachings of Jesus because of the vast amount of Scripture that is read in church Sunday after Sunday. We are wrong to value our reading aloud in worship so much. One reason that we struggle to comprehend the Bible is almost all of what is heard is quickly forgotten. A study conducted by the United States Air Force revealed that seventy-two hours after we hear something read aloud or spoken, we retain only 5 to 10 percent of what we have heard. Therefore, by noon on Wednesday we have forgotten 90 to 95 percent of what we heard in church the previous Sunday morning. In terms of retaining what was read aloud in church, where there are lots of distractions for the eye and ear, the percentage may be lower.

The proof of this inability to learn and retain the Bible through hearing alone comes when church leaders attempt to recruit Sunday school teachers. Many invitees quickly respond, "I cannot teach. I appreciate the invitation, but I simply do not know enough to teach others." My first response is, "We are not asking you to teach a group of Ph.D. candidates, but rather a group of third-graders." Still, their comfort level is low. Most of our members simply do not feel equipped to teach the Bible. We should be concerned.

We Are Producing Non-Contagious Christians

We should see a strong warning sign that our members who have been attending church regularly for decades still lack the confidence to teach the Christian message to a roomful of ten-year-olds. It is just one of many indications that we are failing to engage our members in regularly reading the Scriptures and appropriating God's Word and wisdom for their daily living. One cannot share what has not been fully received. Hence, mainline churches across the country are producing non-contagious Christians, who are like sheep that are incapable of producing lambs. This is a major reason all mainline Christian denominations are shrinking.

Episcopalians are not alone in facing this challenge with reading and understanding the Bible. While the Bible has been the world's best-selling book decade after decade, it often goes unread. The average American owns four Bibles. The average Christian owns eleven, but most of these are gathering dust. They are located in boxes, buried in basements, or tucked away on a shelf somewhere. We do not need more Bibles or even more Bible studies. What we need are meaningful and successful ways to help individuals read through this life-giving and ancient library of spiritual texts that are truly inspired by God.

While the Church of England counts a membership of 26 million members, less than eight hundred thousand are found in worship on an average Sunday. Despite what the Office of Congregational Research notes, I am told that the average Episcopalian now attends worship just once a month. In my parish, we have a large group who attend worship every Sunday. We have a tiny group who attend on both Wednesday and Sunday. We have a large group that attends twice a month on average. We have those who come once every month or two. We also have those who attend twice a year, usually for Christmas and Easter, and we have those who consider themselves members but never darken the door. We will see most of them at some point for a funeral, wedding, major event, or following a national tragedy. All told, when you put these various groups together the notion that the average Episcopalian now attends church once a month rings true from my twenty-five years of experience in parish ministry.

Why is this a problem? The problem is that doing anything only once a month brings little if any measureable result. If we diet once a month, we won't lose weight. If we go to the gym once a month, we won't get physically stronger. If we study a foreign language once a month, we will never master it. If we practice a musical instrument once a month, we will never learn to play. If we do anything just once a month, we can be guaranteed to make almost no measurable progress. To do a thing well, we have to create a discipline that will allow us to participate three, four, or more times a week. Optimally, we will endeavor to create a daily discipline if we truly want to see significant measureable results.

From my experience as a parish priest, worshipers who attend once a month usually arrive with their spiritual gas tank registering empty. They arrive having not read or listened to the Bible or perhaps having done nothing overtly spiritual for the past thirty days to strengthen their souls. They sit quietly and listen as portions of the Bible that are almost completely unfamiliar to them are read aloud. Meanwhile, a child distracts them during one lesson. Their eyes are captivated by a stained-glass window during another. The psalm is sung by the choir, and they enjoy the music but fail to comprehend most of the words. Their mind wanders or they are annoyed by the sound of a swirling ceiling fan and someone wearing a large hat sitting in front of them during the Gospel. Four lessons are read aloud but almost all of the content is completely lost on them. Because the *lectio*nary omits much of the Bible and jumps around a bit, it only adds to the difficulty of understanding how the narrative coheres. Most readings begin in the middle of some unfolding action. Things we don't know about have already taken place, especially if we have not been in worship for several weeks or have not read the Bible.

The experience for most worshipers in an Episcopal church is like walking into a movie halfway through the film and wondering, "Who are the characters? What's the plot? What is going on and why does it matter?" Worshipers sit in church, look attentive, and pretend they comprehend what is being said and find it meaningful, but most who are not regular Bible readers are simply befuddled as lessons from the Bible are read aloud in church.

It's Hard to Preach to People Who Have Never Read the Bible

Most preachers must spend time during the sermon explaining what was just read in one or more of the lessons. Who are the characters? What occurred before this passage of Scripture took place? Why does it matter? What do we need to know about what we just heard? All of this is remedial work. What a biblically literate worshipper would have known from the outset must be explained to those who don't read their Bibles. Our sermons are becoming more and more like explanations or commentaries on an ancient text rather than true proclamations of God's Word that inspire and equip listeners for faithful Christian living.

As if it were not enough to realize that the average worshipper in my tradition attends only once a month, the more startling fact is there is no measureable difference in positive moral behavior found in the lives of those who worship once a week and those who never worship at all. Most mainline churches build their entire ministry around trying to attract people to attend church on Sunday, yet our success has been steadily declining for fifty years. The number of competing activities on a Sunday morning is staggering: soccer games, occasional school programs, family outings, television shows, community programs, and other assorted events. Some families are now selecting Sunday mornings to celebrate birthday parties and invite their children's friends to join them, because this is the *only time* in the week where they can schedule something without too many other competing events. Others claim that Sunday is the only day in the week when their family can sleep in, wake up and eat a leisurely breakfast together. I know from our family's experience with three daughters that this has almost always been the case.

Why Filling Our Church with Worshippers Is Not Enough

Trying to fill a church with worshippers on Sunday morning is swimming against the current. Even if we were to succeed and fill our church pews Sunday after Sunday, studies indicate that the people who worship once a week do not have a significantly higher measurable pattern of moral behavior than those who never attend church. If you went to the gym once a week and a friend of yours never went or exercised in any fashion ever, he or she may still actually be healthier than you are. Your friend may have better DNA. Perhaps his or her parents are still alive or lived into their late eighties or nineties. But if you go to the gym four or more times a week and eat healthily, it is likely that your stronger exercise and eating regimen will trump their better DNA and lead you to be healthier and live a longer, more vibrant life.

The same principle applies to building our faith. If a person attends church once a week, he or she may well be surpassed in moral behavior by someone who is an inherently fine moral person who learned excellent values from his or her parents. But studies reveal that those who engage Scripture four times or more each week demonstrate a noticeably stronger positive set of moral behaviors than those who do not engage Scripture at all. This difference can be measured, which is why mainline churches can no longer afford to put all of our eggs into one basket called

"Getting them to church once a week." Even if we succeed in the short term and get more people in church every Sunday, we are likely to fail in the long run, because once-a-week churchgoers' lives are not changed. If, however, we set our goal higher and focus on helping our members and guests to develop a regular lifelong daily spiritual practice of reading the Bible, we can make a great deal of difference in the world, and especially in their world.

CHAPTER 6

Discovering the Power
of a Daily Spiritual Discipline

"Happy are those who do not follow the advice of the wicked, or take the path that sinners tread, or sit in the seat of scoffers; but their delight is in the law of the Lord, and on his law they meditate day and night. They are like trees planted by streams of water, which yield their fruit in its season, and their leaves do not wither. In all that they do, they prosper."— Psalm 1:1–3

"Listen less to your own thoughts and more to God's thoughts."—François Fénelon

"It is a mistake to look to the Bible to close a discussion; the Bible seeks to open one."—The Rev. William Sloane Coffin

•◆•

In his short masterpiece, *The Nicomachean Ethics,* Aristotle stressed that each one of us is a product of our daily habits. We rise in the morning, brush our teeth, shower, make our bed, dress, eat breakfast, and head off to work or school, to visit friends, or to volunteer. We are an amalgam of the things that we do on a regular basis. We are a product of our habits, and our habits create our character. Our habits determine whether or not we are virtuous people.

If we consistently tell the truth, then truth-telling becomes a habit, a part of who were are, and lying can become difficult or almost impossible. If we are generous in each situation where we have the chance to be generous, then the generosity reinforces itself and it becomes easier and easier for us to be generous. If we put the needs of others ahead of ours, then being selfless becomes one of our virtues, which others can see and appreciate. In time, they will come to expect selfless behavior as part of our character.

Aristotle said, "It makes no small difference to be habituated this way or that way straight from childhood, but an enormous difference, or rather *all* the difference." We all start out life governed by desires and impulses. One of the crucial tasks for every parent is to instill in their children a series of healthy habits that lead to a good, meaningful, and productive life. These include getting adequate sleep, eating healthy foods, exercising, cleaning up after ourselves, and taking care of our bodies. Other virtues include studying diligently, nurturing friendships, learning how to share and get along with others, giving and asking for forgiveness, volunteering, working hard, listening attentively, praying, reading the Bible, and attending church. Our childish impulses are never completely eradicated, but over time our souls are brought nearer to a harmonious state that comes from exercising moral virtues. The road to these virtues is not fancy. It begins when parents train a child, often by withholding some desired thing, until a child without virtues begins to behave virtuously. It is what Hamlet describes to his mother during a strange role reversal where a son attempts to train his parent:

> Assume a virtue if you have it not.
> That monster, custom, who all sense doth eat
> Of habits evil, is angel yet in this,
> That to the use of actions fair and good
> He likewise gives a frock or livery,
> That aptly is put on. Refrain tonight,
> And that shall lend a kind of easiness
> To the next abstinence; the next more easy;
> For use almost can change the stamp of nature . . .

Hamlet is talking to his middle-aged mother about lust, but the pattern applies just as well to a child who wants dessert before eating her dinner.

Life Is about Developing Strong Virtues

Aristotle belongs to a long line of ethicists known today as *virtue ethicists*. Virtue ethics sees virtues akin to skills we can develop as an athlete would. All of us have varying potential in life, but virtues can be acquired and developed. We are free agents. Every action is underpinned by free choice. We are free at any moment to choose to act in a faithful and virtuous manner. Each time we do, it becomes easier to do so the next time. We accrue virtuous behavior like an athlete who repeats the same motion over and over again, until she or he hits a tennis ball or golf ball or performs a pirouette on skates in just the right manner.

Saints are people who have perfected their virtues and have performed virtuous acts over and over again. A saint is not an altogether different species of person. Rather, he or she is someone who has developed holy habits and God works through these habitual holy acts and holy people in ways that bring grace to others. Sainthood is therefore a possibility for all of us. Saints are people for whom virtue has become second nature.

Like everything else, reading Scripture requires forming a daily spiritual practice until it becomes a habit. Over the years in my parish, I had started a number of Bible studies and study groups, most of which had a beginning and an end. I was the teacher and enjoyed expounding on a text. I loved to research and prepare my lectures and studies. I delighted when people expressed wonder at how much I knew. My brain is not very retentive, so much of what I shared had to be reviewed before I spoke and came from last minute study to prepare my lectures. The whole enterprise was more akin to spiritual entertainment. I was the actor. My class was full of passive participants. Over time, I have become convinced that this method of learning was only partially successful at best when it came to producing saints and shaping a holy people.

If I may use an analogy, it is akin to having lots of people in a stadium watching two people play tennis. The two on the court are working up a sweat and demonstrating great agility, nerves, and athletic prowess. The hundreds or possibly thousands watching in the stands, however, are getting no workout and are perhaps not even equipped to hit a tennis ball back across the net. In the Church, our goal must be to get more people out of the stands and onto the court so that they can participate and more fully experience Christian living and learning.

The Church's Role is Not to Foster Dependence

Our job in the church is not to fish for people, but to teach them how to fish. The person who fishes for them becomes like the chiropractor whom a person describes by saying, "I don't know what I would do without him. I have to see him at least once or twice a week to feel good." Such a practice may create an unhealthy dependency. Our role in the church is to teach people how to become holy so they may enjoy a lifetime of holy living without depending on us. If we have wonderful skills, they will enjoy learning more from us but our ultimate goal is to make ourselves dispensable so that they can flourish on their own as holy people living and serving in communities of faith and moving far beyond the walls of the church to serve others.

In every church I have served, people already had well-established habits. Most of them got adequate sleep, ate fairly healthy diets, exercised, cleaned up after themselves, took good care of their bodies, studied or worked diligently, nurtured a number of friendships, and volunteered. Most of them also attended church with some regularity.

What most of them did not have is a daily spiritual practice. They had not discovered a satisfactory way to reach out to God each day in prayer. They had no daily practice of reading God's Word. Many had never even opened a Bible on their own. Their spiritual life consisted of attending church, thanking God for their blessings, listening to the Bible being read aloud, attending to the sermon, confessing their sins, singing hymns, receiving the Eucharist, and enjoying Christian fellowship. This is certainly far better than never going to church at all, even if studies suggest that worshipping once a week does not change our moral behavior in any measurable way.

By worshipping regularly, we learn principles that quietly fill our hearts, minds, and souls. The entire process is a Copernican Revolution that turns us inside out. We enter church often very self-consumed with our own problems and challenges. During the course of the service, we are invited to offer prayers of adoration, praise, thanksgiving, oblation, repentance, and petition. We are encouraged to think of others, who are often more needy than we are. Our focus is turned from looking within to looking beyond ourselves. In the process, a quiet grace often fills our hearts and usually leaves us grateful that we came to worship.

On Monday, however, we enter a different world that is often fiercely competitive, where some people cannot be trusted, and where the rules that we learn on Sunday do not seem to apply. Our weekday world seems non-stop. Many of us are bombarded by hundreds of emails, telephone calls, texts, tweets, faxes, instagrams, pieces of mail, delays, deadlines, distractions, conversations, interruptions, appointments, assignments, and complete surprises. By Wednesday, the peaceful moment found on Sunday morning feels like ancient history.

We Need a Daily Spiritual Practice

What Christianity has lost and needs to rediscover is not a better way of celebrating the Sabbath, but a better way of creating Sabbath moments throughout the week. One need only hear about the thousands of messages that bombard us each day from advertisers on television, in newspapers, on the radio, online, on billboards, in trains, on planes and in buses, at the movies, in elevators, on buildings, in junk mail, and spam to realize that the Christian message from Sunday morning is drowned by a week full of very different ones. These more secular messages often have taglines such as "Be all that you can be," "Go for the gusto," "Because you only go around once," "Do all that you can do," or "You'll find happiness for yourself by. . . ."

They leave us convinced that the secret to joy and happiness is found in purchasing certain goods, acquiring particular possessions, becoming wealthy, developing the body of a fashion model or a body builder, driving a fancy car, living in a mansion, or taking fancy vacations. If this were the case, then most Americans would be much happier than they are. Yet we see higher levels of depression, eating disorders, and general lack of contentment as our material wealth increases. We were not designed solely to be consumers who take in possessions and hold onto them. We were designed to receive love and pass it on to others.

In order to stay in synch with God and be reminded that we were formed to love and serve God and discover our deepest joy, we need to develop a habit of connecting with God every day. Our schedules vary, but it usually works out best if we can find some God time first thing in the day. This allows us to reset our spiritual compass before the day unfolds.

Coptic Christians in Ethiopia have a practice of setting a small bowl of water by their bedside. When they awake in the morning from an evening of sleep, they touch the water with their fingers and place a small amount on their forehead, each shoulder, and chest as they trace the cross upon their body and say, "Into thy hands I commend my spirit this day, O Lord." That simple practice is a way of turning oneself inside out. Many of us wake up each morning as a pagan. Our first thoughts are often, "What do I want to do this day?" or "What will make me happy?" When we carve out time for God first thing in the morning or early in the day, we reorient out perspective. A morning spiritual discipline of prayer or Bible reading or a combination of both reminds us that we are Christians. It is not what we want to get out of this day that matters most, but rather how God desires to use us this day to bless others. Our deepest joy is found in serving others.

Daily Bible Reading Is the Best Spiritual Practice

For a spiritual practice to be effective, we need something that goes well beyond touching our fingers in a small bowl of water, although this is a fine way to start out. A good practice is to read scripture each day in an organized manner that allows us to make progress and move through the various books of the Bible. It is vital not to read the Bible as if it were a scientific or historical document, but rather as a love letter that God has personally written to us, the readers. Some sections of the Bible are very historical, but they were often written well after the events occurred. Their deepest intent is theological, namely communicating truths about God and about human beings. When we read the Bible as a love letter from God written specifically to us, we shift our focus from "How do I know that this is accurate or historically true?" to "What word does God have for me today to carry within my heart and to share with others I encounter?"

We are wise to read through each book of the Bible from beginning to end rather than picking out pieces here and there. A good reading plan can guide us through a portion of the Old Testament, a psalm, and a chapter of the New Testament each day, which is a healthy spiritual diet. Some parts of the Old Testament are so dry and lacking in spiritual flavor that a friend of mine, an incredibly charismatic rabbi, says that he would never recommend that his congregants read all of the Hebrew Scriptures. Yet, even these dryer bits can yield spiritual wisdom. I recall reading through the Book of Leviticus last year and finding it much more interesting than I had ever found it before. In reading the details of the law, it dawned on me that God pays attention to the details of our lives: what we eat and what we drink, who we eat with and how we eat, what we wear and how we wear it, what we purchase, and how we store it all matter to God. God is in the details of daily living. How we make our choices each day matters greatly to God because it creates our character and has an impact on all of our relationships.

Discovering Spiritual Food for Daily Living

While even Leviticus can yield spiritual treasures, we do well to vary our spiritual diet each day. Leviticus can be as boring as eating meatloaf for forty days in a row, and it can be offset by a side salad of a psalm, followed by a chapter of the New Testament, as spiritually tasty as eating a dessert. The combination creates a full, varied spiritual meal that keeps us interested

While on a recent church mission trip to Honduras, I was visited by the Rev. Pascual Torres, the Dean of the Theological Training Program at the seminary in San Pedro Sula, the founder of an HIV/AIDS ministry, and the Chancellor of the Episcopal Diocese of Honduras. Pascual meets each day with eleven men, who are "empleados" or laborers in San Pedro Sula. Together, they are reading through the entire Bible using our Read the Bible in One Year Reading Plan from The Bible Challenge, and discussing the meaning of the text and the significance of it for their own lives. Pascual noted that in the seminary they taught an intellectual approach to the Bible, which is much needed, but just as crucial was the experience of reading the Bible each day for our own spiritual welfare and sharing with others what we were learning from God. "Our hearts come alive during this experience," explained Pascual. "We have nine to eleven people every time we meet," he noted. "It is the ideal size for a group like this." He continued: "At first the men were not sure that they wanted to do this. Now they look forward to it every day. It is like spiritual food for them. They eat and drink and work and sleep each day and visit with their families and friends, and now this has become something that they greatly look forward to that gives each day its meaning. In Central and South America, we have base communities, and this is exactly what this is. It is a chance for people to read the Bible on their own and to discover what God is telling them and revealing to them in their own lives." I was struck by the fact that a ministry that I had started in my church outside of Philadelphia was now making an impact on the lives of twelve men in Honduras and had spread to over twenty-five hundred churches in more than forty countries. God works in amazing ways.

Pascual has shared The Bible Challenge with his Lutheran colleagues in Honduras, and they are benefiting from it as well. It is wonderful to see Christians sharing a ministry across denominational lines. God's Word has the power to break down walls and to build bridges across the divides of race, gender, sexuality, economic status, educational levels, ethnicities, nationalities, and age groups. Sadly, the Church has become fragmented into thousands of broken pieces. As Diana Butler Bass notes, there are roughly twenty-two thousand Christian groups and denominations in the United States. Many have very different ways of holding worship, viewing the sacraments, and establishing ecclesiastic order and governance. Yet, at the heart we are all united by turning to the Word of God to inspire and strengthen our lives for Christian living and service. This Word transcends all the words that we can utter or write, and we must turn to it daily for our own transformation in Christ.

Allowing the Mind of Jesus to Be Formed within Us

In one of the most beautiful passages in the Bible, St. Paul writes, "Let the same mind be in you that was in Christ Jesus, who, though he was in the form of God, did not regard equality with God as something to be exploited, but emptied himself, taking the form of a slave, being born in human likeness. And being found in a human form, he humbled himself and became obedient to the point of death—even death on the cross." (Phil. 2: 5–8) I love the words, "Let the same mind be in you that was in Christ Jesus . . ." How else can the mind of Jesus be in us unless we prayerfully read the words of Jesus on a regular basis and let the Word of God infiltrate our souls, working within us to accomplish what we cannot achieve on our own? Through engaging the Word of God daily we begin to speak like Jesus, think like Jesus, feel compassion like Jesus, serve like Jesus, and live humbly like Jesus.

Developing a daily spiritual habit of reading the Bible is the number-one way by far to "let the same mind be in [us] that was in Christ Jesus." Paul goes on to say, "Therefore, God also highly exalted him and gave him the name that is above every name, so that at the name of Jesus every knee should bend, in heaven and on earth and under the earth, and every tongue should confess that Jesus Christ is Lord, to the glory of God the Father." (Phil. 2:9–11) Paul knew all of the apostles benefited from obeying Jesus and being in his presence; in Jesus' physical absence, they had to "work out [their own] salvation with fear and trembling; for it is God who is at work in you, enabling you both to will and to work for his good pleasure." (Phil. 2:12–13)

Most mainline Christians I know exude a far more tepid sense of faith. They experience Jesus' absence and wonder what it would be like to have been regularly in his presence. They are aware that they must work out their own salvation with fear and trembling, but they struggle to find a vibrant and solid faith that would lead them to turn to Christ and with a sense of certitude exalt him as their Lord. Yet, this is exactly what Scripture calls us to do, proclaiming "at the name of Jesus every knee should bend, in heaven and on earth and under the earth, and every tongue should confess that Jesus Christ is Lord. . . ."

Running on Empty

The chief reason such devotion is so hard for so many of us is that we rely far too much on Sunday morning to fill our spiritual tanks. It simply does not work, any more than if we were to eat only one meal a week and have it sustain us for seven days. We rely on the Church to do much of the spiritual work that we must do. We come to church often running spiritually on empty, having done nothing all week or perhaps all month to connect with God and with Jesus. Our spiritual gas tank is pinned near the red mark. We are running on fumes. Life has beaten us down. What do we do? We turn to the worship service, to hymns and lessons being read aloud that we have never read on our own, and to a sermon based upon a Bible that we barely know to do everything for us. If the hymns being sung are not our favorites, if the lessons seem strange and irrelevant to our daily life, and if the sermon does not specifically address what we personally are facing and most concerned about, then we are likely to sigh and say, "Going to church does little for me."

At various points in my ministry, I have felt as though I was a personal trainer working in a gym watching a crowd of people entering the gym each Sunday who have done no exercise all month. They entered saying, "I am twenty-five pounds overweight and my daughter is getting married this coming week, and I have to fit into my tuxedo that I wore thirty years ago and look great as I walk her down the aisle. You have one hour to make it work." If someone were to enter a health club and tell that story to a personal trainer, she or he would laugh out loud. It's impossible to accomplish, shy of having a surgical tummy tuck! Yet, this is the kind of equation that people bring to church without realizing it, and solving this kind of equation is what we as clergy have come to believe is our job.

The Greatest Gift That We Can Give Our People

The best thing a Christian leader can do is not to act as a Christian entertainer with sermons that are witty and full of fascinating illustrations in order to fill the pews. Even if we offer practical illustrations and gripping stories and make great use of Scripture quotes, there is something more powerful. The greatest gift we can give our people is to help them become seven-day-a-week Christians. As George Herbert notes in the words to the hymn whose tune is known as *General Seminary*, "Seven whole days, not one in seven, I will praise thee. . . ."

If we successfully teach our members how to develop a daily spiritual practice that has substance and, yes, makes demands upon their time and schedules like anything else meaningful in life, we shall once again begin producing spiritual athletes. We shall transform people into articulate, committed, and contagious Christians who desire to share the Word of God with their families, friends, classmates, colleagues, and neighbors. They will be inspired to start new ministries. They will come to see their own work as a ministry rather than a job and their profession as a vocation. Their relationships will be strengthened and will be viewed in a different and more meaningful light. They will have more desire to attend church, and when they come they will understand what is happening far better. When the lessons are read, they will listen attentively because they will recognize what is being read and will not feel as though they have walked into a movie halfway through the film. When the preacher begins to preach, they will sit alertly waiting to hear God's Word, praying others may have their hearts touched by the message, instead of running on spiritual fumes and expecting the sermon to be about precisely what they are contending with in life at that exact moment. They will follow the words of the sermon and the texts to which the preacher alludes. Some will perhaps even wonder why the preacher did not refer to another text in the Bible that would have corroborated the sermon's topic.

As they worship, they will recognize phrases of Scripture in the hymns that they sing. They will look around church with a smile and hope that God will introduce them to someone who has come to worship that day carrying a heavy heart so God may use them to lift up that person spiritually. They will leave renewed and ready to serve, looking forward to returning the following week, because everything is not completely dependent upon what the church will do for them. When the collection plate passes they will give more generously. Their hearts will have been touched on not just one day, but on seven days a week. As they lead increasingly mobile lives and are not always in town to attend church, they will know their church has given them an incalculable treasure they can carry with them wherever they go. They will read God's Word three hundred and sixty-five days a year, and God will be there to help them every day and every hour. There will be a partnership of a Christian working hand in hand with God.

What I witnessed in my own ministry as we began to teach people how to read the Bible and develop a daily spiritual practice, was each one of us was becoming more at ease with the Bible and finding time each day to connect with God. As a result, we were becoming more spiritually centered. We looked forward to our time with God each day, and if a day passed where we could not read Scripture, we missed it like a runner who misses his or her daily run.

Let me conclude this chapter with the words of some Bible Challenge participants who have developed their own daily spiritual practice of engaging God's Word. Their words express the power of what daily Bible reading can do for each of us.

> *I wanted to let you know that as of Friday, December 9, I have finished reading my Bible! I was in Logan Airport when I finished and I wanted to jump up and down as if I were crossing the finish line of a marathon, but decided that that was probably not the appropriate place to share my joy and excitement.*—TRICIA

> *I think that I have finally realized what a mistake I made in my determination to read the Bible from cover to cover. I have recently been following The Bible Challenge's Read the Bible in a Year reading plan and found that it makes a great difference. For me, ending each day's reading in the New Testament is a world*

of difference; I actually look forward to the next reading and end with a positive feeling. Thank you.—NEAL

I've been thoroughly enjoying working my way through the Bible in one year, using The Bible Challenge. I've been highlighting the most meaningful verses, writing down the words from those verses that speak most clearly to me, and then sometimes putting them together into a prayer poem with the best of the best for that day.—ELIZABETH

Vaccinations put a small dose of a disease into one's body to stimulate an immune response. . . . When this is happening one can't feel it. It cannot be heard or viewed from the outside. . . . This is the closest analogy I can think of to describe what has happened to me as I have read (or listened to) the Bible for the last three years. I am being changed in a way that defies description. It embodies the "peace which passes all understanding." Each day a small dose of God's Word is entering my body, "God's temple of the Holy Spirit," and the transforming power of God is meeting it there and fortifying me. . . . God's peace has come as a response to my "vaccinations" and my prayers. Sometimes I worry about this or that but I quickly realize that I have been immunized and I get right back to work.—BARBARA

Initially I felt that "challenge" was an apt descriptor of the degree of difficulty involved in slowly slogging through the daily readings, but when I abandoned my decades old King James Bible in favor of a study Bible recommended by a fellow parishioner my enthusiasm for The Bible Challenge soared. Freed from the archaic (though beautiful) language, and illuminated by thoughtful annotations and historical context, I am now enjoying every minute of my voyage through the Bible. My faith has deepened by reading the Bible in sequence, as a story, and my understanding of God's direction and compassion has grown significantly. I am seeing so much more clearly how things tie together, and how the seeds of the New Testament are scattered throughout the stories of the Old Testament. And I am learning that reading the Bible is a personal journey of discovery. I am grateful for the structure provided by The Bible Challenge program.—LYNN

I truly appreciate being a part of the first year celebration of the "Read." . . . I started this year with the New Testament and have remained faithful to the process and look forward to my daily visit with the Scriptures. My daughter Virginia Frances says that she plans to have her Bible read by the end of the year.—STARR

The Spiritual Leader Must Lead
with a Passion for God's Word

"Come to me, all you that are weary and are carrying heavy burdens, and I will give you rest. Take my yoke upon you, and learn from me; for I am gentle and humble in heart, and you will find rest for your souls. For my yoke is easy, and my burden is light."—MATTHEW 11:28–30

"I know not a better rule of reading the Scripture, than to read it through from beginning to end and when we have finished it once, to begin it again. We shall meet with many passages which we can make little improvement of, but not so many in the second reading as in the first, and fewer in the third than in the second: provided we pray to him who has the keys to open our understandings, and to anoint our eyes with His spiritual ointment."—JOHN NEWTON

"I want to know one thing, the way to heaven: how to land safe on that happy shore. God himself has condescended to teach the way; for this very end he came from heaven. He has written it down in a book! Oh, give me that book! At any price, give me the book of God! I have it: here is knowledge enough for me. Let me be: 'A man of one book.' "—JOHN WESLEY

"I began to read the Holy Scriptures upon my knees, laying aside all other books, and praying over, if possible, every line and word. This proved meat indeed and drink indeed to my soul. I daily received fresh life, light and power from above."—GEORGE WHITEFIELD

· ◆ ·

In his wonderful book, *The Contemplative Pastor,* Eugene Peterson asks, "How can I lead people into the quiet place beside the still waters if I am in perpetual motion?" It is a great question for spiritual leaders to explore. Today, clergy are pulled in countless ways. We are bombarded by countless communications and asked to handle an extraordinary number of differing demands. In a book about clergy burnout, the former Duke University Chaplain Will Willimon notes clergy do not burn out from doing too many great things. They burn out instead from doing a countless number of small tasks, each of which someone in their parish or in the community believes to be important. At times, it feels as though we are being nibbled to death by ducks. As a result, spiritual leaders can lose their ability to see what God has planned for their congregations and for them; what is most important; and what will build committed, contagious, and compassionate Christians. Ultimately, spiritual leaders who are pulled in a myriad of different directions lose their balance and focus and fall flat. When that happens, the church drifts without a spiritual compass. Those participating in the faith community are given little direction about what is most important in becoming a committed disciple of Jesus and thereby fail to make significant progress on their spiritual journeys. The result is that lives are not changed.

Staying focused and spiritually grounded is a key task for every spiritual leader in the Church. In their book *Follow Me: What's Next for You?* Greg Hawkins and Cally Parkinson assert, "It is the goal of every church leader: To guide followers in the footsteps of Jesus, to point them toward growth and transformation, healing and wholeness, intimacy with God and others, to help them move from where they are to where they want to be." While this sounds obvious, it can be hard to carry out in an environment where everyone is trying to get the spiritual leader's attention.

The Struggle to Stay Focused on What Is Most Important

Religious leaders are often pecked to death by a million peripheral concerns that have little to do with creating disciples for Jesus. A committee is concerned about using Styrofoam cups instead of recyclable paper cups or ceramic mugs during coffee hour. Someone else insists on having the church make all sorts of special concessions for their daughter's wedding or a family member's funeral. A parishioner mails in a check directly to the religious leader hoping to receive a personal thank you rather than sending it to the bookkeeper. All day long there are a million little tasks, obscuring the big focus with hundreds of emails ricocheting through the office.

A wise leader and a smart church will build as many clear systems and procedures as possible to insure that these small tasks do not monopolize his or her time so he or she can deal with the larger vision. Spiritual leadership of a church cannot be abdicated to another person on the church's staff or to a committee in the church. The spiritual well-being of the church must always start with the church's spiritual leader. He or she must set the tone, chart the direction, and communicate to the congregation or diocese what the true spiritual priorities are. In order to do so, the leader must stay deeply grounded in his or her own spiritual journey and be a person of deep prayer, passionate about developing a relationship with God, and consumed by making disciples for Jesus. The leader must model a life completely surrendered to Christ as a servant leader. In his book *Good to Great*, Jim Collins says "Level Five Leaders" are those who demonstrate "the paradoxical combination of deep personal humility with intense professional will." Such leaders "routinely credit others, external factors, and good luck for their companies' success." A great spiritual leader will most certainly be humble and will give credit to God and to others for the success of the ministry in their parishes or dioceses.

He or she will strive to live a balanced life, be surrounded by other spiritual leaders, and enjoy regular Sabbath renewal. Above all, the leader will have a daily practice of reading God's Word prayerfully for personal spiritual growth. The leader will not just read the Bible in order to prepare for teaching others. They will read the Bible so God can teach and prepare them. Their regular engagement with Scripture will shape them. It will inform and inspire all of their ministry and actions, shaping words and deeds for many months to come.

The prayerful practice of daily Bible reading is far different from preparing for Sunday's sermon or to teach a Bible study. To read the Bible in preparation for something else or in order to share its wisdom with others is to use the Bible as a means to an end. There is nothing wrong with doing so. Preparation is crucial for preparing sermons and talks, but it is not what sustains the soul of a spiritual leader. A true spiritual leader must read the Bible each day to see what God wants to reveal to him or her. Unless the spiritual leader is first a disciple who listens to what God has to teach, he or she has no right to lead and teach others.

In order to sustain their own souls, spiritual leaders must devote time each day to listen to what God is saying to them. What Word does God have for me this day? Where am I weak or blind, stubborn, prideful, callous or uninformed? What truth is God trying to tell me? How is God's love trying to fill my heart and give me the mind that was in Christ Jesus? What does God want me to see and learn so that I may be a better disciple? It is only through spending time quiet and alone in the prayerful reading of God's Word that they earn the right to stand before others and serve as spiritual leaders. After all, we cannot produce in others what we are not allowing God to produce in us. Spiritual leaders must first be grounded in God's Word in order to help others be grounded in Jesus' love, grace, and hope.

How does one stay grounded? What enables a leader to go deeper in the journey of faith? What inspires someone so they may inspire others? The answer is to develop, sustain, and build a profound relationship with God. God does not want a portion of our lives. God will never settle for 50 percent of who we are. God will not even be content with 95 percent. God demands our entire being, doing, thinking, feeling, and existing. The spiritual leader has to be moving constantly in the direction of giving more of his or her life to Christ and being thoroughly transformed in order that God might use her or him to transform the lives of others.

We Need to Share Our Spiritual Practices with Others

I am fortunate to know many superb priests and bishops who are diligent about tending to their spiritual lives. Most, however, are very humble and, unfortunately, they rarely share a great deal with others about how they manage to stay close to the Lord or about their own daily spiritual practice to draw close to Jesus. Clergy often preach sermons from a third person perspective, speaking about what others need to hear, see, and do. What is most powerful, however, is when we become transparent and share aspects of our own spiritual journey, our successes and failures, and talk about our struggles and successes in following Jesus. People are not looking for greatness in their spiritual leader. They are looking for someone who is like them: who is a work still in progress and who is striving to give their all to God.

I once attended a preaching conference with the Rev. Barbara Brown Taylor, who is one of the finest preachers that the Episcopal Church has produced in the past twenty-five years. Her sermons were the works of a master wordsmith and someone with a great ability to read the Bible carefully and breathe new life into old passages. I had gotten to know her over the years and took the liberty of handing her a few of my sermons to see if she might offer some advice for preaching. Her response caught my attention. She said, "I bet that your congregation would be shocked if you offered them a personal illustration."

Her words struck a chord. I was seeking affirmation for my preaching; instead she brought to bear a set of laser beam-like eyes that could see through my words to their greatest failure. I was writing sermons for the ages that could be read decades from now and sound timeless, yet they lacked power because they were not personal. I was not in my own sermons. They were generic thoughts about leading the Christian life. Phillips Brooks, who was perhaps the finest preacher that the Episcopal Church has ever known, defined preaching as "truth mediated by personality." The problem with my sermons was that there was no personality. There was no "me." People need a transparent spiritual leader who is not afraid to share his or her failings and lessons learned from such encounters with God and others.

Since receiving Barbara's wisdom, I have found that the most important part of my preaching, teaching, or communicating to my parish and to others beyond often comes when I tell a personal story about my struggles to follow God. When I share my attempts and my failures, my dreams and my regrets, God speaks most powerfully through me. People want to know their leaders are human like them. They want to know clergy do not get it right all the time. They want to hear that ordained leaders have doubts and blind sides, weaknesses, and pride that gets in clergy's way at times and that church leaders are still learning as they are, being humbled and forgiven, getting lost and being found by God's grace. Transparency is a spiritual leader's greatest tool.

Thankfully, many spiritual leaders take time for prayer and reading God's Word each day. This daily spiritual practice makes all the difference in their lives. The problem is that they rarely ever share what this is like with those who follow them. Perhaps they take for granted that others in their congregation are doing similar things, employing similar holy habits. Most of them are not. Most of their listeners have no clue where to begin. The vast majority of mainline Christians have no daily spiritual practice, which is killing our churches and producing anemic believers whose own faith is too weak to spread effectively to the next generation.

Spiritual leaders are often functioning at the graduate level while their listeners are in the basic course. Many of those in the pew have yet to take baby steps to move forward on their spiritual journey. There is an enormous gap between what many spiritual leaders are doing, comprehending, and receiving to feed their hearts and souls and what people in the pew are practicing. Bridging that gap and helping to equip others to have a profound personal relationship with Jesus is why God has called clergy into spiritual leadership. This, after all, is the main area where people long to learn from their spiritual leaders. Their occupations and commitments take them in many different directions, drive them to make difficult and often painful decisions, exact their best energies, and leave them little time to focus on their relationship with Jesus. They are not coming to our churches to know more about the authors of the books of the Bible, when and where each of the gospels was written, or whether a particular passage was inserted at a later date. They are looking to find meaning and purpose in their lives. They come because they want to improve their relationships, be better parents, and maintain or revitalize their marriage with the person with whom they once fell madly in love. They seek sanity in the midst of chaos. They long for clarity in a world of moral ambiguity. They need to know God cherishes them despite their glaring imperfections, their history of taking wrong turns, their selfishness, and their sin.

What they need more than anything else from us is regular teaching about how to enter the presence of God and how to draw close to Jesus. They need to know how to pray and how to listen as God speaks through the Bible, prayer, and the events of their lives. They need to know that they are not wasting their time trying to establish a relationship with Jesus. They need to know no one will ever know them better, love them more, or forgive them more fully than God. This is not rocket science, yet it is so basic that we forget to teach and share it. When we do teach it, we often tower above others, instructing them like a teacher speaking a foreign language. What people need most from their spiritual leader is an authentic model of holiness, someone who practices and can speak about holy habits that he or she follows each day. They need someone who will invite them to walk alongside. So often it feels as though we are trying to fill classes, build attendance, and increase pledging units in our church. People do not want to be used as a means to an end. They are reluctant to respond to anything that is not a true call to faithful Christian service. As religious leaders we often invite others to take classes, go on pilgrimages, participate in worship, and care for those in need, but we rarely say, "I am doing this for the sake of my own soul and would love to have your company on the journey. Let's walk side by side, and together we will grow in Christ."

When we say to people, "You should get a spiritual director," or "You need to join a Bible study," we are often towering over them and telling them what they need to do in their lives while they remain clueless as to what we are doing.

When we invite people to join us on a journey that we are taking for our own spiritual welfare the invitation is quite different. It is a way of climbing down from the pulpit and walking beside others as a transparent servant leader who can admit, "I need this just as much or perhaps more than you do. Let's do it together, and it will draw both of us closer to Jesus." People do not need a religious expert to lead them, but a fellow pilgrim who will accompany them on a long, slow, beautiful spiritual journey. Those who walk this journey together learn, share, and experience growing in Christ.

What Does It Mean for People to Follow Jesus and to Follow Us?

As ministry leaders we must be impassioned to share Jesus with others. That's what John Wesley and George Whitfield had to offer as they helped to lead The Great Awakening in America and a similar movement in England that awakened complacent churchgoers scattered across the countryside and in cities. Every member of the clergy has experienced something profound in his or her own life that led him or her to give up some pursuit and dedicate his or her life to serving Jesus and sharing his love with others. We constantly stand before the members of our churches and say, "Follow me." But where are we going? What are those who follow us seeking? Why did they call us into leadership? What are the deep needs of their hearts and souls?

In their book *Follow Me: What's Next for You?* Greg Hawkins and Cally Parkinson note that after hearing from over eighty thousand people in more than two hundred churches, they have learned the number-one thing that people are seeking from their church is not fellowship, worship, or service opportunities. They are seeking for the spiritual leader and the church to challenge them to grow and take the next step in their spiritual life. "They didn't say that they come to our churches to hear great preaching or to meet new friends. They want to be challenged. They want to grow. They want to take the next step on their spiritual journey and make some progress. The people in your church really want to grow closer to Christ. And they're looking to you—their leader—wondering if you can help them."

St. George's Church in Nashville, Tennessee was the first church that I served after being ordained as a deacon and later as a priest. It was a large church with over twenty-six hundred members served by several priests and retired clergy. One of them was the Rev. Julien Gunn, a former Episcopal monk. He was truly a holy man and a delightful human being who was dearly loved by the church. Julien volunteered to teach me how to read the Bible in Greek. We met each day and he tutored me. He taught me many things, but what I remember most is what he said: "Unless you spend time in prayer each day with God, you have no right to stand before the people and speak to them on behalf of God or stand at the altar and represent Christ to them. You will be no different than a dentist or an accountant, who are pulled in countless directions and find little time for God. You must be different, and your difference must begin by living a life grounded in prayer."

I will always remember his words. They are ingrained in my heart. I would add unless a church leader grounds his or her life in the prayerful reading of God's Word each day, a minister has no right to stand before a congregation and say, "Follow me." Throughout his ministry Jesus used these same words, "follow me." As he began his ministry beside the Sea of Galilee, he uttered those words to Peter and Andrew, two fishermen who were plying their trade: "*Follow me*, and I will make you fish for people." (Matthew 4:19) The Bible says that they "immediately" left their nets and followed Jesus. (Matthew 4:20) I suspect that there was more to the story. What workers would leave livelihoods that supported their families and follow a complete stranger? My suspicion is Peter and Andrew had heard about Jesus' wisdom and reputation as a holy person long before meeting him. Like most of us, they were struggling for answers and seeking meaning in their lives. When Jesus offered his invitation, they were ripe for change and chose to follow.

When the religious authorities later doubted Jesus, he said, "My sheep hear my voice. I know them, and they *follow me*." (John 10:27) After he had entered Jerusalem for the last time and his own death was approaching, Jesus told his followers, "Whoever serves me must *follow me*, and where I am, there will my servant be also." (John 12:26) With following comes responsibility to walk in the leader's steps, however. It was not enough for someone to say, "I know Jesus" or "I like Jesus." Jesus accepted nothing less than a person's total devotion. As he predicted his own death and resurrection, Jesus said, "If any want to become *my followers*, let them deny themselves and take up their cross daily and *follow me*. For those who want to save their life will lose it, and those who lose their life for my sake will save it." (Luke 9: 23–24) After he was crucified and resurrected, Jesus repeated the same message. After meeting the risen Christ, Peter, who had denied Jesus three times, declared that he would never forsake Jesus and would always love him. "Lord, you know everything; you know that I love you." Jesus had compassion on Peter and forgave him and told Peter three times, "Feed my sheep." He concluded by saying, "*Follow me*." (John 21:15–19)

Our mission is to follow Jesus. He alone is the ultimate Word of God. How can we follow Jesus if we do not "read, mark, learn, and inwardly digest" the Word of God each day? I have come to believe that regular engagement with God's Word is the single best spiritual tool God has provided. Reading the Bible daily can transform our churches and our lives, but only if we as clergy commit ourselves to reading the Bible prayerfully each day and inviting others—both within and beyond our church—to share this rich experience with us.

We Need to Be Our Community's Number-One Evangelists

Our members and our friends listen to our voices. They trust us to lead. They will emulate our models, but only if we go first and lead the way, committing to a daily spiritual practice, sharing our experiences, inviting others to walk alongside of us and share the journey, listening to their questions, and learning as they share what they are experiencing. The first task of a spiritual leader is to step out in front and to lead spiritually by example. The Bible Challenge encourages clergy and bishops to reach out to their friends and acquaintances from high school and college, friends with whom they play golf or tennis, travel, or socialize and invite them to join them in reading the Bible in a year. Often these invitations will include people who never go to church or who do little to stimulate their own spiritual life, though they often hold their clergy friends in great admiration. When a priest or bishop invites his or her own friends outside "the Church" to engage regularly in reading God's Word together, the spiritual leader is modeling evangelism for the entire church or diocese.

What they experience is what every evangelist experiences: the joy of having someone take small steps in faith and ask simple, but powerful questions that put them in touch with the heart of the Christian faith. Something about sharing our faith with others makes our faith grow deeper and more alive. Every spiritual leader is where he or she is because of others along the way. When they reach out to someone who trusts them and invite that person to walk alongside, he or she is grateful for the offer and together they learn much from one another.

The priest or bishop is a church's or diocese's number-one evangelist. They must lead by example and encourage their church members and fellow clergy to follow what they are doing. Knowing that others are following and depending on their leadership helps them to stay faithful to the journey and give it their best. The Bible Challenge invites spiritual leaders to write about what they are learning as they engage the Bible each day. Many parishioners are surprised and gladdened to hear their priest or bishop is discovering new things in God's Word and does not have all the answers. It gives permission for lay persons to become learners and to ask simple questions when they know that their leader is also a student, though more experienced and knowledgeable. Both are still being formed in Christ. No one is the complete finalized Christian product. We are all on a journey.

Leading Laterally: Sharing Ministry Side by Side

Last fall I spent five weeks walking the Camino to Santiago de Compostela. I started in the small French town of St. Jean Pied de Port, crossed over the Pyrenees Mountains, and walked more than five hundred miles to my destination in Santiago de Compostela in the northwest corner of Spain. Along the way I stayed in albergues and refugios, where there were often as many as twenty to one hundred people sharing a large room. I learned to get up early, travel light, and walk in a relaxed manner.

Along the way, I spoke French, Italian, and Spanish with other pilgrims. I have a love for languages and it was great fun to speak with people from different parts of Europe. I usually mentioned that I was an Episcopal priest on sabbatical and was walking the Camino as a pilgrimage. Mentioning I was a priest opened the door to all sorts of interesting conversations. People felt free to share their thoughts about the Church and about God. They asked me about forgiveness, sin, suffering, death, heaven, Jesus, and the Bible. Sometimes I felt like I was offering spiritual direction. I received more from those whom I walked beside than I could possibly have given. One of the most important lessons I learned was the power of walking beside another person. Most of my ministry has been spent walking in front of others. Sometimes, I got too far in front. Now I have little interest in doing so. What I enjoyed most about walking side by side was feeling so free and satisfied. We were dressed in similar ways. I did not look like a priest. In fact, I wore a French beret. Because I spoke French, I was often mistaken for being French. There was no hierarchy on the Camino. We were all pilgrims walking beside one another, sharing stories and food, listening, laughing, and enjoying being together. It significantly changed my outlook on ministry and leadership.

I regret, however, that there was somewhat of a mad rush each morning to get up and set out on the Camino. People were scurrying in and out of the bathroom. There were sleeping bags to be rolled up; lotion to be applied to feet that would be carrying us on our twenty mile hike; clothes, books, flashlights, food, water bottles, toiletries, and rain gear to be placed carefully inside backpacks. There was no time to sit quietly and read the Bible and have time to pray. That had to be found later in the day. I greatly missed being saturated in God's Word first thing in the morning. I managed to get through five weeks without starting my days with Bible reading, but had I continued my life would have been impoverished for lack of beginning my day with an infusion of God's truth, light, and joy. Being steeped in the Word is like being recharged with a great night's sleep, a fresh cup of coffee, and something terrific for breakfast. It is the best way that I know to begin the day, whether one is a leader, a follower, or a pilgrim.

Charles Simeon: A Man Immersed in God's Word

One of my favorite illustrations of someone deeply steeped in Scripture is Charles Simeon. In 1783 he was called, at the age of twenty-three, to serve as Rector of Holy Trinity Church in Cambridge, England. He was unknown and inexperienced. He was nearly forced out of his own church during his first year by the Church Wardens who wanted a different man to lead them. Nevertheless, Simeon persevered. In time, he won over his congregation and went on to serve as Rector of Holy Trinity Church for a remarkable 54 years. He was a faithful, inspiring leader, and God used him to build one of the great churches of his day.

In 1833 Simeon produced a twenty-one volume collection containing over twenty-five hundred of his sermons. The collection went through several editions in his lifetime and produced vast royalties. Simeon used the proceeds to establish and fund the Simeon Trust to further the work of the Church and hire evangelical preachers to preach throughout England. He would purchase the rights to name the Rector of a congregation and would then place someone in leadership whom he knew to be deeply engaged in reading the Scriptures so any church they served might thrive from sermons steeped in a prayerful reading of the Bible. In his own ministry, Simeon labored at least twelve hours in preparing each sermon. In time, he became the leading preacher of his era. The most distinctive feature of his preaching was his faithfulness to Scripture. Simeon arose daily at 4:00 a.m. and devoted four hours a day to Bible study and prayer. As result, he knew the Scriptures extraordinarily well. He was saturated in the Word of God, and his sermons therefore exuded the love and grace of God.

Simeon read the Bible more than any other book and believed that the preacher's task was to let the Scriptures speak to people: "My goal is to bring out of Scripture what is there, and not to thrust in what I think might be there." He wrote that the true test of a preacher's work was for one's sermon to "humble the sinner . . . exalt the Savior . . . and promote holiness." By daily immersing himself in prayerfully reading the Bible, Simeon was transformed that he might transform those who listened to him. He remains a powerful role model for every preacher.

I Learned by Making Countless Mistakes

I have served three churches since being ordained. The first, as I mentioned, was St. George's Episcopal Church in Nashville, Tennessee. My second church was St. James's Episcopal Church in Richmond, Virginia. I greatly enjoyed serving both of them. For the past nineteen years, I have served as Rector of St. Thomas' Episcopal Church in Fort Washington, Pennsylvania, a lovely suburb of Philadelphia. We have about fourteen hundred members. Our church is three hundred and sixteen years old. We began as a little log cabin on one acre of land in 1698. Thomas Clayton, the rector of Christ Church, Philadelphia, rode his horse to visit St. Thomas' in the Whitemarsh Valley and regularly led the poor farmers in worship. By all accounts, Clayton was a wonderfully educated and intelligent spiritual leader. In 1710, the small group of farmers, which included a handful of Dunkards, Presbyterians, Lutherans, and members of the Church of England, voted to join the Church of England, and our church was born. Over the years, we expanded and acquired forty-two more acres. We now have a campus with nine separate buildings, one hundred and fifty years old on average. We operate one of the most stunning and expensive to maintain campuses in the Episcopal Church.

When I arrived as Rector, I had never supervised a single full-time employee. My learning curve was vertical. The church took a big risk in calling me. I had been an assistant in my first two churches and had never led a church. For the first few years the verdict was out as to whether they had made the right decision. The biblical literacy in the church was very low. One of the leaders in the church told me that he had traveled to Italy and, while looking at a painting in Rome, realized Thomas was the disciple who doubted that Jesus had risen from the dead. I was shocked that a leader from a church called "St. Thomas" had to go to Rome to learn that fact. I had my work cut out for me.

The church had fallen on hard times, and I felt as though we were building an airplane as we flew it down the runway. Much of the infrastructure of the church had been allowed to decline or disappear altogether. Everything appeared to need fixing. I had come from two extremely well-run churches and could see many of the things that needed to be added or changed. Few members seemed to notice what I saw. Looking back on it, I should have exercised far more patience in making changes; I made plenty of mistakes.

After five years, I was called to lead one of our largest Episcopal cathedrals as Dean, but had to decline because that same week my wife, who is a very accomplished attorney, was made partner at her law firm. She had already left a partnership with a major law firm in Virginia to move to Pennsylvania so I could lead my own church. We decided not to move. The result was I stayed and went much deeper with one parish and learned some great lessons that I might never have learned had I continued to move from church to church. Most of what I learned I gleaned from making mistakes. My first decade in our parish was a time of great rebuilding. Our fifteen acre cemetery was overgrown with grass and filled with broken tombstones. We could barely afford any staff to lead our ministries. Our relationship with the diocese was remote. We had no written policies for how to conduct our ministries, weddings, or funerals. Our newsletter was cut and pasted together by a volunteer. The church lacked a strong sense of community. Sunday worship sometimes felt like a drive-in movie theater, where people came and left.

I told friends that I was trying to build a decent-size southern church in the north. What I meant was I wanted a church with a deep sense of community where we gathered to develop our closest friendships, share our joyful moments, and turn for strength when we faced life's losses. Bringing this about was a long-term challenge. Our giving was paltry. I am convinced much of this had to do with our anemic spiritual focus. There was not a single ongoing Bible study in the parish. It was an outward and visible sign that we were a collection of buildings on a vast property with wonderful people, but lacking in spiritual direction and vitality.

More Challenge than I Could Imagine

The church was still recovering from forcing out its rector of twenty-five years. During his tenure, the church shrank from two thousand five hundred members to under one thousand. The wardens fired the only secretary on staff; she could photocopy but not type. The church had no committees to oversee their finances, worship, pastoral care, cemetery, or buildings and grounds despite having one of the largest campuses in the Episcopal Church. Worship was stuck in the Fifties. We did Morning Prayer three Sundays a month and Baptism without the Eucharist. No small groups were permitted to compete with what had once been a large Sunday Forum, which had hosted renowned figures including Bishop Fulton Sheen, Archbishop Desmond Tutu, and Will Willimon. The Forum was struggling to average twenty attendees by the time I arrived.

The average pledge was so low that our parish finances were on life support. We were starving for money, lay leaders, and confidence. I told colleagues we were like the Columbia University football team, which at the time had a record of zero wins and twenty losses. Most of the football players had never experienced the thrill of winning a college football game. Our parish was no different. Our members could not imagine God doing something significant in our church. Our vision had shrunk, our confidence waned. Worst of all, many of our members had become hypercritical. They were quick to point out any error or change. Many of our healthiest and most gifted members had drifted away. If a person were on a significant spiritual journey, he or she would have starved spiritually or left. If a family with children had visited, they would have found little reason to stay. Children left worship three minutes into the service and were gone for almost two hours. It was ideal if parents wanted time without their children, but we were failing to attract young families.

We Tried Everything to Grow Spiritually

For the next fifteen years we did everything we could to transform the parish spiritually. We brought in some of the top spiritual leaders, preachers, and teachers from across the country including Basil Pennington, Thomas Keating, Stanley Hauerwas, Walter Brueggemann, Luke Timothy Johnson, Barbara Brown Taylor, George Regas, Terry Waite, Sister Helen Prejean, Dan Matthews, Bishops Paul Moore, and Fred Borsch, and many others. Every year for twelve years, Frank Griswold, the XXV Presiding Bishop of the Episcopal Church, joined us for Christmas Eve or Christmas Day to preach or celebrate the Eucharist. His wife, Phoebe, grew up in our church.

People started flocking to our church from other churches and other places to hear these great speakers. We developed a reputation as a church where you did not have to check your brain at the door. Our members were stimulated, inspired, and entertained, but we were unconsciously training them to be passive learners.

Lyle Schaler, church consultant and author, consulted with our church twice. He told us that New Jersey, New York, and Pennsylvania were the three lowest-commitment states in the country in terms of worship attendance and giving. We wondered what we could do to make our church come alive. We started all sorts of programs: Education for Ministry (EfM), the Disciples of Christ in Community (DOCC), and Alpha. I created and taught The Spiritual Classics Book Club, Basic Christianity, The C.S. Lewis Book Club, A Spiritual Life for the Over-busy, A Bible Brush Up, Where is God in *The Philadelphia Inquirer*?, and The Monday Connection: How to Connect Sunday to Monday. I gave lecture series on world religions, heaven, ethics, Jerusalem, Celtic Christianity, Islam, and the Lord's Prayer.

All of these things helped to raise the bar of understanding and belief in our parish. DOCC did more than anything to build Christian community. Most of our future leaders went through it and found a sense of community greater than anything they had previously experienced. Alpha helped people to speak freely about their faith, something that few had done before we launched the program. EfM helped people learn how to read the Bible carefully, learn about church history and theology, and how to reflect on their lives spiritually. We developed several ongoing Bible studies, but found most people wanted to attend a large Sunday Forum and hear a top speaker or one of their clergy speak on a relevant topic. There was a strong resistance to joining small groups for adult Christian learning and to weeknight gatherings. I think this is characteristic of our region of the country where few churches have a large number of thriving small learning groups.

Developing a Deeper Focus

After the theological chaos in the Episcopal Church as a result of the General Convention of 2003 following the election of the first openly gay bishop, we decided to have our parish focus on annual themes. We realized we had to go deeper and that the only way to do that was to stop flitting from one topic to another and concentrate on a single aspect of Christianity. We had to get back to basics. We chose "Read, Mark, Learn, and Inwardly Digest the Word of God," taking a line from one of Thomas Cranmer's most famous prayers. That year we asked biblical scholars to join us and help us to go deeper in our knowledge of God's Word. The following year we focused on prayer, examining "Prayer: a Conversation with the Ultimate Partner" as our theme, using the words from William James' book, *Varieties of Religious Experience*. Then we looked at our own tradition and the theme "Unabashedly Anglican;" the next year was an examination of "Ethics in Daily Life." Again, we had great speakers and lectures and received wonderful feedback.

Our themes were successful at helping our folks to focus and go deeper. Many of the speakers and sessions were engaging and entertaining. Our members were on a learning curve. They brought their friends. Occasionally, they bought books published by our speakers, read, and discussed them. Their minds were engaged, but their hearts were rarely touched. There was limited time for discussion and interaction around the tables. The speakers, for the most part, came and went and most of our members continued to be passive Christian learners. We were not helping them to develop daily spiritual practices, and they rarely read their Bibles

George Müller: A Leader Devoted to the Bible

After leading the parish for sixteen years I discovered what others found long before I did. One of my forerunners was George Müller, who was born in Germany in 1805. He later made his way to England where he served as a preacher, evangelist, and the Director of the Ashley Down orphanage in Bristol. He died in 1898 at the age of ninety-three. During his lifetime, he established one hundred seventeen schools that offered a Christian education to over one hundred and twenty thousand children, many of whom were orphans. He was a remarkable man, a person of deep prayer with great commitment to Scripture. He wrote:

> I saw that the most important thing I had to do was to give myself to the reading of the Word of God, and to meditation on it. . . . What is the food of the inner man? Not prayer, but the Word of God; and . . . not the simple reading of the Word of God, so that it only passes through our minds, just as water runs through a pipe, but considering what we read, pondering over it, and applying it to our hearts.

My work as a minister was far from what he described. I was pouring all sorts of Christian content into my brain and heart and soul, but much of it was diluted. I was reading words, but not being transformed by the Word of God. Everything I read from spiritual writers, mystics, and theologians was less than God's Word. I felt I had chosen not to digest the healthiest spiritual food available. While I consumed a large amount of spiritual content, it was less invigorating and left me less spiritually alive than I could have been had I allowed myself to become saturated in God's Word.

I am reminded of what colleague and friend Miroslav Volf wrote in *Captive to the Word of God: Engaging the Scriptures for Contemporary Theological Reflection*:

> Certainly, Christian communities draw on other sources of nourishment as well—some of which provide them with spiritual junk food (such as pop psychology), and others that yield solid nutrients (such as the responsible study of the human psyche, to stay with the same intellectual "food group"). They also draw on rich theological and spiritual traditions. But even the best of these sources—whether intra-Christian or extra-Christian—cannot substitute for the

Scriptures. These others are important side-dishes; the Scriptures contain nutrients indispensable for the growth of the individual Christians as well as ecclesiastical communities. The Scriptures represent the critical link to Jesus Christ as a site of God's self-revelation. Take the Scriptures away, and sooner or later you will "un-church" the Church.

Müller was someone who knew, lived, and shared this with others. He appreciated the power the Bible alone possesses to transform our lives. Though he passed through a dissolute stage of life, which included heavy drinking, in time he became a fervent Bible reader and began to pray regularly. In 1828, Müller was offered an opportunity to study Hebrew with the London Society in order to promote Christianity among the Jews. During his time in England, the twenty-three-year-old Müller became gravely ill and convalesced in the country in Devon, where he befriended a man named Henry Craik. Their friendship transformed Müller and lasted for thirty-six years. Müller was so inspired by the stories Craik told, that when he returned to London he decided he would stop reading books about the Bible and read only the Bible itself. Once he had read it in its entirety, he would start at the beginning and read it again. The more he read the Bible, the more he was changed. God began to show him the power that comes from engaging Scripture regularly and allowing the Holy Spirit to reveal God's truth.

When Müller returned to London, he exhorted others to join him every morning for prayer and Scripture reading from 6:00 a.m. until 8:00 a.m. He spent several hours in prayer during the evening, even praying late into the night. Sometimes he was unable to sleep due to the joy of his deep communion with God. As he spent more time in prayer and reading Scripture, Müller felt called to leave the London Society in 1830 to pastor a small congregation. That same year he married Mary Groves. Müller abolished pew-rents and refused to take a fixed salary or to appeal for contributions towards his support. Instead, he simply placed a box at the door of the church for freewill offerings.

In 1832, Müller moved to Bristol where he spent the remainder of his life. Here Müller served a congregation and founded the Scriptural Knowledge Institution. In one year's time, Müller became responsible for educating nearly seven thousand children in England, Spain, India, Italy. It was in Bristol that Müller began working with the orphans. In 1836, he opened his first home with twenty-six children. Over time, he opened four more orphanages. From 1848 and 1874, Müller went from caring for one hundred and thirty orphans to over two thousand. Often Müller lived day to day, wondering how he would meet the orphans' needs, praying for divine help.

In 1841, however, he had a paradigm shift in what he believed to be the ultimate purpose of his life. He had learned a great deal about how to transform the spiritual lives of others by allowing God first to transform his own spiritual life.

Müller published a short booklet called "Soul Nourishment First," in which he summarized the thoughts that gave birth to his fruitful ministry. They illustrate the power of a spiritual leader who is grounded in prayerfully reading God's Word.

> I saw more clearly than ever that the first great and primary business to which I ought to attend every day was to have my soul happy in the Lord. The first thing to be concerned about was not how much I might serve the Lord, or how I might glorify the Lord; but how I might get my soul into a happy state, and how my inner man might be nourished. . . . Before this time my practice had been, at least for ten years previously, as an habitual thing, to give myself to prayer, after having dressed myself in the morning. Now, I saw that the most important thing I had to do was to give myself to the reading of the Word of God, and to meditation on it, that thus my heart might be comforted, encouraged, warned, reproved, instructed; and that thus, by means of the Word of God, while meditating on it, my heart might be brought into experiential communion with the Lord.
>
> I began therefore to meditate on the New Testament from the beginning, early in the morning. The first thing I did, after having asked in a few words the Lord's blessing upon his precious Word, was, to begin to meditate on the Word of God, searching as it were into every verse, to get blessing out of it; not for the sake of the public ministry of the Word, not for the sake of preaching on what I had meditated upon, but for the sake of obtaining food for my own soul. . . . How different, when the soul is refreshed and made happy early in the morning, from what it is when without spiritual preparation, the service, the trials, and the temptations of the day come upon one.

Early on in his Christian life Müller would shut himself in a room to pray and meditate over Scripture. He recalled he had "learned more in a few hours than . . . during a period of several months previously." Throughout his life he exhorted others to read the word of God as often as possible that God might teach them though the Holy Spirit.

> . . . the Spirit explains the Word by the Word. . . . Above all, he should seek to have it settled in his own mind that God alone by His Spirit can teach him, and that therefore, as God will be inquired of for blessings, it becomes him to seek God's blessing previous to reading, and also whilst reading. He should have it, moreover, settled in his mind that although the Holy Spirit is the best and sufficient Teacher . . . we may have to entreat Him again and again for the explanation of certain passages; but that He will surely teach us at last, if indeed we are seeking for light prayerfully, patiently, and with a view to the glory of God.

Müller's dependence on God to meet his needs is inspiring, especially when one considers how large his needs were. In 1874, he needed $264,000 a year to support twenty-one hundred people, assist one hundred eighty-nine missionaries, support one hundred schools with nine thousand students, and provide 4 million tracts and tens of thousands of copies of the Bible. Between 1875 and 1892 Müller and his wife traveled around the world preaching and sharing with amazing faithfulness. They traveled two hundred thousand miles over seventeen years. He preached his last sermon on March 6, 1898 and died four days later. His funeral was one of the largest events Bristol had ever seen as tens of thousands of admirers lined the streets.

According to Müller, the key to living the Christian life was to know and trust God. To know God one must spend time reading God's Word each day. The reading must be done prayerfully, for Müller was convinced that the only way for the Word to truly transform was by the power of the Holy Spirit. In trusting God, one should turn to God for every request and ask God to provide every need. Müller explained how he set out to complete this step of the process:

> I seek at the beginning to get my heart in such a state that it has no will of its own in regard to a given matter. . . . The Spirit and the Word must be combined. If I look to the Spirit alone without the Word, I lay myself open to great delusions also. If the Holy Spirit guides us at all, He will do it according to the Scriptures and never contrary to them at all, He will do it according to the one without the reflection, I come to a deliberate judgment according to the best of my ability and knowledge.

It has taken me a long time to realize what Müller had learned at thirty-six: the Holy Spirit and the Word must be combined, and it is the Holy Spirit that truly opens the Scriptures to us when it knows that our hearts are set on the glory of God. It is a joy to encounter a Christian whose heart and soul are alive with the love of God, who has a bright, articulate, and joyful faith and an abiding sense of inner peace. The combination is captivating and makes such a person's faith contagious. That very faith is what we need to transform lives and build a dynamic Church for the twenty-first century.

CHAPTER 8

Bridging the Gap to Help
People Read the Bible

"The grass withers, the flower fades; but the word of God will stand forever."—Isaiah 40:8

"Faith comes from what is heard, and what is heard comes through the word of Christ."—Romans 10:17

"The first and almost the only book deserving of universal attention is the Bible."—Thomas Jefferson

"The Bible is the most thought suggesting book in the world. No other deals with such grand themes."—Herrick Johnson

• ➤ •

Herb O'Driscoll, the former dean of the Church of Canada Cathedral in Vancouver, British Columbia and former Warden of the College of Preachers at the Washington National Cathedral, is a mesmerizing Irish storyteller. He often tells the story of watching Charlton Heston play Moses in *The Ten Commandments*. Heston looked bigger than life as he stood atop the mountain surrounded by an ominous sky waiting to receive God's commandments etched in stone. As O'Driscoll watched the film, he overheard two moviegoers in the row behind him. One asked the other, "Did this take place before or after Jesus?" O'Driscoll says overhearing that conversation was an epiphany. He realized most preachers were preaching significantly over the heads of those who are listening. They assumed their audience knew more than they did. Elaborating on this theme in a preaching class, O'Driscoll said, "Most preachers mount the pulpit and start to build a biblical skyscraper for their audience. The only problem is that the first ten floors are missing for most of those who are listening in the pews."

No One Wants to Be Biblically Illiterate

When it comes to mainline churches, O'Driscoll is correct. Most of us tend to preach above the heads of those in church. It's as though we have been asked to coach a little league baseball team and then try to train our players as though we were coaching the New York Yankees. Few churchgoers, however, will tell us that our sermons are pitched beyond their reach or focus on issues that generally do not concern them. No one wants to appear biblically illiterate. Few want to appear unappreciative. Most are afraid that they are the only ones in the pew who know as little as they do about the Bible.

The idea of joining a Bible study is even more challenging. At our previous church in Richmond, my wife and I started a Bible study with several other couples who were close friends. We had a great time together. Our discussions deepened our friendships. Soon, however, one of them confessed how little she knew about the Bible. It was as though she had committed a crime. She struggled to say it. Thank goodness she did. It allowed us to focus our discussions in a different way, and it turned out that she spoke for most of the group. It was hard for her to confess how little she knew. I could tell she assumed that everyone in the group knew more about the Bible than she did. Actually, most of the group was right there with her. That moment was my epiphany, much the way overhearing the conversation between the moviegoers was for O'Driscoll.

Teaching the Bible Need Not Be Rocket Science

More recently in my ministry, we invited a wonderful teacher of the Bible named Helen White to lead a two-part series in our Sunday Forum called "An Outrageous Romp through the Old Testament." The following Sunday, she led "An Outrageous Romp through the New Testament." Our parish has had some remarkable speakers from across the country and even from overseas. We have had distinguished authors, leaders, and Trappist monks who have taught prayer to large audiences, and many speakers with doctorates. Helen, who never authored a book nor earned an advanced degree, attracted the largest audience the Forum had had in years.

I watched from the back of the room as well over a hundred people sat at round tables listening intently. She was humble and excited. Helen spent over forty years helping groups in our area to read through the Bible, with special focus on reading the Synoptic Gospels and studying the differences in the texts. Her reputation preceded her. Some church members had encouraged friends, neighbors and family members to attend. There were too many people present for that alone to account for the crowd; the audience was mostly church members.

Looking over those in attendance, I saw a husband and wife seated side by side. He was educated at an Ivy League school and was one of the best-known lawyers in Philadelphia. She had served as the chair of several school boards and had earned a reputation as a bright, well-organized leader who got things done. I could not recall seeing them in any of our previous Sunday Forums. Why were they there? Helen was not a celebrity speaker. This was not an exploration of some important aspect of daily living or how to communicate better or how to foster a better relationship. This was Bible 101.

Then it dawned on me. Despite all of their education and successes, these two bright Episcopalians were probably biblically illiterate. We offered a safe setting in which they could overcome their illiteracy without having to confess to anyone how little they knew about the Bible. We had Bibles at each table, which was something rarely seen in an Episcopal church. Helen began by asking everyone to open to the first page of the first book. "Now thumb through the pages until you come to the end of that first book. What is the name of the first book of the Bible?" She asked.

Someone shouted out, "Genesis."

"Wonderful," she said. "You are absolutely correct. Now what is the next book called?"

"Exodus," said another member of the audience.

"Right. Now thumb through the pages until you come to the next book of the Bible."

This went on until they had paged through the first five books. "Now I want you to hold in your left hand the first page of the first book of the Bible and in your right hand the last page of the fifth book of the Bible. What do they call this section of the Bible?" she asked.

Someone shouted out, "The Torah."

Another asked, "Isn't it also called the Pentateuch?"

Then another called out, "I thought it was also called the Law."

Helen said, "You are all correct," and she began to explain to them when and where and how it was put together. She then moved on to the next thirty-four books of the Old Testament, doing something similar for each section of the Bible. As she spoke, I thought to myself, "I could have done this with the group. I did not need to invite an outside speaker to come in and teach at this level. I could have done this with almost no preparation." That was the very issue. Had I done this, I would have tried to dazzle folks with my knowledge. I would have spent a lot of time preparing a talk. It would have been a lecture, not a show and tell or a simple teaching. It would have been someone with a master's degree in divinity and with a clerical collar speaking to an audience of people who had probably never taken so much as a course on the Bible in college.

Helen met them exactly where they were. She did not begin at the eleventh floor of the biblical skyscraper, to use O'Driscoll's analogy, while they were still wondering whether God gave Moses the Ten Commandments before or after Jesus died. Rather, she met them on the first floor of a great adventure called "Discovering What The Bible Has To Offer." Indeed, Helen was a magnificent teacher of the Bible who created a safe, exciting place where people could begin the adventure of learning about the treasures that the Bible contained. No one felt intimidated to ask even the most basic question. Helen has a great gift, and I learned a lot from watching her. I left that session realizing the ground floor was where we in the mainline church need to begin when we teach about the Bible.

Creating a Safe Place to Overcome Biblical Illiteracy

If we could create a safe setting where the members of our congregations feel comfortable sharing how things truly are for them when it comes to knowing God and understanding God's Word, we would be humbled and perhaps shocked by the basic questions they need to ask. We are wiser to create a safe place where others can come and ask honest basic questions as we listen attentively and respond at a basic level rather than preparing tour de force lectures and addressing things that may of little or no significance to our audience.

Where do we start? The first thing people need to know about reading the Bible is how to choose a translation. Many clergy would be surprised to learn half of the people who enter a bookstore to purchase a Bible leave without having bought one because they are overwhelmed by the number of choices. "I thought that there was only one Bible," people have told me. "I went to the bookstore to buy a Bible and found dozens of different Bibles and different translations and even different kinds of Bibles. There was a Women's Bible and a Green Environmental Bible and Teen Bibles and big print Bibles and Red Letter Bibles, and I did not know which one to purchase. So, I left without buying one."

The first thing, therefore, most Christians need to know is which translation to read. This might sound self-evident to most clergy, but it is not obvious to many who attend church, and it's even harder for most people who do not attend. Most bookstore chains have greatly reduced or completely eliminated their religion sections. They may have a section on the occult, or self-help books, New Age books, a mixture of philosophy, religion, and meditation books, but inevitably they have a selection of Bibles. The Bible continues to be the best-selling book in the world.

Which Bible to Read?

Selling Bibles is such a big market for publishers and those who own the rights to the New Revised Standard Version (NRSV), the New International Version (NIV), the King James Version (KJV) and other translations, that they have spawned new ways to package the Bible to increase sales. Major publishers now offer women's Bibles, women's study Bibles, One-Year Bibles, men's Bibles, men's study Bibles, teen Bibles, teen study Bibles, children's Bibles, big picture Bibles, Bibles with large sections of maps, Bibles with concordances, contemporary translation Bibles, thin-line Bibles, large-print Bibles, travel Bibles, group-study Bibles, Bibles with discussion questions, archeological study Bibles, stewardship and financial Bibles, poverty and social justice Bibles; the list goes on. What translation should we suggest that they read? The Center for Biblical Studies and I recommend the *New Oxford Annotated Translation of the Bible*, which comes with excellent study notes and is a NRSV translation. It is an English translation of the Hebrew and Christian Scriptures, including the deuterocanonical books or Apocrypha, which are books included in Anglican or Episcopal Bibles such as the Oxford Annotated NRSV. These sections are also included in Roman Catholic and Orthodox Church Bibles and are actually used by these Churches for establishing doctrine. I like this version of the Bible because it is a reliable translation and the study notes are very helpful without being overly erudite or esoteric.

The NIV is another excellent translation. Once again, it is another reliable translation that is easy to read and offers very good study notes. The Common English Version (CEB) is a fine translation and has become a personal favorite of mine since its release in 2011. The CEB was created to be at "a comfortable reading level for over half of all English readers," hence the name "Common English Bible." One hundred twenty scholars—men and women—from twenty-four different denominations in American, African, Asian, European, and Latino communities worked on it. The CEB represents the work of a diverse team with broad scholarship. The translators' goal was to produce a rendering of the Bible at the same reading level as the *USA Today* newspaper.

A similar careful process was followed by the creators of the NRSV, the NIV, and the CEB translations. None of these Bibles was translated by a single individual. Each was translated by teams of expert translators, who had an outstanding understanding of the nuances of ancient Hebrew, Greek, and other languages. Each had various teams of translators check the translations of other teams. An enormous amount of time and careful work went into each translation. What makes the CEB unique is that it attempts to substitute more natural wording for traditional biblical terminology. For instance, where most Bibles use the term "Son of Man" in the Old Testament (e.g. Ezekiel 2:1) the CEB translates it as "human." In the New Testament where Jesus uses the Greek version of this term for himself—probably with messianic overtones—the CEB renders it "the Human One." Another example of common English is the substitution of "harass" for "persecute": "If the world harassed me, it will harass you too." (John 15:20).

Bible readers cannot go wrong with the *New Oxford Annotated Version of the Bible*, any of the NRSV translations, the NIV, or CEB. Their easy readability can enhance personal Bible reading and study and help those who are discovering the Bible for themselves for the first time by removing the stumbling blocks of outdated language and expressions, which can make first-time Bible reading more challenging than it needs to be.

Thou Shalt Not Read the King James Version

While there are many fine translations of the Bible, the Center for Biblical Studies and I encourage first-time Bible readers not to use *The King James Version* (KJV) because it is a more difficult text to read. The KJV, or "Authorized

Version" as it is known, makes reading a book that has three thousand year-old passages even more difficult to read. I occasionally encounter someone who has a deep love for the cadences of the English language who has disregarded my advice. Later, they often say, "I didn't follow what you said about *The King James Version* and I tried to read through it on my own, but I got bogged down. Now I am reading a more contemporary translation and it's made all the difference."

I must confess in 2012 I started to read the KJV with the hope of reading through it entirely that year, since 2011 had been the four hundredth anniversary of the translation of this classic English version of the Bible. I, too, got bogged down with the translation like so many others and switched to the CEB. It only reinforced to me the advice that I had given to others.

Listening to the Bible

Many people are now harnessing the power of technology and are reading the Bible using their iPad, iPhone, Kindle, or Nook or are listening to the Bible as an audiobook or on CDs. The NIV Bible is readily available on CDs. *Audio.com*, Faith Comes through Hearing—a Bible reading ministry in New Mexico, and other resources offer wonderful ways of listening to the Bible. Many people are not strong readers or lack the time to sit down for a half hour each day to read. Others may commute for thirty minutes or more daily to work or school, or have time to listen in a volunteer setting or while walking the dog. They could easily listen to the Bible being read aloud. Faith Comes through Hearing offers an MP3 player with the entire New Testament. An individual can listen to the twenty-seven books of the New Testament in just twenty-eight minutes a day for thirty days. This is very useful, as one of the chief reasons people give for not reading the Bible is that they simply do not have enough time to do so.

Richard's Story

One of the members of my church decided to listen to the Bible during the course of a year. He told our congregation it transformed his year. All sorts of good and unusual things started to occur in his life, which he attributed to his commitment to listen to the entire Bible. He heard about our Bible Challenge and became quite excited. "Might I improve my spiritual life?" he wondered. He envisioned it might impact the quality of his life and even improve how he handled money and dealt with issues at work. Would it "make me more generous?" he wondered, "and make me shout less at my boys? Would it be 'Value for time?'"

In the past he had found reading the Bible not to be a good use of his time. It was too wordy. The pages were too thin. The words were too small. There didn't seem to be much of a story as far as he could tell. He failed miserably within thirty days of trying to read through it. He later stumbled upon listening to the Bible, and it made all the difference in his spiritual journey. His experience was so positive that I invited him to preach a sermon to our congregation about his experience.

He is a British actor and a native of London. His accent is as lovely as he is charming. His testimony was so powerful that several women in the parish later told me that their husbands, who never read the Bible, went home, downloaded it on to a mobile device, and started listening to it. Sometimes all it takes is one individual telling another how to do something that has created enormous benefits in his or her life. Years ago I heard a great definition of the word *evangelism.* "It is all about one beggar telling another beggar where to find bread."

The role of clergy is to give voice to the people in the pews and let them share their story about how they read the Bible and how it came alive and transformed their life. Too often, clergy monopolize the life of the congregation by doing all of the talking and communicating. The Bible Challenge recommends having someone in the congregation be invited to write an article each month for the church newsletter about his or her experience of reading the Bible and how it transformed their life.

We gave Richard our British actor a platform to share his story about listening to the Bible during the course of a year, and here is some of what he had to say.

> I had a rather odd, narrow view of who actually reads the Bible—clergy, old ladies and farmers' wives. I remember growing up thinking no one in their right mind would actually read the Bible when you could be watching TV, reading proper books, playing sport, traveling. My own ignorance to this day astounds me. But then, I thought about the John Adams HBO series I had caught up with on TV. I was bowled over by the brilliance and accomplishment of the man and in particular struck by his relationship to the Bible. John Adams wrote to his son: "I have myself for many years made it a practice to read through the Bible once every year. I have always endeavored to read it with the same spirit and temper of mind which I now recommend to you; that is, with the intention and desire that it contribute to my advancement in wisdom and virtue. . . . My custom is, to read four or five chapters every morning, immediately after rising from my bed. It employs about an hour of my time, and seems to me the most suitable manner of beginning the day."
>
> I mean, once is enough, surely! But this guy read it for several years running— once a year! And so it came to pass that I gave myself a break. Through a friend of a friend I met a woman who was very religious. I decided to share and lamented that I had, in fact, failed my own church's Bible Challenge the year before. She went to her car immediately and presented me with a book called *Jesus Calling*, a devotional for every day of the year kind of book. It was comforting to read the

passage each morning and I decided to investigate the *audible.com* Bible apps that in the past I had thought would be kind of cheating. I replaced this [Bible] with this iPhone! It cost ten dollars and was narrated by Bob Sauer. I like the sound of his voice. The total time was sixty-nine hours fifteen minutes—which works out to about fourteen cents per hour. If you want to do this, you have to identify time and place, or both, where you have ten to twenty minutes of spare time. I opted to listen in the car, which turned out to be more productive than I had imagined. Once my boys were safely on the bus, I would jump in the car going to wherever I was heading and listen to at least fifteen or twenty minutes of Audible.

At first it was tough. I'm a news junky and love to listen to BBC World Service in the morning. I also had numerous *audible.com* titles that were going to suffer as I became determined to get through the Bible and complete The Bible Challenge as quickly as possible so I could get back to Daniel Steele, Ken Follet, William Boyd, Tom Rob Smith and Bob Woodward, all waiting patiently in my audible library. The Old Testament is tough. The language is dense and old fashioned. I had never read it from cover to cover. The obsession with human reproduction and circumcision without, in my opinion, even much back story or characterization was difficult to get into. After all my Church of England education, I knew bits of the Bible but was never able to fit them all together and I was looking forward to doing just that.

I listened to the Bible every day. I began to get used to and even look forward to reading the Bible. There was a progression of sorts and, yes, my curiosity was being fulfilled. I found the origin of many biblical names, passages, and references quite fascinating. I began to think, "Yes, this makes sense. You have to read the Bible to know God. How can you not?"

As I listened daily, it wasn't so much what was going on in the Bible, but what was going on outside that was interesting. It was as though the very vibration of my intention—a good, honorable intention or goal—was rubbing off on daily life. Good things began to happen.

He went on to speak about how his life was transformed by reading the Bible and how blessings started to be showered upon him. Richard worked for QVC, selling products on television. He started selling a hot buttered croissant and the sales began skyrocketing. Richard attributed much of his success at work and at home to his Bible reading or Bible listening, which he said was transforming him as a parent, spouse, and employee. His wife noted that he was much calmer. His sons benefited from his increased patience and gentleness. He was more at peace at work. Something inside him felt deeply fulfilled and balanced and this radiated outward into every aspect of his life. His witness was phenomenal.

Like many others, Richard sent me a personal email immediately after completing The Bible Challenge. It was as though he had gotten to the top of a mountain that he had climbed and wanted to share the achievement and good news with me. Here is what he wrote:

> Having started January 1st, I have just finished "reading" the Bible on my *audible.com* app for the first time. In fact, my eighty-three-year-old mother was in the car with me when I got to the end, a special way to finish. It's been a great year, and I am convinced that The Bible Challenge was behind the blessed time we have enjoyed this year. I shall probably start listening to the Bible again soon. Apart from the spiritual food for the soul, it was also fascinating to see how so many literary and cultural references all came from the Bible.
>
> *Thank you—Richard*

90 Percent or More of Our Members Are Not Reading the Bible

One of the problems with church is that clergy rattle on week after week "explaining" what the Bible says and why a particular passage that was read in church has a significant meaning for those who have been listening. This does next to nothing to encourage people in the pews actually to pick up and read their Bibles. While surveys show there are a fair number of Bible studies in Episcopal churches and a large number of respondents claim to read the Bible, I would venture from my experience in colleague groups with rectors of large churches that only 5 percent or less of our members on the church rolls are regularly attending a Bible study.

Perhaps 10 percent are reading the Bible regularly using materials by the Daily Lectionary or a publication like *Forward Day by Day*. The vast majority are doing no regular Bible reading at all. But put someone like Richard in the pulpit and let him tell his story and then give another person a similar chance and another person and let others tell their story in writing through the parish newsletter and you begin to transform a church into a Bible-reading congregation and God's Word begins transforming lives.

The Word of God triumphs over all words. Even the mystics who have experienced direct encounters with what the German theologian Rudolph Otto called "the mysterium tremendum ad fascinens," are less compelling, healing, renewing, and inspiring than the Bible. Listening to the most spell-binding preacher is less transformative than sitting quietly and regularly reading or listening to the Bible on our own. Too many mainline Christians are substituting being spiritually entertained or stimulated by a spiritual book or a captivating or not so captivating preacher for encountering God's Word directly. I am not suggesting that we stop going to church or listening to sermons or reading books by great spiritual writers. They are all important resources for the Christian life. I am suggesting when a person sets aside time on a regular basis to spend with God either to read or listen to the Bible, lives are changed.

God Honors the Time We Spend with His Word

God honors our setting aside time to say, "God, I want to be with you. I want to be in your presence and be blessed by reading your Word. I am open to change and allowing you to mold and shape me, like clay in the potter's hand. May our time together be a blessing for me that I may be a greater blessing to others." In The Bible Challenge, we encourage our participants to utter such a prayer before they begin their daily Bible reading, rather than merely pick up the Bible and race through it as though they were reading the newspaper.

St. Paul, after all, tells us, "Faith comes from what is heard, and what is heard comes through the word of Christ." (Romans 10:17) Readers of the Bible need to enshrine the Bible in their homes so that it might be enshrined in their hearts. I try never to let anything sit on top of my Bible. I do not put a cup of coffee on it. I try not to ever let my Bible sit under a stack of other books on my desk. My Bible is not a book among books, it is the Book of Books.

The late Fr. Basil Pennington was a remarkable teacher of prayer. A photo taken of him sits in my office. I met him on the day after my wife and I were married. Our wedding was on a Saturday in Richmond, Virginia, and we were not scheduled to depart for our honeymoon in Paris, France until Monday. I asked her if she would mind if I went to a retreat center in Richmond to meet with Basil for an hour, and she agreed. Basil and I met for an hour of spiritual conversation, and thus began one of the most important and influential spiritual relationships in my life. He later came and spoke at each of the churches where I served on five different occasions. I learned a tremendous amount from him.

One of his stories I will always remember is about people in the Ozark Mountains. Basil spent time with people in that part of Arkansas who would "enshrine" the Bible in their homes. Every night, they would read a portion of the Bible before going to bed. Then they would put the Bible on their slippers below their bed. That reminded them to pick up their Bible first thing in the morning before they put on their slippers and read it again. After reading a portion of the Bible immediately after getting up in the morning, they would make their bed and place the Bible on their pillow. This reminded them to pick up the Bible before going to bed and spend some time reading it before they slept. The ritual made it clear to themselves and to their family that the Bible took precedence in their lives. It was not just another book or a book among books, but it was the Book of Books, the fountain of life and source of eternal wisdom. I believe God honors us when we honor God's Word. When we honor God by taking time to engage God's Word each day, God bestows special blessings upon us and helps us to grow in the

Word. Most Episcopalians do not talk like this or think like this, but I believe it is absolutely true. God bestows many blessings upon us as we faithfully engage the Word.

Reading the Bible Is Not Easy

Along the way, I have found some persons who have tried and who have truly struggled to read the Bible. Many try again and again and finally something clicks. The first time I tried to read Fyodor Dostoevsky's masterpiece *The Brothers Karamazov* I failed. I got bogged down in all the Russian patronymics. I was confused. The variations of names used to identify the same person seemed baffling. I started all over again and again was frustrated. It was only on the third time that the book began to make sense, and I could follow the storyline. It was worth it, as I fell in love with *The Brothers Karamazov*. I found riches in it that I would never have discovered had I allowed myself to give up easily in reading it. Reading the Bible is similar. It is not an easy task. Clergy and lay leaders need to be upfront with those whom they encourage to read the Bible. It is a challenging book to read, and reading the entire Bible is akin to climbing a mountain. It is a true spiritual feat, but one well-worth doing for the rewards are incredible.

The Story—A Helpful Option

Some individuals, however, who have tried reading the Bible and failed miserably, may enjoy reading *The Story*, a seamless collection of Bible stories woven together and published by Zondervan who own the rights to the NIV translation. *The Story* omits genealogies, dietary codes, and other portions of the Bible deemed boring and less critical to read. *The Story* looks like a novel and to some extent reads like one. The Old Testament and New Testament are each reduced to about 250 pages which means the Old Testament is reduced by about two-thirds. Any redundancies are removed. You read about one good or bad king once.

The Story is very accessible for people not used to reading the Bible, but it is not the full Bible, nor is it a true translation of the Bible. Hence, it is not my first choice to recommend to someone interested in reading the Bible. One Episcopal rector whom I know and greatly respect has encouraged his entire parish to read *The Story* with the hopes that this will make the Bible more accessible to them and stimulate his church members eventually to read the entire Bible. I prefer to start people on reading the Bible itself and point to *The Story* as a good alternative for those who have struggled to read the Bible and failed.

The Message—A Help to Many

Some clergy highly recommend reading Eugene Peterson's engaging contemporary rendering of the Bible known as *The Message*, which has helped many people who have struggled to read the Bible and access its ancient message for readers who live in an entirely different culture. Even long-time Bible readers will find it a refreshing book that captures the Bible's message and breaks it open in fresh, new ways.

Both *The Story* and *The Message* are not true translations of the Bible, so we recommend not focusing on them initially. The Center for Biblical Studies and I recommend introducing them as you re-launch The Bible Challenge for people who tried but struggled in reading the Bible in the previous year. They are fine options. Overall, I believe that regularly reading of the Bible is the single best way to grow in faith. Here is what a few recent participants in The Bible Challenge had to say about their experience of reading or listening to the entire Bible:

> *I completed reading the Bible last year and now read and meditate on the daily readings from Forward Day by Day. Plus we have started a Scripture study class at Trinity and it has opened a whole new world of meaning. Scripture is central for me now and I thank you for keeping me focused.*—SHARON FROM SAND SPRINGS, OKLAHOMA

> *There is certainly a hunger in many for a better understanding of the Bible and a thirst for a relationship with God. I wonder if that is the reason that The Bible Challenge has caught fire. For me, reading the Bible in a year was transformative. I hadn't realized how beautifully it was written and how profoundly the stories would affect me. To say that it deepened my faith is an understatement; it really changed it. My prayer life opened into a quiet conversation with God where I felt heard and not alone. I had two intense religious experiences during services for healing that have sealed my belief. I know God is with me. And I know that started when I read the Bible in a year. Thank you for extending such an invitation.*

> *So, yes, I continue to read the Bible. When I read again, I perceive it differently so it almost feels new. I find it immensely peaceful; it is my sacred time. This time around, I don't read it in order, and I don't read it every day. My Bible is on my bedside table, and when my mind is quiet, I know it's time to read. I downloaded the Bible onto my iPad, and I read it while traveling or waiting, when I have time alone to ponder its meaning. I purchased The Bible Companion by John Bowden which clears up or puts into context any confusion that I have. Every other book that I purchase is spiritual, and I try to see life through someone else's eyes. When we go to Trinity Church, Boston, I always find something to read about the Bible in the church bookstore. In these ways I keep my Bible reading active and current. Church and prayer are my havens.*—PRISCILLA FROM BOSTON

I am almost done with my second Bible challenge in a row! It is a great feeling to set out on a journey that can't be rushed, one that has to be taken by small steps each day and to finally reach the destination. I feel the first time I read the Bible I was only skimming the surface and this time I went slightly deeper beyond the stories and more into the meaning. I can only hope each time I continue to read I get more insight and wisdom.

*I have been working on my Bible Challenge each day. I fell behind early because I didn't really start until mid-April. Despite this, I realized that I really had no excuse not to complete The Bible Challenge. The thing that most people complain about is a lack of time, but that is not a problem I have. So recently I have been pretty diligent about reading each day. I am trying to find a balance between reading slowly to absorb the text and meditate on it and reading at a clip to make sure I finish before the end of the year. I am currently reading about ten pages each day I read, which is about 4–5 times per week. I feel that completing this undertaking will give me a great sense of accomplishment and make me a better Christian.—*ROB, A PEACE CORPS WORKER IN COLOMBIA

*Well, we are over half way through the Bible and I am still with you daily. As an individual I tell others, but the journey is mine alone. After being a lifetime member of an Episcopal church that is now in transition as far as the congregation is concerned, I seek God daily from this Bible Challenge ministry. I am reminded that I have followed the liturgy faithfully. Familiar words resound in my head with every reading. Now they have more meaning, rooted in history and guiding me to keep the faith with my young grandchildren.—*LAURIE

I thought you might like to know that after about two years and two months, and plenty of stops and starts, I finally finished The Bible Challenge. I got slogged down in the prophets and the Apocrypha, and ended up skimming through a good bit of that, but I finally made it through.

I'm sorry to say that I wasn't real good about steadily reading every day for a few minutes, but rather tended to do it in bunches. Your earlier advice about mixing in some psalms, gospels and epistles with a dose of Old Testament each day was very helpful.

*I found much of the Old Testament tough to take, which I guess is one reason why we don't dwell too much on it in most churches these days. I feel good that I completed the challenge, and I think I learned a few things in the process. The Bible is indeed an amazing book with just about every kind of writing in it imaginable. Thank you for inspiring me to do this.—*RANDY

I am so in favor of reading the whole Bible. I have kept a personal record of the times I've read through all the biblical books since 1989, and I led an electronic Bible study from 2006 to 2010 in which we read through books of the Bible at a rate of one chapter per week. Your program seems beautifully structured and well resourced—I have learned a great deal just from reading your description and tip sheet. Because it looks like you'd like parishes to consider joining, I will share information about your Bible Challenge with my home parish, the parish where I'm currently serving as deacon, and the parish where I served as an intern.—THE REV. DR. CAROLYN SHARP—PROFESSOR OF OLD TESTAMENT AT YALE DIVINITY SCHOOL

We enjoy reading the Old Testament, New Testament and a psalm each day and meeting once a week to discuss it. I like the group and the format. We all particularly like the daily mediations that do an excellent job linking the daily Old Testament, psalm and New Testament readings. I think there are 100 people pledged to this program in our parish. Pretty good numbers for Episcopalians!—ELIZABETH FROM VIRGINIA

CHAPTER 9

Reading an Ancient Text
with Modern Eyes

"Do not be conformed to this world, but be transformed by the renewing of your minds, so that you may discern what is the will of God—what is good and acceptable and perfect."—Romans 12:2

"Take away, O Lord, the veil of my heart while I read the Scriptures." —Lancelot Andrewes

"Reading the Bible without meditating upon it is like trying to eat without swallowing."—Anonymous

• ❖ •

The Bible is not an easy book to read. It is very difficult to begin at the first page and try to read straight through to the last page despite generations having tried to do so. I suspect that only one in twenty persons who attempt this today make it to the end. Most readers bog down somewhere around Leviticus and never make it into the first chapter of the New Testament. Somewhere, while struggling to get through the Old Testament, they conclude that the Bible is a tedious book full of too much irrelevant information and they quit reading it. Bible readers need some help and encouragement. This chapter is designed to give first-time readers some basic insights to help them get started and to remind church leaders of what people in our churches need to know in order to succeed. The first thing to know or to teach others before they read is the Bible is perhaps the most complicated book anyone can attempt to read. It is unlike anything else that we will endeavor to read and comprehend. It is not meant to be read as a novel, a scientific manual, a historical text, a book of poetry, or a biography. Yet, it has many of these elements in it. The word "Bible" comes from the Greek word *biblos*, which actually means "books" rather than "book." Hence, it should be called "The Good Books" rather than "The Good Book."

While deeply treasured, it is complex. It is not a single book, but a library of sixty-six individual books placed side by side, thirty-nine in the Old Testament and twenty-seven in the New Testament. They were written over the course of about a thousand years, so the style of writing varies greatly. The process of compiling these books ended about eighteen hundred years ago. These are ancient texts and reflect archaic practices, beliefs, and patterns of living. A person must learn to be a savvy reader of the Bible, which takes time and comes only through practice, reading, discussing the Bible with others, reading books about the Bible, and, most of all, sitting with the Scriptures and letting God's Word reveal to us what is vital and what is dispensable or irrelevant to our lives. No one else can decide this for us.

In reading the Bible, we discover both inspiration and information. The biblical stories are not written for amusement or instruction, but are set down as episodes of history that clearly reveal that God is active in our world. Throughout history God has endeavored to reveal himself to us. God longs for self-disclosure, and God wants a relationship with each of us. Like works of classic literature, Greek tragedies or the writings of Plato and Shakespeare, the Bible has the power to speak across the centuries. No book has had greater influence or impact on humans. It is older than the Quran, which has also exercised a wide impact across the centuries. Today, there are two billion Christians and over one billion Muslims in the world. Thus it can be argued that the Bible has made the largest impact of any book in history.

The books of the Bible are not arranged chronologically. The Book of Genesis was not the first book written. They were written in many places ranging from Israel to Rome to Ephesus by a wide variety of authors of differing ages and backgrounds and intended for widely differing audiences. What binds them together is the Church's belief that God has spoken to us through the various writings. They comprise God's revelation to us.

One of the great things about reading portions of both the Old and the New Testament together is we can see echoes across time that reveal how God acts in history. In the Servant Songs of the prophet Isaiah we see the prefiguring of Christ as the crucified and suffering Messiah. In reading about the sacrificial system in the Hebrew Scriptures, we learn the significance of how the Early Church first came to understand and appreciate the power of what Jesus did upon the cross for our salvation.

In reading a psalm each day, we begin to appreciate the longest and one of the most influential books in the entire Bible, a foundation for Christian worship and prayer for almost two thousand years and a spiritual resource for the Jews going back even farther. Every emotional and spiritual experience seems to be captured within the covers of the Psalter. These prayers, which were set to music and meant to be sung, range from thanksgivings, praises, enthronement psalms, and laments to angry rants at God, shocking for their candor and honesty.

The Thirty-Nine Articles

Episcopal Church doctrine is spelled out in *The Thirty-Nine Articles* found in the back of The Book of Common Prayer. The *Articles* have been revised numerous times throughout their history, but the basic intent is to articulate what members of the Church of England believe about vital aspects of Church doctrine. As regards Scripture and what we believe, Article Six states,

Holy Scripture containeth all things necessary to salvation: so that whatsoever is not read therein, nor may be proved thereby, is not to be required of any man, that it should be believed as an article of the Faith, or be thought requisite or necessary to salvation. (p. 868)

The key here is that the Bible "containeth all things necessary to salvation," but not all things found in the Bible are necessary for salvation. In fact, there is much in the Bible that seems irrelevant to salvation. A young graduate of a prestigious university, who took up the challenge to read the entire Bible in a year, recently asked if he could meet with me. I invited him to send some of his questions in advance so that I could give them some thought and our conversation could be more fruitful. He wrote,

Does God predestine us and have our whole life planned out? Why does God create those who will not be Christians? How can non-Christians be so good and many Christians still be so selfish and evil? At what point do you think God saves us and what does it look like to submit to Him? Why did Christ need to die for us? (why couldn't God just forgive us on His own accord?) Why is there a lot of text in the OT that is not timeless? (the creation of the tabernacle, offering rituals, etc. . . .)

These are great questions. Episcopalians do not believe in predestination. We do not believe that God has scripted out our entire future. Rather, God is working constantly with us to help us make the most of what we have done in the past and what we can do in the future with our lives. God does not purposely create people who will reject him or decide not to be Christian. God gives us free will to choose to follow God or not. Each person has the choice, if they are introduced to Jesus and God by someone else. Christ died for us to atone for our sins and to build a bridge of forgiveness between God and all of humanity. Jesus made the ultimate sacrifice in order that we might know God and experience abundant life, being forgiven for all of our failures and sins and living with hope and grace.

The young man's questions reflect what a lot of readers of the Old Testament feel. There is so much there that seems ancient, outdated, and irrelevant to our ordinary lives that one who attempts to read the Bible from cover to cover often puts it down within a matter of days and stops reading it altogether, which is why the Center for Biblical Studies and I suggest reading a chapter of the New Testament each day, along with a psalm and a portion of the Old Testament. Neophyte readers will be helped to know how the Bible is divided into sections. The Old Testament is composed of the Law, the Prophets, and the Writings. Israel saw God being revealed through historical events as well as proclamation and judgment. The New Testament is composed of gospels, the book of Acts, letters called "epistles," and finally the mysterious and apocalyptic book of Revelation. Brief teachings on these categories can give readers a foothold as they read through Scripture.

Bible readers will benefit from learning about the similarities of the Synoptic Gospels of Matthew, Mark, and Luke and how they can be read and studied together, while the Gospel of John stands apart as a thing of utter spiritual beauty and vastly different structure. In John's Gospel, Jesus makes the great "I am" claims. The story follows a very different timeline from the Synoptics. Jesus enters Jerusalem to share the Passover one time in the Synoptics but three times in John, indicating that his ministry lasted for three years as opposed to one. The Synoptic Gospels place the cleansing of the Temple shortly before Jesus' crucifixion as a sort of cataclysmic event which brought the religious authorities down on Jesus. The author of John's Gospel, by contrast, places it at the beginning of Jesus' ministry. All of the gospels concur Jesus was executed on a Friday, but the Synoptic Gospels maintain that it was the Day of the Passover, while the Gospel of John states that it was the Day of Preparation, preceding the Passover itself. The Day of Preparation is the day on which the lambs were slaughtered as sacrifices to be eaten at the Passover Seder. It was a most fitting day for the Son of Man to surrender his life for the sins of the world and the salvation of humanity.

In his book *Encountering Scripture: A Scientist Explores the Bible*, John Polkinghorne, one of the world's great particle physicists and a Church of England priest writes,

> A central task for the Christian interpreter of Scripture is to discern what in the Bible has lasting truthful authority, rightly commanding the continuing respect of successive generations, and what is simply time-bound cultural expression, demanding no necessary continuing allegiance from us today. (4–5)

While many in the past fifty years have pointed to passages in the Book of Leviticus to support their thoughts about homosexuality, few have pointed to Leviticus 19:19 or Deuteronomy 22:11 that forbid the wearing of two differing fibers. These passages, if taken seriously, could destroy the worldwide garment industry, which depends on the mixing of various fibers in order to produce clothing. Furthermore, the admonition in Leviticus not to touch the skin of a pig would be enough to ban football from ever being played. Of course, we do not apply these literally. The challenge is to determine which passages to apply literally to our lives and which are to be read and pondered, but not applied to our daily living.

Read the Bible as if God Wrote It for You

St. Augustine encouraged everyone to read Scripture like a series of love letters from God written directly to them. An outside source will not teach us how to read the Bible. Rather, our best teacher will be to listen carefully to our own conscience guided by the Holy Spirit as we engage God's Word regularly and strive to comprehend its overall message, seeking the value of each passage and how it applies to our daily lives.

Over time, many passages that were once deemed important, shaping Christian customs in previous eras, have since been found outdated and unnecessary to living our faith, such as Paul's emphatic insistence that women cover their heads while worshipping. (I Cor. 11:2–16) Meanwhile, passages like I Corinthians 13, which Paul wrote to the church in Corinth, remain powerfully influential for generation after generation of Christians.

> Love is patient; love is kind; love is not envious or boastful or arrogant or rude. It does not insist on its own way; it is not irritable or resentful; it does not rejoice in wrongdoing, but rejoices in the truth. It bears all things, believes all things, hopes all things, endures all things. (I Cor. 13:4–7)

One can begin reading the Bible with one, two or three chapters of Genesis, a psalm and a chapter of the New Testament each day, beginning with the Gospel of Matthew. In this way, all of the books of the Bible are read in sequence. The reader will hear echoes of the Old Testament in the New Testament. He or she will begin to understand the serious focus on sin and forgiveness that permeates the entire Bible. The history of sacrifice and the way it changes will be understood far differently and will illuminate our understanding of God, the people of God, and what it means to follow God.

If a reader reads three chapters of the Old Testament, a psalm and a chapter of the New Testament each day and does no readings on Sunday in order to spend time hearing the Scriptures being read aloud in church, she or he can read through the entire Bible in a year. This varied diet of Bible readings ensures there will always be something spiritually enlivening in any day's readings to sustain a disciplined reader and help her or him continue reading profitably through the entire Bible.

The Bible is not meant to be read as a guidebook for charting our daily life by simply opening its pages and acting on whatever we read. There is an old joke about a man who was in great despair, when it dawned on him that the Bible was a book full of great wisdom and truth. He thought, "I will pick up the Bible and read it and do whatever it says." So he picked up the Good Book, opened it randomly and read the words, "Judas hanged himself." Not feeling inspired in the way that he expected, he decided to give it another try. He closed the Bible, then randomly opened it again and placed his finger down on the page and read, "Go and do likewise." Clearly, this is not how the Bible is meant to be read. As Polkinghorne writes,

> To use an analogy that comes naturally to me as a scientist, the Bible is not the ultimate textbook in which one can look up ready-made answers to all the big questions, but is more like a laboratory notebook, in which are recorded critical

historical experiences through which aspects of the divine will and nature have been most accessibly revealed. I believe that the nature of divine relevation is not the mysterious transmission of infallible propositions which are to be accepted without question, but the record of persons and events through which the divine will and nature have been most transparently made known.

The Bible began in an oral culture where stories were told rather than written down. Over time the story expanded and changed and there were various accounts of the same story related by different people in different places. Everyone knew the stories did not always correspond exactly to fact. The oldest piece of literature in the New Testament is Paul's first letter to the Thessalonians. It was probably written about twenty years after the death and resurrection of Jesus to a small, struggling community on the coast of the Mediterranean in what is now called Greece. Twenty years, however, is a long time for something to be told and retold, memorized and altered in various ways, before it was set down on parchment and possibly altered again by those who transcribed it. What is remarkable is not that this or any text of the Bible is the literal truth or inerrant, but rather that God has spoken to individuals and communities for centuries through these texts and continues to do so today. No book on earth has altered the course of humanity more than the Bible. Hence, it is the Book of Books.

Oral tradition and the lag time between what occurred and when it was written down is one of the reasons why the four gospels show inconsistencies. The four gospels were written by four different authors over a span of possibly sixty years. Much like today we can view things differently in recounting the same event. If you have ever been involved in a car accident, you know that no two persons see it in quite the same way. The two drivers each have very different perspectives. A witness watching from another car or from the sidewalk may offer a completely different account of how the accident occurred. If you allow several months or years to lapse, the memory of the incident will probably be vastly altered or barely remembered.

Ancient artists sometimes depicted various authors of the Bible listening intently as an angel dictated words or a bird told them what to write as though they took dictation directly from God, but this is not how the Bible was composed. It was written by human beings inspired by God who were convinced that they had received divine revelation and had to write it down for others to read and benefit. With the exception of the letter to Philemon, the four gospels and all of the letters of Paul were written for *communities* rather than *individuals*.

For a long time, biblical scholars influenced by other areas of the humanities and scientific analysis attempted to view the Bible through an historical critical method searching rigorously for veracity. Scholars attempted to date and place texts to determine if there was more than one author or if other writers came along later and edited the text. While intellectually stimulating, this process turned the Bible into a vast sea of clues for detectives seeking to solve one mystery after another. The Bible was treated like a cadaver to be carefully examined by the scholar's scalpel. Fortunately, biblical scholarship has moved on recently and the focus today is more on contextual matters and readings.

Unlike the Quran, which is full of teachings and sayings, the Bible is full of stories. For that reason alone, it is easier to read even by a neophyte to religion. The Christian Scriptures offer some of the most engaging stories ever written in any form of literature. The Bible cannot be read as one might read *The New York Times*. As a former reporter, I still love reading the newspaper. The front page is usually full of "hard news." There may also be a "feature story" on the front page, which offers an entertaining or uplifting tale amid the day's more painful or disturbing stories. Inside the paper are international, regional, and local news stories; editorials which convey a writer's opinion; theater, orchestra, restaurant, and movie reviews; obituaries; weather forecasts; comics; sports stories; classified ads, large print ads, and more.

Different Genres of Literature

The Bible is composed of many genres of literature. Just as it would be a mistake to read the comics as if they were "hard news" or an op-ed piece as if it were a blow-by-blow account of what transpired in an event, we need to be aware of the varieties of literature found within the Bible. There are myths, legends, laws, letters, parables, poetry, prose, etiologies, theophanies, songs, hymns, history, dietary codes, genealogies, biography, building and design specifications and instructions, autobiographical information, and apocalyptic literature found within the various books. Some of it can be skimmed quickly, especially in a first time reading through the entire Bible. There are portions that are mystical in nature, such as when the prophet Ezekiel experienced an overwhelming vision of God beside the banks of the river Chebar (Ezekiel 1), or when a fiery chariot pulled by four strange living creatures escorted him to heaven.

We do not need to read every word of a long genealogy, but we should realize then, just as now, family matters. We are a product of those who came before us. We are part of a family system, and we carry on a family name with pride and respect. We do not need to read every word of the long and sometimes very boring dietary codes in order to understand that what we eat and how we eat and who we eat with matters to God. God is in the details of our lives. God cares about our ordinary actions and activities. While what we eat and who we eat with today may differ widely from what the book of Leviticus suggests, there are commonalities that still speak to us. The most unlikely passage of Scripture can be an instrument through which God communicates today to an attentive reader.

The Bible Is Not a Scientific Manual

The Bible often employs metaphorical and analogical language. The Psalms are hymns that were meant to be sung: poems set to music. We no longer have the music, but we have the words. Most of the Bible is not meant to be read like an essay or a factual report or a scientific treatise. God is beyond all understanding. God defies the constraints of human logic, reasoning, and language. Hence, we need imagery and metaphor. That's why artists and composers have done as much as biblical scholars and theologians to illuminate the nature of God. No scholar has contributed as much to shaping our concept of heaven and hell as Dante in his *Divine Comedy*. We fail the Bible by sitting down to read it as a factual account of creation and history. T.S. Eliot wrote in *The Four Quartets*, "You are not here to verify." The same applies to the Bible. When we read, we must suspend some of our historical, scientific mindset that is trained to look for verifiable and reliable facts. The Bible is not a collection of facts. It is revelation from God given to humanity through fallible authors.

The Church Fathers—Origen, Clement of Rome, Augustine, and Gregory of Nyssa—understood that the "days of creation" were not twenty-four hour periods of time. They were metaphorical segments of time. Likewise, when it rained forty days and forty nights on the earth, killing all the life that was not aboard Noah's Ark, it was a metaphorical period of time that seemed as though it would never end. The number forty is a Hebraism for a time that seems unending. Hence, Moses spent forty years living in Pharaoh's house, forty years working as a shepherd for his father-in-law Jethro and forty years wandering in the desert leading an exodus of Jews from Egypt.

Adam was said to have lived to be nine hundred and thirty years. Noah lived longer and died at the age of nine hundred and fifty. Could this be true? Certainly it is not. Church leaders need to assure Bible readers that we are not meant to take every word literally. Parts of the Bible must be accepted on faith. We have to learn which parts to keep and apply to our lives today and which parts to consider metaphors, myths, legends, or rules that applied to an ancient culture. To say that Adam or Noah lived a very long life is to say that God blessed them and honored them with the gift of years. It is not, however, a factual statement suggesting that some people lived nine centuries in biblical times.

Portions of the Bible are told in the form of myths. Many of these were influenced by tales from other cultures, especially by Babylonian myths like the Epic of Gilgamesh. This myth of an epic flood exercised significant influence over the author of the book of Genesis. Myths were the primary way to describe our relationship with God or the gods. They were not factual reports. Snakes, for example, do not speak. This again is metaphorical rather than scientific language. To read myths as scientific reports destroys the capacity of well-educated, rational beings to appreciate and follow the timeless teachings of the Bible. In the creation narrative in Genesis, for example, the birds come too early to have been created, yet plants arrive before the sun exists to fuel them with photosynthesis. The creation narrative is not a blow-by-blow account, but a myth which reminds us God designed the universe and brought it into being. The handiwork of God is all over creation. When we appreciate and care for creation we discover God and serve our Creator.

The story of Adam and Eve is also a myth. Like the story of creation, it was never intended to be taken as a factual account because it does not hold up to any reliable scientific scrutiny. For example, the sources of light were created after the light itself according to Genesis. Likewise, Genesis 1 and 2 tell two very different accounts of the creation of Adam and Eve: in Genesis 1 they were created together; in Genesis 2, Adam preceded Eve, and Eve was made from a rib in Adam's side. It is helpful to realize that in the Hebrew mindset the more accounts of something the better. Each sheds new light on the subject, even if they differ. Hence, two differing stories about the creation of the first two human beings on earth posed no problems.

We in the West, however, are shaped by a Greek mindset that requires there can be only one truth, explanation, or answer. One story must be correct and the other story must be false. Many biblical literalists read Genesis 1 and 2 and try to argue that there are no differences in the stories in order to maintain that the Bible is inerrant. This is a fool's errand at best. The Bible is full of revelation, but humans wrote down the words, and scholars have helped us to see that there are numerous inaccuracies in terms of names, dates, and places mentioned, as well as direct contradictions or stories told in completely different ways.

I remember eating lunch in a restaurant in Richmond, Virginia with a bright lawyer who had expressed interest in possibly joining our church. We met through a funeral or a wedding conducted at the church, and he seemed genuinely interested in faith. As we spoke, however, he said, "I cannot accept Christianity as real because of the whole Adam and Eve thing."

"What do you mean?" I inquired.

He responded, "It's inconceivable to me to accept that story of Adam and Eve or Noah's Ark and many of the other stories found in the Bible and believe that they are true." I agreed with him that they were not true, or if true, then they had been embellished. I explained to him the various genres of literature in the Bible and noted that it was a mistake for anyone to read Genesis as a factual account of how creation occurred. That was not how the Bible was meant to be read. What struck me, however, was that vast gap in knowledge and awareness between what this bright lawyer had received in his legal training and his almost neophyte understanding of religion, the Bible, Christianity, and literature. He had little or no appreciation for myth and legend and the various genres of the Bible. Perhaps he studied Greek mythology in elementary school or junior high, but no one had ever explained to him the nature of the stories of Adam and Eve, Noah and the flood, the Exodus, or the burning bush and Moses.

The gap prevented him from accepting Christianity and taking even baby steps along the spiritual journey. In dismissing the stories after a superficial reading, he lost the opportunity to appreciate the deeper messages beneath the surface. The story of Adam and Eve, for example, is about boundaries and order. God established a quintessential environment for us to inhabit and set boundaries for our own sake. When humans violate these boundaries, there is punishment. We spend most of our lives rediscovering this story in our own lives. When we transgress the boundaries, there is always a price to pay. It is not a story about two actual people at the beginning of time. It is a story about us today, and the same lesson that has applied to billions of people across time applies to us today. We have freedom, but must respect constraints and limitations on that freedom in order not to hurt ourselves or others.

Sin erupts anytime a human being selfishly demands to "do it my way." A breach in the created order occurs, and inevitably someone is hurt. St. Paul speaks in Romans 5 about Jesus as the "second Adam." "Just as sin came into the world through one man, and death through sin, and so death spread to all because all have sinned," notes Paul, so "much more surely has the grace of one man, Jesus Christ, abounded for many." God has restored humanity to a just relationship with God through Jesus' sacrifice upon the cross. It is this truth above all that we preach and hold to be true as Christians. It is the North Star that leads all of us on our Christian journey. As a result, Scripture is not a collection of dead facts in an ancient document to be picked and probed like a cadaver. Rather the Bible is the greatest repository of living faith and a font of eternal wisdom, healing, forgiveness, and grace that continues to inspire and transform lives around the world today.

The Nature of God in the Bible

Even the depiction of God varies greatly from book to book and sometimes even within a particular book of the Bible. One of the most common things that we have heard at the Center for Biblical Studies is, "I really like the God of the New Testament. He is patient, kind, loving, and forgiving and slow to anger or punish anyone. The God of the Old Testament, however, seems mean and wrathful, has a short fuse and is quick to seek vengeance. Do we follow one or two different gods?" The answer is we follow one God, but this very God has revealed his being in different ways to different people across the centuries.

Some believe that God evolved over time and became more patient, loving, and forgiving. Others maintain that God was angry and wrathful as noted in the Old Testament. Still others believe that human understanding of God evolved over time from an almost barbaric overseer to a loving father figure that was more compassionate and loving as expressed in the New Testament. Each person must decide for him or herself what to believe. I personally opt for the latter viewpoint. I believe that humans have projected much of their own violent outlook and angry judgment upon God. Over time, we humans have come to a far clearer view of God, which is that of a loving, compassionate and forgiving Creator. We must remind ourselves as well that Judaism was the first religion in history to conceive of one God. This monotheistic concept was an enormous breakthrough in the understanding of God and humanity.

Even in the New Testament we find stories that seem to give God's reputation a black eye. Take the story of Ananias and Sapphira as told in Acts 5:1–11. The couple sold some of their property and pretended to give all of their proceeds back to Church, while secretly withholding some of the money for themselves. The husband was struck dead for his actions. When the wife returned home, she was informed that her husband was just carried out dead, and she immediately died as well. Did God really strike people dead because they did not return 100 percent of what was available to them to share with the Church?

As Walter Brueggemann writes when speaking about the Covenantal promise between God and humanity, the story of God's relationship with us "tells us something about God, that God is not a remote, self-serving agent who is for God alone; God is for us, characteristically involved on behalf of all creatures." (*The Bible Makes Sense*, 17) Hence, one of the benefits of reading the Bible as a daily spiritual discipline is over time we develop a healthy concept of God that is not formed by sound-bites, but is assembled from a more nuanced reading of the entire book allowing us to discover the true God who is actively involved in each of our daily lives and is our ultimate counselor, comforter, healer, forgiver, and source of love, hope, and faith.

What Do We Make of Violence in the Bible?

Another very troubling aspect of the Bible is violence. Most of the violent passages are removed from "One Year Bibles" sold in bookstores that are a compendium of Bible lessons arranged to be read each day throughout the year. The same holds true of the Common Lectionary, which mainline churches share and read together in church each Sunday. It is composed of a portion of the Old Testament, a psalm, a selection from one of the epistles or the book of Acts or the book of Revelation, and a reading from one of the four Gospels. In almost all cases, the Lectionary omits violent sections of the Bible. As a consequence, when mainline Christians read through the entire Bible they are often aghast at the amount of violence, especially in the Old Testament. They are shocked by the amount of suffering and vengeance that God seems to instigate, sanction, or disregard.

> Hear, O Israel! Today you are drawing near to do battle against your enemies. Do not lose heart, or be afraid, or panic, or be in dread of them; for it is the Lord your

God who goes with you, to fight for you against your enemies, to give you victory. (Deut. 20:3–4)

Time and again, God seems to have chosen sides. God championed the Israelites against their enemies and at other times supported Israel's enemies and allowed them to gain victory or destroy Jerusalem and the Israelites in order to punish the Hebrews for failing to keep God's Covenant. In 1 Samuel 15, God rebuked Saul for not obeying his command to "utterly destroy the sinners of the Amalekites, and fight against them until they are consumed." (I Sam. 15:18) How was God acting justly here? Is this the God we worship and follow?

Indeed, portions of the Old Testament read like holocaust chronicles. What I have found interesting is how those who have read the entire Bible often begin to see a strong similarity between what they came across in some of the more troubling portions and what they read or heard in the daily news. The parallels made the Bible seem more relevant. It mirrors the problems, the anguish, and the tragedies that plague our world today. Indeed, the Bible is relevant. It is not just a book about saintly people behaving in saintly ways. It tells the stories of people who frequently did despicable things, who were punished many times by God and who often recognized their incredible shortcomings and need for grace, love, and forgiveness. The people in the Bible are more like us than we have ever imagined.

By reading the entire Bible and not just the more sanitized portions, readers are challenged to wrestle with questions of theodicy: Where is God in the midst of pain and suffering? Why do bad things happen to good people? Where does evil come from and why does God permit it to occur? Does God himself commit evil? We need to wrestle with these important questions, but One-Year-Bibles and the Common Lectionary omit some of the most powerful biblical stories, making it far more likely that we will not engage these questions.

There are other stories that cause us to question the nature and character of God. One is the binding of Isaac, which is known by Jews as the *akedah*. Did God really command Abraham to take his son atop Mt. Moriah, bind his hands and feet together, and offer him as a human sacrifice upon an altar? Scholars believe this story is an etiology meant to instruct the Israelites that God was forbidding the practice of child sacrifice, which was common when the story was first told. The neophyte Bible reader, however, will struggle with this story, and rightly so. Would God ever exact this sort of sacrifice from us? What does it mean to live sacrificially? How much will God require of us? Is God just, ruthless, or malevolent? As we read through the Bible each one of us must gather information prayerfully and use it to shape an accurate and healthy understanding of God that will guide us to lead faithful, compassionate, and loving lives. Often it is the violence within us that is being projected back onto God. One of the most shocking texts in the Bible is Psalm 137, which begins with a poignant opening line

By the rivers of Babylon—there we sat down and there we wept
    when we remembered Zion.
On the willows there we hung up our harps.
For there our captors asked us for songs,
and our tormentors asked for mirth, saying
    'Sing us one of the song of Zion!' (Ps. 137:1–3)

As the psalm continues, it takes a turn from sorrow to zealous anger and a passionate desire for vengeance. The psalmist concludes,

O daughter of Babylon, you devastator!
Happy shall they be who pay you
    back what you have done to us!
Happy shall they be who take your little ones
    and dash them against the rock! (Ps. 137:8–9)

It might do us a world of good to recite an entire psalm like this in church and to acknowledge there are moments where we would like to kill or hurt or at least punish someone who has harmed us or others. The Lectionary neuters this psalm; it is never read aloud in its entirety in church. Once again, good manners and tactfulness triumph over the ability to read the entire Bible and examine our own humanity more fully

Old Testament scholar Pete Enns helped me as I launched the Center for Biblical Studies to share The Bible Challenge around the world. He said,

We as Christians have the good fortune to read the Bible knowing how the story will end. We read the Bible backwards knowing that Jesus will be crucified and die before being resurrected on the third day and ascending into heaven. This is the ultimate testimony of God. Any account or Bible teaching that portrays a God who will not have mercy and offer forgiveness, healing, hope and life is therefore to be questioned.

The Characters Are Not All Saints

One of the shocking aspects of reading the entire Bible is we discover a whole medley of imperfect and sometimes shockingly immoral, deceptive, and downright dastardly characters. Are we supposed to emulate these people? Yes and no. Many of the greatest characters in the Bible are shown for what they are: deeply flawed characters. One of the great things about the Bible is it rarely attempts to cover up human imperfections. We discover brothers who fight and kill one another, sisters who plot against each other, husbands who are despicable, and wives who are selfish and sinister.

There is a lot of ambiguity in the Bible. Characters are rarely black and white. The truth comes in many shades of grey. When God promised Abraham would become the father of a great nation with more descendants than stars in the sky, Abraham got itchy and couldn't wait. He fathered Ishmael by his Egyptian slave Hagar (Genesis 16) instead of waiting for his wife, Sarah, to become pregnant. Later, when he feared that King Abimelech might kill him in order to appropriate his wife, Abraham passed her off as his sister. (Genesis 20) Is this the man who is the Father of the Jewish people? Jews, Christians, and Muslims all look to Abraham as one of their great pioneering figures. Yet, Abraham was far from flawless.

Likewise, Moses was a murderer. Long before he led the Jewish people to freedom, escaping slavery in Egypt and trekking across the desert, Moses killed an Egyptian, who was threatening a Jewish slave. In an impulsive act of retribution, Moses took the law into his own hands and killed an Egyptian taskmaster in cold blood. In the book of Exodus, we read, "Moses' anger burned hot. . . ." (Ex. 32:19) After learning that the Israelites had manufactured a golden calf while he was on Mount Sinai meeting with God, Moses smashed the Ten Commandments, then ground the golden calf into dust and made the Israelites drink it. Moses next commanded the sons of Levi to exterminate brothers, friends, and neighbors, purging the people of all who have been seduced by other gods. The sons of Levi obeyed Moses, and "about three thousand of the people fell on that day." (Ex. 32:28) It is one of the worst massacres in the Bible. Did Moses indeed cause the death of three thousand Israelites? What rings true today is bad religion and misguided leaders are the cause of thousands of deaths every year to this day. The Bible has much to teach us about the use and abuse of religion.

Although King David is perhaps the most iconic of all Jewish figures and his kingdom is still viewed today as the high water mark of the Jewish golden age, David was a mixture of good and evil. His well-known plot to kill Uriah the Hittite, husband of Bathsheba, after he had gotten Bathsheba pregnant, is one of the most despicable stories found in the Bible. David knowingly tried to live above the law. He used people as pawns. After starting out as a leader with unparalleled humility and integrity, David stayed behind when his troops risked their lives in battle. David then seized upon one of his soldier's wives, after spying her bathing on a rooftop.

David's grasp over the kingdom soon began to spin out of control. After one of David's sons raped his daughter Tamar, David did not lift a finger to punish the assailant. Later, despite his son Absalom's fierce opposition and willingness to destroy his father, David could not bring himself to rebuke Absalom. On his deathbed, David urged his son Solomon to kill Shimei as soon as possible in order that Solomon might avoid a coup from within his own court. David was clearly a mixture of good and evil, compassion and malice. The Bible paints an honest picture of a man who had excellent attributes and also succumbed to temptation and monstrous actions.

Themes of God Intervening in Human Lives

The Bible is full of wonderful themes. One of the greatest is the notion that "God is with us" or "Immanuel." God intervenes in human lives and makes an incredible difference as God transforms ordinary people into extraordinary figures. Throughout the Bible we find "call narratives," where people who were not even seeking God are found by God.

In almost every case there are similarities that appear again and again. One is the element of surprise. God comes in unexpected ways to people one might not expect to attract God's attention or curry God's favor. God came to Abraham in his old age. God appeared to Moses after he had committed murder and wasted forty years working for a deceiving father-in-law as a shepherd, which was the lowest job that anyone could find in the Ancient Near East. God came to David, who was the runt of a litter of boys belonging to Jesse.

God asked Jonah to serve as a messenger to warn Jonah's enemies in Nineveh, which was the last thing Jonah had in mind. God called Jesus from a backwater town called Nazareth. Jesus called Peter, a bumbling character, to serve as the foundation stone of his Church. God intervened and struck blind a man named Saul, who was hunting down "people of the Way" and putting them to death, and transformed Saul into Paul, a giant of Christianity and the Church's first theologian.

Over and over again, God came in surprising ways to people whom we would least expect. In almost every case, God offered a promise of something significant if the person would accept God's invitation to service. In most cases, the recipient of God's grace had an initial reaction to flee or to refuse God's call. The individual struggled with the cost of following God. Finally, there was a moment of surrender when the recipient came to understand and accept what was being asked of him or her. In that moment, they uttered words such as the prophet Samuel spoke when Eli instructed him to say, "Speak, Lord, for your servant is listening." (I Sam. 3: 9–10) This was the beginning of the spiritual journey. It is a pattern that repeats itself over and over again in the Bible and it occurs again and again in each of our lives today. The Swiss psychologist C.J. Jung called recurring stories like these "archetypes." They speak profoundly about the human experience and serve as narrative road maps to help us understand what it means to be created in the image of God and to serve Jesus.

So What Do We Believe?

We believe in miracles. There is much in the Bible and much in the Christian faith that we must accept on faith. Bible readers must determine what to make of "angels." Are they feathery creatures with white wings, or are they merely "messengers," as the Hebrew word means, which come to us bearing words from God? Each of us must decide for ourselves.

I believe there are people who act as God's agents in profound ways who appear at our side as angels when we most need them. I tell people coping with major illnesses or beginning to mourn the loss of a loved one that there will be angels who will come and minister to them. Sometimes those whom we expect to come to our aid do not, but there are others whom we would never have expected to care for us who arrive like angels in disguise, much like angels the Bible says ministered to Jesus after he spent forty days and nights praying and fasting and being tempted in the wilderness. God also sends angels to care for us.

An angel is a miraculous being. The Bible is full of miraculous actions that speak to our daily lives today. Jesus' first miracle was to transform water into wine. Bible scholars speak about the six stone jars of water used for purification rites as representing the Old Covenant that God had with the Jewish people and the six jars full of new wine as representing God's New Covenant with the Christians. Their interpretation may be true, but I tell couples in pre-marital counseling sessions that the miracle of transforming water into wine actually speaks powerfully to today's marriages. Water, after all, is a common beverage. A vintage 1982 bottle of Chateau Lafitte Rothschild, however, is extremely special. So, too, marriage is somewhat commonplace. Most people eventually get married, but when you start to think of truly great marriages you know you can probably count them on one hand. Extraordinary marriages are rare.

The point I make to couples is if we allow Christ to be at the center of our marriage, God can transform our relationship from something as ordinary as "just another marriage" into something truly extraordinary. God and Jesus can help us to be more forgiving, gentle, kind, loving, faithful, and generous than we would ever be were Christ not actively present in our lives. If we allow Jesus to guide our relationship we can have one of those rich and wonderful marriages that people long for and admire. The entire wedding service suggests that our marriage relationship is "in Christ," "by Christ," and "through Christ."

Scholars read all sorts of things into Jesus's transformation of water into wine: Jesus' transforming the water into wine was a symbol that the Jewish law was being replaced by Christ's message of grace and forgiveness. Perhaps more importantly, it signifies that with Jesus all things are possible. God can take the most ordinary thing in life—like our marriage—and transform it into something extraordinary, life-giving, and loving. In the end, we would be wise to ponder the words found in the Gospel of John, "These things are written so that you may come to believe that Jesus is the Messiah, the Son of God, and that through believing you may have life in his name." (John 20:31) The purpose of the Bible, after all, is to point us to God in order that we might see ourselves more clearly and lead the sort of life that God created us to lead.

The Bible is not meant to be an ancient text or a dead repository of literature. It is a source of the water of life that God freely gives to us to transform our lives eternally, if and only if we prayerfully pick it up and read it carefully and put into practice what we have read. I wish to close once again with words from those who have participated in The Bible Challenge.

In my opinion, The Bible Challenge points to a vitally important topic related to the social value and future of the Episcopal Church and that is accountability among membership. Think about it. What successful and sustainable organization, such as Apple Computer, the Boy Scouts of America, the Mormon Church or an excellent school or university does not have "accountability" deeply woven into its corporate values and vision statement. Even if it is painful at times, I think the leadership of the Episcopal Church must promote and demand accountability throughout the Church as if our very existence depends upon it.—FRED

I have appreciated the opportunity to read the entire Bible through, once again, this past year. The discipline involved in daily Bible reading has been an anchor and strength in my life for many years. I appreciate the comfort of reading the many familiar passages that have been so important to me, especially in times of difficulty. I continue to seek God's direction and guidance for my life and my Bible reading is an essential tool as I seek to connect with God's purpose for me.—ELISA

I did it!!!! I just finished reading the Bible. I am so glad you got me involved. It was a wonderful and very enlightening experience. As I mentioned to you, I am now going to start the NIV version. Thank you so very much.—GRETTA, NOW A STUDENT IN EfM

I have been reading through the Bible since January. I have found it wonderful, tedious, irritating, challenging, and profoundly moving. I have become reacquainted with things I had half forgotten, and introduced to passages that I had completely forgotten.—MARK, A PARISH PRIEST IN PENNSYLVANIA

So far so good, I'm listening to the Bible on CD's every morning while exercising. I'll finish Numbers this weekend, and I've lost five pounds! Go Bible Challenge!—DAVE

Reading the Bible every day has had a tremendous impact on my life. I've just completed my first read through (took me about 14 months). I found a book at Barnes and Noble: Halley's Bible Handbook and that has added another dimension to my understanding, and helps me be more reflective and read the Bible more slowly.—JUDY

I want to thank you for getting me started on The Bible Challenge. I am enjoying it. Somehow on the 3rd or 4th try it is sticking. I do 10 minutes here and there. I am still in Leviticus, but enjoying it for the literature as well as the wisdom.—DOUG

We were in Russia earlier this month and of course went to the Hermitage in St. Petersburg. (breathtaking!!!). I was in awe of Rembrandt's painting The Return

*of the Prodigal Son. . . . it was so calm and peaceful. Could have stood there for hours I think. We had a young Russian guide with us explaining some of the paintings. She wasn't too familiar with the stories or characters in the paintings depicting biblical scenes especially from the Old Testament, but having just finished reading the Old Testament (on the train from Moscow) as part of The Bible Challenge, I was able to help her out !!! I loved taking my Bible to Russia and reading it there.—*MARGOT

*I am about to begin Samuel 2—Samuel 1 was hair-raising and poignant. I am beginning to see the Bible in long arcs of human history, rather than isolated smidges. First there was creation, then the great patriarchs, and now the kings. All along the way, listening to God and obeying His will is the hardest thing for us. Over and over again, we think we can do it all by ourselves. I am especially intrigued by how much New Testament, and especially Jesus, I hear in the Old Testament now.—*ANNE

*. . . watching ospreys, eagles soar, examining the gorgeous sea urchin, mussel shells, feeling the warmth of the stones from the beach on my face, lying on the spongy mosses, lichen with my grandchildren asking what cloud creatures they see. Showing them that God is EVERYWHERE! Because of reading the Bible, I am now so much more aware of HIS gifts to ALL of us and how much fun is it to teach my family to "observe."—*CYNTHIA

*I am moving forward with The Bible Challenge and enjoying spending some time in the scriptures. I began in February and have now gotten through Day 25. I often don't have time to do all of the readings for one day. So I just read a few chapters in the Old Testament at breakfast, and check off what I have read. The next day I will move on to the psalms, or the gospels. Sometimes I find that I prefer to read 8 or 10 chapters through in one book before going on to another book. It helps me get the flow of the storyline so that I can meditate on it during the day.—*KIT FROM THAILAND

A couple of weeks ago on a Thursday morning, I was reading in 1 Chronicles 19 a story about two brothers, Joab and Abishau, who were leading two armies into battle. The one brother says, (I'm loosely paraphrasing) " You go fight those guys and I'll go fight the others. If you need help, I'll come to your aid, and if I need help, you come to my aid. We'll leave the outcome up to God". That afternoon, I got a call from my brother that two tumors were back and test show that they were "hot." I left the office, went home and packed my bag and went to Lexington, Kentucky, drove through the night so I could be with him the next morning for a 9 a.m. appointment where they prepared him for his radiation treatment that began last week. I told him about this story of Joab and Abishau, along with another story about Moses holding his arms up in prayer as Joshua fought a battle, as Moses grew tired and his arms began to descend, Joshua started losing the battle; so two men went to help Moses keep his arms up in prayer until the battle was finished. I like that story, because it touches on action (doing the things we need to do) coupled with prayer and then is topped off with people helping people when they become spiritually tired. It seems to me we all at times become spiritually tired and it's great to have someone step in and help us keep our arms up. —STROUD

I am very much enjoying reading the Bible. I am currently reading Nehemiah, where he is rebuilding the temple. I have found this to be a wonderful, thought-provoking experience. What I find most intriguing so far is the continuous cycle of reward and punishment, where God rewards those who follow Him with power, sustenance and children, and then punishes those who don't follow Him with death (often violent) or affliction. My vision of an all-forgiving God is somewhat challenged at this point, although there are certainly examples of forgiveness to those who repent. I am also surprised at the vast amount of sacrifice to God or other gods, which I know was common among all peoples in that era. Thanks for encouraging this Bible Challenge. I can see why people say it is a life changing experience. —BARBARA

I happen to have flown from my home in Seattle, WA, to be in Dallas, TX this weekend visiting my daughter who gave birth to her first child last weekend. I am thrilled to have the birth of my grandson be the spiritual drive to my current Bible Challenge. His future depends on how people of the past (like me) and people of the future (like him and his generation) pass down and carry on Christian covenants. In spite of all the present issues with church communities, this history depends on Scripture, tradition and reason. When we hit pivotal faith issues we must take up the Bible and dig deeper into what meaning our spiritual selves live with. I pray every day, through the Old Testament, Psalms and New Testament readings, that I will somehow see the world differently due to God's work. I want my grandson to have the depth of the Gospel message on which to plant his little feet day after day for his whole life. —LAURIE

I just wish to thank you sincerely for making this Challenge available to me here in the U.K. . . . I have just completed my Lent to Lent reading of the Bible and found the experience both uplifting and instructive; so much so that I have bought myself a copy of the Life Application Study Bible (NIV) and intend to re-read the Bible, not this time in the given order of the OT/NT, but starting with those books I struggled with most. I have now given myself the duty of (gently) persuading others to take up this challenge, as I know that their lives and understanding will be all the better for doing so. —MRS. NEAL

CHAPTER 10

Engaging the Bible
with Children and Teenagers

"Jesus said, 'Let the little children come to me, and do not stop them; for it is to such as these that the kingdom of heaven belongs.'"—Matthew 19:14

"Apply yourself wholly to the Scriptures, and apply the Scriptures wholly to yourself."—Johann A. Bengel

"Once we truly grasp the message of the New Testament, it is impossible to read the Old Testament again without seeing Christ on every page, in every story, foreshadowed or anticipated in every event and narrative. The Bible must be read as a whole, beginning with Genesis and ending with Revelation, letting promise and fulfillment guide our expectations for what we will find there."—Michael Horton

•◆•

I left the Yale Divinity School and the Berkeley Divinity School at Yale with an incredible education, but remarkably I did not take a single course about how to help instill faith in children and teenagers. I had courses on systematic theology, historical theology, the Old and New Testament, ethics, church history, preaching, pastoral care, world religions, Anglicanism, liturgy, and worship. I took no courses about human development or faith development or how to help children and youth grow as Christians. None was required and few were offered.

Perhaps most seminaries assume that clergy will learn about these things as they progress in their ministry or hire people on a church staff to do them. They are wrong. Almost all of my peers in ministry were excited and focused on leaving seminary to preach and teach classes for adults, lead worship, and connect with people who were older and well-educated. Very few of us were focused on reaching children and youth. Many of us did significant youth ministry prior to entering seminary; we were ready to move on to focus with adults.

About one person in ten thousand who has not been raised in the Church comes to accept Jesus Christ as their savior and lead a strong Christian life as an adult. In other words, we spend a tremendous amount of effort trying to attract and retain adults to our church. If we were truly looking to make the largest impact on society, we would do far better to focus on transforming the lives of children and youth in our congregations and equipping their parents to teach them at home. Parents, after all, are the single greatest influence on their children's spiritual lives.

I remember attending a cocktail party with parents from our daughters' school, when a parent who did not go to church asked me if children who are not brought up with religion have a higher chance of becoming zealous about religion later in life. I told her that only about one person in ten thousand goes on to lead a strong Christian life if they have not been raised in the Church. The mother breathed a sigh of relief and said, "Oh, you have really helped me. You see my husband and I don't like religion and so we haven't exposed Michelle to any religion in the hopes that it would not warp her. I was afraid, however, that perhaps when she became an adult that she would rebel and become some sort of religious zealot to make up for all that we did not expose her to. You have made me feel much better!"

I was a bit astounded. Helping our children develop a healthy worldview is one of the most important things a parent ever does. This entails helping our sons and daughters understand life and death and come to believe that there is more to life than what can be measured, comprehended by the senses, or scientifically replicated. Love is the driving and unifying force of the universe, yet love cannot be measured or proven scientifically. If we had to discard all things that are not replicable in experiments then we would have to rid ourselves of love, truth, honesty, compassion, forgiveness, grace, generosity, kindness, patience, and self-control, which are what create relationships and give life its ultimate meaning.

As Our Clergy Focus on Adults, the Church Shrinks

Most clergy spend the majority of their time assisting adults, when we would be far wiser to help our churches become bastions of strength in terms of leading children and youth to develop a profound relationship with God. Our failure to focus on helping young people to engage the Bible regularly and appropriate a deep Christian faith that will carry them successfully through a life of service and discipleship with Jesus is deeply troubling.

According to church historian Diana Butler Bass, in 2009 there were more than twenty-two thousand Christian groups and denominations in the United States and only four of them were growing: Mormons, Jehovah's Witnesses, and two Pentecostal groups. Everyone else was shrinking. This is frightening. Christians of all denominations must sit up and take notice. We are at grave risk of losing the next generation of believers. All it takes is losing only one generation to cause Christianity to spiral downward. The largest growing religious group in the United States is a group that self-identifies as "former Roman Catholic." They are not Episcopalian, Methodist, Lutheran, or Orthodox, but merely former Roman Catholics. Many left and joined the Episcopal Church and other denominations, but the largest portion have simply stopped attending church and nurturing their spiritual lives. They are stalled or sputtering on their spiritual journey.

For the first time since 1950, there are now fewer than 2 million Episcopalians in the United States, despite the fact that our nation's population has more than doubled in that timeframe. Something is occurring that is not allowing us to grow or even replenish our numbers. The problem crosses virtually every denomination. In 2012, over 30 percent of twenty-five to thirty year olds in the United States self-identified as being "of no religion whatsoever," the largest percentage of young adults in history to do so. While the number of believers remains as high as it was twenty years ago, according to Gallup polls, the question used to measure that has now been broadened to read, "Do you believe in God *or a higher power?*" Formerly, it read only, "Do you believe in God?"

The typical pattern in the Episcopal Church is that young parents come to our churches after the birth of their first child, seeking to have their son or daughter baptized. Each additional child is baptized. The parents develop friends in the parish and the children are raised and confirmed in the church. Mom or dad may teach Sunday school, serve on the altar guild or as an usher or lay reader, and perhaps even join the Vestry. By the time the children have become teenagers, most demonstrate a growing reluctance to attend church. "Do I have to go?" they ask.

Parents struggle to get them to continue to attend, especially if there is no youth group or young parish priest who understands and connects well with teenagers, or a worship service that allows teenagers to participate actively and help lead worship. Eighty percent of Episcopalians who are confirmed as teenagers stop attending church almost immediately thereafter. Confirmation has become an exit ritual for most teenagers, rather than a major step forward in accepting adult responsibilities of being a Christian and sharing in leadership of a church.

My Own Experience of Feeling Lost at Church as a Teenager

I can recall being confirmed as a teenager and having no interest in confirmation or worship. I had a crush on a girl named Holly in my confirmation class. Being in the same room with her was the only thing that interested me about attending. Learning about sin, salvation, redemption, heaven and hell, the Bible, and prayer did not feel relevant or important. I was concerned about how I looked, whether my acne would put Holly off, and if she had any interest in me.

On the day of my confirmation, I had a huge battle with my parents about what I was to wear to church. I came down the stairs dressed in a pair of faded blue jeans and an old shirt, which I thought looked sufficiently "cool." My parents sent me back up to my room to change into something "proper." I put on clothing that was slightly more presentable, but it was not enough. After coming downstairs for the second time in unpresentable apparel, my parents raised their voices and demanded that I dress in my grey-flannel pants, a white button-down shirt, a tie, and my navy blazer. They wanted me to look like a model straight out of the Brooks Brothers catalog. The sole concession I was able to negotiate was I was allowed to wear a pair of my father's old loafers, which were somewhat worn, instead of my brand new shoes that were too shiny to be cool. The problem was my foot was a size eight and my father's foot was a size twelve. As I walked down the aisle alone to kneel before the bishop, I had to slide my feet on the carpet in the church like I was doing the moonwalk to keep my father's enormous shoes from sliding off my feet. My only thought was if I walked out of his shoes while the entire congregation was watching, and Holly in particular, I would never get over it.

Shortly after being confirmed, my parents informed me I was an adult and had made an adult decision to be confirmed; therefore, the choice was now mine as to whether or not I wanted to attend church on Sunday mornings.

"Do you mean that I can stay home and sleep in and watch cartoons instead of going to church?" I asked.

"Yes, if that's what you want to do," they replied.

"Perfect," I said, deciding then and there to stop going. It was not a wise move. I was thirteen or fourteen and heading into some of the most troubling years of our family's history and my own personal development. My parents separated while I was in high school, and my home life was full of tension. Church was nowhere on my radar screen. God was a distant reality. At the time I most needed a supportive faith community, I opted out.

No Group Needs Our Focus More Than Teenagers

Teenagers need the Church more than anyone else. Studies indicate that the highest rate of eating disorders in the United States occurs among teenagers. The highest rates of depression in our country occur among teenagers. The highest suicide rate in the United States occurs among teenagers. In addition, the highest rate of divorce takes place among parents of teenagers. Parents of teenagers are coping with aging parents, stresses from work, home life, and their teenage children, who sometimes seem more complex than a Rubik's Cube.

Teenagers often are exposed to alcohol, drugs, pornography, and pre-marital sex on top of the social pressures to fit in, be popular, develop self-confidence, establish friendships, be successful in athletics and academics, and come to terms with their own sexuality. Emotions and hormones are raging, and the last thing on many teenagers' minds is developing a spiritual life unless their church is fortunate to have made a major commitment to creating a strong youth ministry and offering worship and ministry opportunities that are compelling and exciting for young people.

One in twenty teenagers will attempt suicide. Three out of every twenty teenagers engage in promiscuous behavior. Four out of five teenagers do not read Scripture. One out of three teenagers feels that religion is unimportant. Our children are growing up in a civilization that is more akin to the first century than any other century since. We live in a culture awash with hedonism, video games, cyber traffic, immorality, drunkenness, paganism, magic, cults, and family break-downs. The good news, however, is there are strong similarities between our culture today and the culture in which Christianity was born and flourished.

It was in a culture similar to ours, as the Holy Roman Empire began to break apart, that a young student named Benedict, who grew up in a small town north of Rome called Norcia, was sent by his parents to study in Rome. He was so shocked by the immoral behavior of his fellow students that he decided to quit school, leave Rome, and live in a cave in Subiaco, a town about twenty miles to the west. Benedict spent two years there devoted to prayer, fasting, and reading the Bible. He went on to found the Benedictine order and write a book called *The Rule of St. Benedict*, which some maintain is the second most influential book in Christianity. There is something about an immoral society that both drives individuals to seek ultimate values and drives them into the arms of God.

My own lack of experiencing ultimate values and developing a strong relation-ship with God led me to experiment with things in high school and college that I wish that I had never tried. I drank feverishly and tested every boundary that I could. I survived a handful of irresponsible driving incidents that could have ended my life; it's only by the grace of God that my friends and I survived those years. My parents' marriage, however, did not. We were one of those classic cases of a family where the parents announced to their teenage children that they were getting a divorce, but it took several years to become a reality. In the meantime, the pain and tension in the household led me to act out and self-medicate. I was swimming in a sea of emptiness with no sense of absolute truth instilled in my heart and no personal relationship with God. I was like a lot of American teenagers. Our family enjoyed financial pros-perity and lived in a lovely suburban neighborhood, but something seemed terribly lacking. My soul ached for that something which was missing.

We Leave Our Faith Behind as We Head to College

I was a classic Episcopalian. Like most college students I put away my Bible and Book of Common Prayer as I headed off to college, leaving them somewhere in the house where they eventually disappeared. Over the next few years I made all sorts of important decisions without ever consulting the source of the deepest values found in these two books. I was a normal mainline American Christian teenager. Like most young adults who go to college, I envisioned Christianity as a straitjacket of rules that said, "Thou shalt not" and put a damper on life and the things that were fun or interesting to my friends and me. Like many of my peers, when I did things that violated the values with which I had been raised, I experienced feelings of guilt and remorse, which only drove me further from any interest in faith. In the midst of guilt and remorse, I, like many others, felt that God was the last one I wanted to turn to for comfort, help, and guidance.

Parents are the most formative influence on the faith journey of their children. They exercise a far more important role than Sunday school teachers or preachers. This is true not only for Christians, but for Muslims, Jews, and other religious groups. Next in terms of influence are friends within a youth group. Third are friends outside of a youth group. Fourth are youth leaders. At the bottom of the list are other adults in church. We have found, however, that pairing our youth with adult mentors in confirmation has created strong bonds and offered a wonderful resource for teaching and mentoring to our youth.

In surveys, college students indicate that three of the top challenges they faced at college included developing friendships, dealing with being alone, and finding a church. Many kids were part of a youth group, but they did not necessarily feel part of a church. Studies show that the more actively involved students were in intergenerational worship during their teenage years, the better they did in college. Their participation helped to make their faith stick and remain useful to them when they found themselves wrestling with important moral decisions in college.

Many parents view church like a dry cleaner, where they drop their children off and pick them up after Sunday school, polished with Bible lessons, and ready to go forward and lead a more moral life. Unfortunately, that rarely works. Kids learn best from what their parents model. Our church has worked with Ministry Architects on several occasions to develop a high impact, excellent, long-term, consistent youth ministry. They are now working with other churches to help them do the same thing with children's ministries and Sunday school, which is vital because when a church hits a home run with children and teenagers, the church prospers and has a wonderful future.

One of our consultants was an old friend and colleague from my newspaper days and a long-term youth minister named Jeff Dunn-Rankin. I will always remember Jeff telling us about his approach to encouraging his own children to read the Bible.

I don't tell them to read it or make them memorize verses or study the Bible. If I did, I would be virtually guaranteeing that they never read the Bible. Instead, I would lie down on the couch and read the Bible for my own spiritual benefit. Sometimes, my kids would see me doing that and ask, "What are you reading, Dad?" I would answer, "I'm just reading the Bible. It gives me a lot of interesting ideas and helps me to think about life and figure out some answers to problems." That is all that I had to say. The next thing I saw is that they started to read the Bible on their own for the very same reason. They figured that if Dad got something out of it, then maybe they could get something out of it.

Youth learn from relational values. If they have a positive relationship with a parent, youth leader, coach, mentor, instructor or teacher, then they will learn from that person. If these same individuals do not take time to develop a relationship with teenagers, then the youth will resist any of their attempts to teach them.

Bible Reading among Teenagers

So what impact does Bible reading have on children and teenagers? The Bible continues to enjoy a strong reputation in American society. Many view it as the most important book ever written or given to humankind. In response to an open-ended question in 2008 about what books they consider to be sacred or holy, 84 percent of respondents named the Bible. The next closest book on the list was the Koran with 4 percent, followed by the Book of Mormon with 3 percent and the Torah with 2 percent. At the same time, many people have never actually read the Bible.

Not all generations approach the Bible in the same way. According to studies conducted by the American Bible Society in conjunction with the Barna Group, nine out of ten Baby Boomers (44 to 62) and Elders (63 and older) named the Bible as sacred, compared to eight out of ten or 81 percent of Busters (25 to 43) and just two out of three Mosaics (18 to 24). Young adults are more likely to express skepticism about the origins of biblical manuscripts than older adults.

Among Mosaics, 56 percent believe the Bible teaches the same universal truths as other sacred texts, compared with four out of ten Busters and Boomers and one third of Elders. Studies also reveal that Mosaics and Busters are far less likely than Boomers and Elders to read the Bible in a typical week. The overall picture is that youth and young adults view the Bible as less sacred, exercise more skepticism, view it as part of something with greater universalism, and engage less with the Bible than older generations.

To hearken back to my friend and colleague Jeff Dunn-Rankin who allowed his children to watch him reading the Bible rather than instructing them to read it, we know that just because mom and dad tell us to turn to the Bible for answers does not insure that we will. In fact, the chances are becoming smaller with each generation. Younger adults, for example, are less likely than older Americans to say that their parents' outlook on life, truth, and morality encouraged them to accept the Bible's teachings: 37 percent of Boomers and Elders compared to 30 percent of Busters and Mosaics. An amazing 45 percent of Mosaics and 30 percent of Busters said their parents simply "expect them to figure it out on their own," compared to 19 percent of Boomers and 21 percent of Elders. Mosaics were the least likely to say their parents expected them to adopt the same point of view.

While churches remain the primary conduit of Bible teaching and engagement, children and youth today are growing up in a digital environment. They are technology natives, growing up with computers and other devices that further the speed and the scope of gathering and sending information. Boomers and Elders embrace two types of online behavior as mainstream, where Busters embrace four online activities, and Mosaics regularly rely on eight digital expressions (email, search, texting, instant messaging, posting on blogs, maintaining a social network page, watching video, and downloading music). As a result, Mosaics do more non-linear thinking, are involved in new styles of relating and self-expression, are exposed early to a greater amount of the dark side of life, and have greater access to spiritual resources.

Just as regular Bible reading greatly affects the moral behavior of adults who engage the Bible four times or more each week, the same holds true with teenagers. When the Center for Biblical Engagement examined the spiritual disciplines and risk behavior among teenagers, they discovered a somewhat different picture from the research with adults. Teens that read or listen to the Bible are significantly less likely to engage in risky behaviors. Those who engage in reading Scripture four times or more a week have the lowest rates of risky behavior in all of the behaviors measured except for pornography.

Regular Bible Reading Shapes Teenage Souls

Among adults, prayer and church attendance are not as strongly correlated with risky behaviors as among teenagers. Among teens, the CBE found no effects for church attendance and prayer in alleviating risky behaviors. Identifying as a born-again Christian is the only significant predictor for lowering the odds of getting drunk. The CBE found Scripture engagement to be the best of the spiritually-based predictors. Those who read or listen to the Bible at least four days a week have significantly lower odds of smoking, getting drunk, or engaging in any of the risky behaviors examined than their peers who do not read the Bible at all. Similarly, teens who engage Scripture one to three days each week are slightly less likely to smoke, get drunk or participate in risky behavior than those who do not engage in Scripture at all. As with adults, there appears to be a strong tipping point that occurs in moral behavior as a result of engaging Scripture four times or more each week.

The CBE findings demonstrate that Bible engagement is the best spiritually-based predictor among thirteen to seventeen year olds, significantly predicting three out of the five risk behaviors examined. The normal Episcopal model of attending church and listening to the Scriptures being read once a week, therefore, makes little or no measureable difference in the moral behavior of teenagers. The average Episcopalian now attends church only one time per month. Furthermore, as noted previously, studies conducted by the United States Air Force demonstrate that we forget ninety to 95 percent of what we hear within seventy-two hours.

Thus, we should have modest expectations of the impact our worship will have on the moral behavior of our children, teenagers, and adults. It is not that our worship necessarily needs to be overhauled or what we are doing in our liturgy is wrong. Rather it is predicated to work in an environment where churchgoers read Scripture four times or more a week and are thus exercising a daily spiritual practice which improves their moral behavior. This is the key that we need to recognize and implement in our parishes and in youth ministries.

In my own experience of leading a large youth group in Nashville and watching and supporting youth ministries in Richmond, Virginia and Fort Washington, Pennsylvania, the average teenager probably attends worship once or twice a month. Many rarely attend. Most teenagers do not regularly read Scripture on their own. Our biggest challenge therefore is to help encourage our children and youth to read the Bible four or more times each week on their own.

The good news is there is a real hunger among children and youth to read and learn from the Bible today, though they will appropriate it in very different ways from Elders, Boomers, and even Busters. Just as students now "pirate" term papers from the internet and go to Google to learn about subject matter while writing high school and college essays, the digital revolution has now put thousands of Bible resources at their fingertips. The opportunity for young Christians to learn and grow in their faith is enormous, and the Church must be part of the digital revolution if it wants to reach them.

Two of the challenges of our digitized world are information overload and the increasing reliance on digital tools as opposed to reading books in a slower, more meditative fashion. Jesus and the message of the Bible are getting lost in the data stream flowing through the minds of young people today, passing in and out of their ears and across the screens of their devices.

The study by the American Bible Society and the Barna Group also notes that youth and young adults desire more participation in the learning process today than previous generations. Children and teenagers do not want to be face-forward-to-the-blackboard learners. Godly Play and The Catechesis of the Good Shepherd are excellent hands-on ways for children to learn the Bible stories. Teenagers are more interested in new, experimental learning styles, gleaning insights from addressing social justice issues and serving the poor. Churches are wise, therefore, to connect Scripture with the deep impulses for social justice, mission work, and serving the poor that captivate the interest and hearts of so many young people today. In the process of doing so, children and youth can become co-creators of the Church of tomorrow.

CHAPTER 11

Getting Practical: How to Help Children Read the Bible

"Point your kids in the right direction—when they're old they won't be lost."—PROVERBS 22:6

"Love the Lord your God with all your heart, all your being, and all your strength. These words that I am commanding you today must always be on your minds. Recite them to your children. Talk about them when you are sitting around your house and when you are out and about, when you are lying down, and when you are getting up . . ."—Deuteronomy 6:5-7

"Ignorance of the Bible is ignorance of Jesus."—St. Jerome

• ◆ •

"I want my children to know the Bible" is the emphatic statement clergy and Christian educators hear often from households. We want to know scripture, and we want our children to know it as well. There are plenty of programs such as Godly Play and Catechesis of the Good Shepherd that help children enter into the Bible stories and exercise their own imaginations. These are excellent programs, and fortunately they are widely used within the Episcopal Church. If, however, we want our children to read through the Bible and develop a life-long spiritual discipline of daily Bible reading then we need to do more than have them participate in programs such as these. The Center for Biblical Studies and I recommend that parents and children participate in The Parent/Child Bible Challenge and become a Bible reading household.

Think about it for a moment. The average church only has 40 hours in a given year to influence the life of a child. The average parent has 3,000 hours per year to influence a life. As a parent, we are our child's most influential spiritual teacher. The gift of our time will build our son's or daughter's confidence and faith in God. We need the support, encouragement and expertise of a good church to help us be our child's primary spiritual influence. But without our commitment and attention, the church can do little to make a spiritual impact upon our child.

A study of households who regularly attend church found that few parents discuss spiritual issues with their children. In another survey of 80,000 people, 87 percent claim it is of great importance to understand the Bible. Throughout the Bible God uses families as a way to tell a story of love, forgiveness, reconciliation, and healing. The Bible is God's family story. The Center for Biblical Studies and I invite parents to learn how to read the Bible with their children and emerge from God's story as people of God, changed, and excited to do God's work.

The purpose of The Parent/Child Bible Challenge is to:

- invite families to become fully engaged in The Bible Challenge
- explore how the church can support families in reading an age appropriate Bible
- share how the church and families grow together and are strengthened in their relationship with God through regular Bible reading

Reading and learning the Bible together as a family does the following:

- helps families grow closer
- opens communication
- helps kids know that faith practice begins at home
- transforms our lives every day and all the time

You can discover how The Bible Challenge can engage your household by visiting us at: *www.thecenterforbiblicalstudies.org* and signing up to participate in The Parent/Child Bible Challenge.

We often hear from households that want to be grounded in God's Word. They need more guidance, however. Without guidance, it is like the blind leading the blind. Our children teach us much as we participate together. They want to know the Bible. So, why not learn with them?

How do we study the Bible as a family? Here are some steps in helping our children in The Bible Challenge that might help us as well.

Pick a Readable Story Bible

We have to begin by selecting a Bible that is appropriate for children to read. I know a parent, for example, who set out to read through the entire Bible with her children. Each night they would read a portion of the Bible together. At first, this sounds like a lovely thing to do. The problem, however, comes when they get to portions such as the 19th chapter of the Book of Judges. In this chapter we read about an innocent woman who is viciously assaulted and later dismembered; her body parts are sent to the far corners of Israel in hopes that it will insure that such an act of brutality will never happen again. It is hardly good bedtime reading for parents with young children.

Likewise in II Samuel 13 we read the story of the rape of Tamar—another equally disturbing story. In fact, large portions of the Hebrew Scriptures read like holocaust chronicles of the ancient Near East. According to the authors of the Bible, God commands Moses, Joshua, and David to lead the Israelite soldiers into various villages of their archenemies the Edomites and instructs them to kill all of the men, women, and children. I personally do not believe that God ever acted in this way. The problem is that it appears in the Bible, and the authors of various books of the Bible give God the unwanted credit for heinous human acts of brutality.

I strongly believe that these stories are worthwhile for an adult with a mature faith to read through to comprehend the depths of human evil and depravity and to seek God in the midst of such heinous actions. By reading these Bible stories, which are never read aloud in church, readers are forced to confront issues such as those that appear on the front page of the newspaper and to ponder questions of theodicy, which is the study of God and evil and suffering. Children, however, are not ready for this.

The first practical matter for a parent hoping to help their son or daughter read the Bible, therefore, is to select one that is appropriate for the age of their child. Reading an adult Bible with a child is not a wise way to start. Fortunately, there is a rich selection of Bibles now available for children, which are far more engaging than the traditional adult version. The Center for Biblical Studies and I recommend the following children's Bibles:

- *The Spark Story Bible*—This children's Bible is ideal for ages two through second grade. This story book is nicely illustrated, theologically sound, engaging, and thought provoking. Mr. Squiggles worms through every story and keeps children's attention. *The Spark Story Bible* engages both reader and listener with activities and questions. It captures important biblical stories that children can appreciate and avoids stories that are inappropriate for children. Visit: *www.sparkbibles.org* to order it.

- *The Story for Kids*—This seamless collection of Bible stories published by Zondervan has been stitched together into one continuous narrative that reads like a children's book. Boring and repetitive parts of the Bible are eliminated. There is also an adult version of this same book simply called *The Story*, which is excellent reading for any parent. After reading *The Story for Kids* your child and you will have a much better understanding of the Bible. Visit: *www.thestory.com* to order.

- *Deep Blue Kids Bible*—We recommend this new Common English Bible for children 7 to 12. This translation introduces us to a crew of friends, Asia, Edgar and Kat, who dive deep with us in our reading, asking the hard questions, navigating us from place to place, revealing explanations for difficult stories, and helping to equip us with rock solid faith. Visit: *www.deepbluekidsbible.com* to order it.

- *My First Message*—This is a children's version of the best-selling adult paraphrase of the Bible called *The Message* by Eugene Peterson, a pastor and teacher. Peterson brings the original biblical language alive to the modern reader with a retelling of Scripture using contemporary English. Visit: *www.messagebible.com* to order.

- *The DK Children's Illustrated Bible*—This gives us the best known Bible stories appealing to the early reader, told in clear, lively language. Parents will learn as well while reading with their children. Visit: *www.dk.com* children's illustrated Bible to order.

Get Excited about Reading the Bible

Children draft off the emotions of their parents. When we are excited, they share our excitement. Reading the Bible is a spiritual practice that allows us to enrich our lives with our children. We have an incredible, once in a lifetime opportunity to help them know of God's inspired Word and life saving story. Get started with the story of creation in the Book of Genesis. The Old Testament has some of the best stories in the entire Bible. Read tales of struggle and joy and journeys of wonder and delight. Be amazed by the crossing of the Red Sea, Ruth's faithfulness, David standing up to Goliath, and Esther's courage. Let Jesus change our lives with his miracles and compassion.

Take Turns Reading on a Regular Basis

Challenge one another to retell the story that you have just read. Start to learn the names of the books of the Bible as well as names of various parables and stories. Get to know individual books of the Bible and strive to see the big picture of how these books and stories fit together.

Show Them How the Bible Is Like Real Life

Jesus tells us in Luke 6 about ways to live and to love, how to forgive, and how to care for others. In Matthew's Gospel, Jesus tells us, step by step, how to forgive one another. The Bible gives us real life stories and real life solutions so that we can build God's kingdom here and now. The apostles' letters tell us how to care for one another and follow Jesus' way. Join your children at bedtime and read a story each night. Talk about how the story is or is not like real life. Ask how the Bible's teaching helps us to build a better world and become better people.

These are God's stories given to us to show how God brings hope, healing, and love. Sad stories end with joy. Joyful stories are complete with responsibility. We are God's people, loved and cherished by God. Sometimes, the stories don't tell us what we want to hear. If this is the case, then what is God teaching us? If you don't know something, say, "I don't know why this happens in the story." Then ask, "What do you think?" Your children will teach you, and you will grow together in faith.

Read and Retell

Pick a favorite Bible story or verse and read a few verses before and after your selection. Ask some questions: What does the writer want us to know? Where are you and I in the story? What is God asking us to do in this story? How would you feel if you were in this scene? What do you smell, touch, see, and feel? If you could change how the story ends, what would you change? How would you tell this story in your own words? At the conclusion of each reading, ask your child: 1) What do today's readings tell us about God? 2) What did we learn about how to treat other people? and 3) What did we learn about our family and how we should live?

Pick a Designated Time and Get Started

Read in the same place at the same time each day. Bedtime is a great time to read, but do what works best for your family. You may try reading an entire Gospel together, such as the Gospel of Luke, to learn more about Jesus' life. Then try reading the book of Acts to learn about how the Church began. Offer up prayers of thanksgiving for a life renewed and anchored in God's Holy Word.

Keep a Gratitude Journal

Each time you finish your Bible reading, write in your gratitude journal about three things that you are thankful for. Count your blessings and give thanks. This is a great way for parents and children to end the day, reflecting back on events and experiences of the day. Which ones were blessings and why? Roman Catholics practice Examen of Conscience, which is an exercise designed by Jesuits to reflect back on the happenings of the day to see where we acted in accord with God's will and where we failed to do so. Keeping a gratitude journal is a great way to help see the fingerprints of God in the ordinary events of our lives.

Give Space to Talk

How will your children apply these stories in their lives? If, for example, your daughter is sad because she was mistreated by a classmate, in your Bible time you may want to look at stories about love (Matthew 22:34–46), forgiveness (Luke 15:11–32), helping (Luke 10:25–37), and friendship (Luke 19:1–10). You don't have to have all the answers. Reading the Bible stories will give you a safe platform for your discussion. In time, your child might be able to say to her classmate, "I don't know why you had to be mean to me. I want to be friends."

Set Goals

The seasons of Advent and Lent (those times before Christmas and Easter) are often set apart as intentional times to know God working in our lives. Decide to read together Monday through Saturday each week during Advent and Lent. Take Sunday off to listen to the Bible being read in church.

More Options and Going Deeper

Read a One-Year Bible

A One-Year Bible consists of selected readings for each day taken from the Bible, using lessons from both the Old and the New Testaments. This is an excellent way to introduce regular Bible reading as your child grows older. Most One-Year Bibles omit violent and scary passages that may be inappropriate for teenagers. Still, you should review a One-Year Bible before selecting it for your daughter or son to insure that it is right for them. You know your own child best and what they are ready to read.

At the conclusion of each reading, discuss with your son or daughter: 1) What do today's readings tell me about God? 2) What do they tell me about other people? 3) What do they tell me about myself? Ponder these questions alone, with a friend or a group. Google *one year Bible* to find several good options available through *Amazon.com*

Harness the Power of Technology and Download the Bible for Free

Children are digital natives and love technology. Consider downloading the Bible on your iPad, iPhone, Kindle or Nook. Keep the Bible with you at all times. *YouVersion.com* and *bible.com* offer numerous reading plans from read a Bible in a year to suggestions for exploring faith, love, and other topics. The site includes downloads of mobile apps for smart phone, iPad, Blackberry, and Android devices.

Oneyearbibleonline.com offers a reading plan divided into daily segments, each containing a passage from the Old Testament, the New Testament, Psalms, and Proverbs. *Biblegateway.com* is a great searchable Bible with multiple options for finding just what you need. *Bibleresources.bible.com* is another site with good resources. *Amazon.com*, *Zondervan.com*, and *BN.com* offer an array of Bibles and downloads available in Kindle, Nook Reader, smart phone, Blackberry and Android phone, NIV Audio Bible Dramatized, and CD formats.

Listen to the Bible

There are many resources today that will allow your children and you to listen to the Bible as you ride in the car, drive to school, walk your dog, travel, do arts and crafts or relax at home or in bed. For audio learners this is especially helpful. You can listen to the Bible in a variety of translations by using apps and programs from: *Audio.com/Bible, listenersbible.com, BibleGateway.com, YouVersion.com* or *www.faithcomesthroughhearing.com. Faith Comes through Hearing* provides audio programs to listen to the Bible in 692 languages. You can listen to the entire New Testament in 28 minutes a day for 40 days.

Schools are becoming more sensitive to the different ways in which children learn. At our daughters' school in Philadelphia, teachers make every attempt to help each child discover how they learn best. Are they a visual learner? Do they learn best from reading books or listening to lectures or seeing something visual that imprints the lesson or fact in their mind? One of our daughters is less inclined to reading than her sisters. Instead, she loves to listen to Harry Potter CDs for hours at a time. Audio learners will benefit greatly from listening to the Bible on CD or on a digital device such as a Kindle, Nook, iPod or iPad.

Scripture Memorization

Scripture memorization is a great way to develop your faith and increase your knowledge of the Bible. When we memorize something, it becomes part of us. We can recall it, recite it and use it to form our thoughts, guide our decisions and articulate our beliefs. Bible memorization helps to form our character and shape our virtues. There is even an app called *BibleMinded* that helps you to memorize verses on your own or by following one of several plans.

We suggest reading a chapter of the Bible a day and highlighting one verse to memorize. Write it down on an index card. Spend a few minutes trying to memorize it. Take the index card with you and practice reciting it as you drive to school, study or rest. By the end of the day, you should have it memorized. Review your index cards once a week.

Jim Mellado was one of the very charismatic speakers who spoke at the Uncovering the Word Conference sponsored by the American Bible Society that I attended in Orlando, Florida in 2011. Jim had risen to become the Executive Minister of the Willow Creek Community Association, overseeing many of the Willow Creek Church's operations. He told us, "My own spiritual engagement with the Bible is the most powerful spiritual thing that I have ever experienced."

"My family was my first church," Jim told us. "My father was an engineer, and we moved 40 times in 53 years. My mother would read the Bible to my siblings and me every day at the breakfast table. She gave us a verse for every letter in the alphabet. 'L' was for 'Love the Lord at all times.' 'G' stood for 'Greater love has no one than to lay down his life for his friends.' 'C' stood for 'Children obey your parents.' 'X' stood for 'How excellent is thy name in all the world.' I cannot imagine life without the Bible guiding my life and shaping my every decision," Jim told us. His words were powerful and incredibly inspiring.

Read the Gospel of Luke and the Book of Acts

If reading a large portion of the Bible seems too daunting, begin slowly. Read Luke, a Gospel rich in stories about Jesus' life and ministry and full of great parables. This will give you an introduction to the life of Jesus. The book of Acts will teach you about how the first Christians began to spread Jesus' message and love.

Do a Parent Child Bible-Challenge or a Family Bible Challenge for Lent

Commit to reading a children's Bible with your child for the 40 days of Lent and invite other families to join you. Get together for play dates and discuss it. Gather with other parents to share your experience and learn from theirs.

Utilize Different Learning Styles

Because children have different learning styles, engaging the Scriptures using different methods is helpful. Visual learners benefit from watching the Bible stories. Enjoy *Veggie Tales* or your favorite Bible stories on Youtube. Tactile learners enjoy manipulatives. Find a favorite Bible verse, cut it into individual words and make it into a puzzle. Auditory learners appreciate hearing the Word read. Practice various techniques in studying the Bible.

Share Your Joy of Reading the Bible with Someone Else

If you have enjoyed and benefited from reading the Bible on a regular basis, share your experience with a friend or family member. Consider purchasing a Bible as a gift for them. Tell them about The Bible Challenge, or get their permission to sign them up as a participant. Consider re-reading the Bible with them and meeting regularly to share your thoughts and experiences. It will deepen your relationship with one another and with God.

Testimonials

I am always looking for ways to do more things together as a family. My son, Trey, is required to read twenty minutes every night. Sometimes this is a real struggle for him. He loves picture books and I knew he would love The Spark Story

Bible. *Here was an opportunity to kill two birds with one stone—join The Bible Challenge and satisfy Trey's reading requirements. I went home that night with great anticipation and announced that we would be reading the Spark Story Bible for twenty minutes every night Monday through Friday for eight weeks. We often exceed the twenty minute timeframe. At this rate we will have finished the whole Bible before our eight weeks are up. Trey eagerly gets out his reading progress report after we finish each night and records the number of minutes and the number of pages he read.*—KAREN, A PARENT

Something really beautiful that has come of it in my life is a time of Bible reading every morning with my son Seth. After reading one of your Bible Challenge articles I got Seth a new Children's Bible that is age appropriate for his reading level for a Christmas gift. We've fallen into the habit of going out to sit in the car and wait for the bus early each morning, and he reads two or three pages each day. It is something we both enjoy, it is great for his reading, and spiritual development, and a nice bonding time for the two of us.—CAROLYN

I love reading the Bible. I love learning how God reveals God's self through Scripture. Most of all, I love reading the Word with others and watching how God is revealed to them. My five year old grandchildren spent a big part of our week on summer vacation wondering, pondering and learning God's miracle of Moses leading the Israelites from slavery and bondage into freedom. The grandchildren learned that God helps us make good choices, especially in difficult times. Together, we all discovered God's greatness of salvation in God's Holy Word. I'll cherish it forever.—HILLARY, A GRANDPARENT

I love reading the Bible. It is moving. I always say No!! when we have to go to bed (and the Bible story is over). We do gratitude journals after we read the Bible. I like writing about what I am grateful for.—TEDDY, AGE 7

I used to not know a lot about the Bible. I thought it was all about rules. I also used to think it was about compliments. That Jesus was sent to the world to thank people. It's good to learn more about God and Jesus. It's hard for young people to learn about God without reading the Bible.—MARGARET, AGE 9

When you read the Bible you start looking at the world in a new way. A flower becomes a miracle.—CAROLINE, AGE 11

CHAPTER 12

Getting Practical: How to Help Teenagers Read the Bible

"But Jesus said to them, 'My mother and my brothers are those who hear the Word of God and do it.'"—LUKE 8:21

"The Teen Bible Challenge gives me the opportunity to read the Bible in an organized way. With college on my mind and a busy school schedule, having an outline to help me read through the Bible is really helpful to me."—ALEC (AGE 17)

"I am reading away—and using what I'm reading. Just last night, at the Junior Youth Group Meeting, I was able to insert a Bible quote from Matthew at just the right moment; and for a few minutes we had fourteen sixth through eighth graders focus on the question at hand. 'So the last shall be first, and the first last.' It was quiet as they considered the meaning of the quote and how it applied to their lives. We had a focused discussion where no one interrupted the speaker for about ten minutes (which is a Junior Youth Group record)."—JIM (A YOUTH GROUP LEADER)

• ◆ •

My wife, Mims, and I recently dropped our daughter, Marguerite, off at Vanderbilt University to begin her freshman year in college. Vanderbilt does an incredible job of welcoming incoming students. As my wife piloted our rented mini-van onto the campus, student volunteers wearing yellow T-shirts lined the parking lots cheering wildly as if each car were full of movie stars arriving at a glamorous Hollywood function. When two attractive, young volunteers called out, "Welcome to Vanderbilt," I nearly burst into tears. In many ways, I had been dreading this time for years. I adore our daughters and having them leave home was not easy. I had spoken to Marguerite since she was old enough to listen about how I would dread the day when she moved out of our home and headed off to college. I told her that it would be the hardest day of my life. After we went through the teenage years together it became easier.

Communicating with teenagers is not always easy. It often seems as though we speak completely different languages. As I watched our daughters grow and change, I tried to step back and give them space. They needed to become young women and learn to make important decisions on their own, while knowing that we would always be there to help if needed. After I hugged my daughter before leaving, she said, "Good-byes are not easy for me."

I said, "They aren't easy for me either. That's why I'm going to give you one last little bit of advice as you head off to one of the most wonderful chapters of your life. Study hard and learn for learning's sake. Enjoy your education. Take the best classes that you can. Get good grades. Work hard, but most of all learn and grow from what you are learning. Make friends that will last a lifetime. Get to know your professors. Take time to be involved in programs and activities that will allow you to serve and give back. Keep balance in your life and have fun. Follow your bliss. Read a little of the Bible each day. It will help you greatly, and let us keep each other in our prayers every day." She smiled. We hugged again and parted. I flew home to Philadelphia. The next day I caught a flight to Spain and began my sabbatical by walking the Camino, the ancient pilgrim's path that leads to Santiago de Campostela where the relics of St. James the Apostle are said to be buried.

Instilling a love for reading the Bible is one of the greatest gifts we can ever give our children. Once they are out of our daily lives, it is a comfort and joy to know they are still in God's safekeeping each day and receiving wisdom and comfort from God's Word. It will guide them and draw the best out of them every day. Taking time each day to read a little bit of the Bible is the number-one way for teenagers to develop as young Christians. The best way for teenagers to begin their journey with the Bible is to read the New Testament in a year, reading just a chapter a day, which is very manageable. It is a great way for teenagers to develop an understanding of the Christian message, deepen their faith, and encounter Jesus. I also recommend reading one psalm every day. The Psalms are the backbone of the Judeo-Christian spiritual tradition and expose teenagers to the world of the Hebrew Scriptures. Jesus quoted the Psalms more than any other book in the Bible, so it makes good sense to combine reading the New Testament with the hymnal of Jesus, which he knew by heart.

The Center for Biblical Studies and I encourage teenagers to reflect upon the texts they read. Plato said the unexamined life is not worth leading. Likewise, unexamined Bible reading does not lead to deeper understanding. It is like eating food without allowing the body to process and benefit from the nutrition. I once visited Honduras on a church mission trip and picked up a bad parasite. For over six weeks, food passed through me without giving me many of the benefits it was meant to provide. My doctor discovered I was anemic as a result. He prescribed an antibiotic that restored my health. Once again, I began benefiting from each meal. If reading the Bible is like a spiritual meal, then processing what we are reading is crucial to getting the most out of what God wants to communicate. In order to reflect upon what they are reading, the Center for Biblical Studies and I encourage teenagers to ask themselves three basic questions each time they sit down to read the Scriptures: 1) What does this text tell me about God? 2) What does it tell me about other people? 3) What does it tell me about myself? Young people can ponder these questions alone, with a friend, or with a group.

The benefit of reading the New Testament from beginning to end before tackling the entire Bible is it begins to nurture the faith within a teenager. There is no better reading for a young Christian than the Christian Scriptures. However, the Old Testament also has vital content for Christian understanding. Dietrich Bonhoeffer noted near the end of his life that Christians too often skim over the Old Testament and race to read through the New Testament. Every Christian can benefit from regular engagement with the Old Testament.

Given the schedules and the spiritual maturity of most teenagers, I believe it is best for them to comprehend "how the story ends" before starting to read through the entire Bible and discovering large portions that seem very irrelevant to ordinary living. Until someone is formed as a Christian and develops a solid understanding of the nature and ways of God, it can be very discouraging or even spiritually damaging to plow one's way through the Old Testament. For a person with a minimal level of faith, reading stories that tell of how God commanded Moses, Joshua, David, and other figures to commit violence and eradicate their enemies can be very disconcerting, to say the least. A teenager could draw the rash conclusion that religion is at the heart of the world's problems, rather than being a potential solution to many of life's great issues and concerns. While the world of the New Testament is ancient and far different from the one that most modern teenagers experience, the world of the Old Testament is even more estranged. Tribal warfare, concubines, child sacrifices, execution by stoning, the oppression of women, intolerance of homosexuals, slavery, disdain for differing religions and practices, kings killing kings, ethnic cleansings, pagan practices, strange dietary codes, and long boring genealogies can be extremely off-putting.

After they have read the entire New Testament, the Center for Biblical Studies and I encourage teenagers to read a One-Year Bible, which consists of selected readings for each day, using lessons from both the Old and the New Testament. The more difficult, boring, and violent passages, especially from the Old Testament, are omitted. This is an excellent way to go deeper with regular Bible reading. At the conclusion of each reading, we encourage teenagers to ask themselves: 1) What do today's readings tell me about God? 2) What do they tell me about other people? 3) What do they tell me about myself? Once they have read the New Testament on their own, reading and pondering these questions with a friend or with a group is the next step.

Most teenagers I know are far more tech savvy than I am. They live with their mobile devices. They are digital natives. We do well to encourage them to harness the power of technology and find a Bible download. They can find a Bible app for the iPad, iPhone, Kindle, or Nook, which will allow them to keep the Bible with them at all times. *YouVersion.com* and *bible.com* offer several Bible reading plans from Read-a-Bible-in-a-Year to plans exploring faith, love, and other topics. *Oneyearbibleonline. com* offers a reading plan divided into daily segments containing a passage from the Old Testament, the New Testament, Psalms, and Proverbs. *Biblegateway.com* is a great searchable Bible with multiple options for finding what you need. *Bibleresources.bible.com* is a similar site. *Amazon.com, Zondervan.com*, and *BN.com* offer an array of Bibles and downloads available as ebooks, audio books, or CDs.

One of the things that my wife and I appreciated most about our daughters' school was the individualized attention given each student and the ability of teachers and administrators to perceive learning traits that made each pupil unique. Students were taught to discern their own particular learning style and use that knowledge to facilitate their learning. Some students, for example, are visual learners and others are audio learners. For audio learners, listening to the Bible being read is a great way to engage God's Word.

Options for Listening to the Bible

For many audio learners, being assigned or encouraged to read yet another book sounds completely uninviting. Reading the Bible may seem like yet another undesired task, ranking up there with taking out the trash, making one's bed, or doing a mountain of homework. Listening to the Bible, however, is a bit like listening to Harry Potter books being read aloud. Some of the stories are simply magical. Some are downright practical. The teaching is vital and the narratives are some of the best literature ever written.

Many resources today allow you to listen to the Bible as you drive to school, walk your dog, exercise, travel, or relax at home or in bed, which is great for audio learners. You can listen to the Bible in a variety of translations by using apps and programs from *Audio.com/Bible, listenersbible.com, BibleGateway.com, YouVersion.com* or *www.faithcomesthroughhearing.com*, which provides audio Bible programs in nearly seven hundred languages. A teenager can listen to the entire New Testament in forty days by listening just twenty-eight minutes a day—a manageable task for a summer, perhaps. Studies reveal that if a person reads the Bible for twenty-one days in a row, there is an 80 percent chance that he or she will become a lifelong daily reader of the Bible.

Scripture memorization is a great way for a teenager to develop their faith and increase their knowledge of the Bible. When we memorize something, we can recall it, recite it, and use it to form our thoughts, guide our decisions, and articulate our beliefs. Bible memorization helps to mold character and shape virtues. *BibleMinded* is an app that allows people to memorize verses on their own by following one of several plans. The Center for Biblical Studies and I suggest both teenagers and adults read a chapter of the Bible a day and highlight one verse to memorize. It is best to write it down on an index card and spend a few minutes memorizing it. We recommend that teenagers then take the card with them during the day to practice reciting it. By the end of the day, he or she should have it memorized; he or she should review favorite verses once a week.

For teenagers who have struggled to read the Bible, we suggest reading *The Message Remix*, a teen version of the best-selling paraphrase of the Bible *The Message* by Eugene Peterson. It is a great introduction to the Bible for those who struggle with reading Scripture in its original form because it makes the stories come alive in a fresh, new way. Visit *www.messagebible.com* to order a copy. Another option is *The Story Teen Edition*, a seamless collection of Bible stories published by Zondervan that stitches together almost all of the stories of the Bible into one continuous tale that reads like a novel. Long dietary codes, genealogies, and repetitive portions of the Bible have been eliminated. After reading this, a teenager may be ready to tackle the entire Bible or at least the New Testament on his or her own. Visit *www.thestory. com* to order a copy.

For teenagers who have developed a mature faith and have read the entire New Testament, *The Message Remix*, *The Story Teen Edition* or a *One-Year Bible*, we recommend progressing to a Read the Bible in a Year Reading Plan, which can be downloaded from *www.thecenterforbiblicalstudies.org*. This is a way of engaging the Old Testament while not having to engage all of the violent stories found within it. The Center for Biblical Studies and I think that this is a better approach for teenagers. After this, they will be prepared to engage the entire Old Testament.

If reading the entire Bible or even the New Testament seems too daunting, we encourage young people to begin by reading the Gospel of Luke and the book of Acts. It is a great way to begin to understand the message of the Bible and learn how the Church was born. Since Luke authored both Acts and his gospel, the two read like a movie and its sequel. Luke uses a mountain motif throughout. The Gospel of Luke is the story of Jesus' journey to Jerusalem, which is set atop a mountain and climaxes when Jesus is crucified in Jerusalem on a the hill called Golgotha and is resurrected. Acts is the story of the journey of his disciples down from that mountain to carry the message of Jesus' love, his model of servant leadership, and his capacity for healing to people around the world. Luke's Gospel is rich in stories about Jesus' life and ministry and full of great parables. It provides an excellent introduction to the life of Jesus. Acts teaches teenagers how the Church began to spread Jesus' message of love.

After reading a significant portion of the Bible on your own, the final step is to join or start a Bible study. This is a great way to experience the Word of God. It cannot replace reading the Bible on your own, but it helps to strengthen your knowledge and love of it. Bible studies often meet once a week. My recommendation is to read the Bible daily and attend a Bible study once a week. The Bible comes alive when we read and study it with others. The heart of religion is not about having all of the answers but asking the right questions. Bible studies help us to formulate good questions and learn from others. If there is not an on-going Bible study at your church, start one in your home, school or church. Invite friends to join you. Begin by reading a gospel. Then consider reading the book of Acts and Paul's letter to the Romans; move on to his first and second letters to the Corinthians. For the

Old Testament, the Center for Biblical Studies and I encourage you to start with Genesis and Exodus.

I close with a story. There was a couple in my parish who rarely attended church. Their focus was on family, friends, and sports, and finding enjoyment and sharing it with others. They were fine people. I began inviting the husband to get more involved in the church. I challenged him to become a stronger steward, invited him to join a Bible study that I led, and asked him to serve on our Youth Ministry Commission. He plunged deeper into the life of the church and eventually ran the commission. Then one morning he was headed to work with a colleague on an expressway outside Philadelphia when a truck whose brakes were failing ran into his car and immediately took his life. The other person in the car was so badly hurt that it took many operations to restore his body, and he will suffer from the result of his injuries as long as he lives. The church was packed to overflowing with people for the funeral. We ran a cable down to another building on our campus to broadcast the service to two hundred and fifty people who could not fit inside our church. After his death, one of the man's daughters began reading Evening Prayer from The Book of Common Prayer each night at home. She is a young woman of amazing character with a huge heart for serving God and others. Sometime later, I encouraged her to join The Bible Challenge to continue to build her faith and spiritual life. She gladly accepted and in time read through the entire Bible. It had a transforming impact on her life. She has always had a heart for service, but now her heart continued to be honed to serve God in a way that was inspiring to everyone around her. She could articulate her faith and her reasons for serving in ways she could never have done before. In high school she won the distinguished service award in our community and went on to the University of Pennsylvania with a special scholarship for service work.

I believe that she was headed in this direction because of the goodness of her spirit. Reading the Bible, however, gave her a heart of gold, an ability to connect her love of others with serving God, and the faith to trust that her father is watching over her from heaven and she will one day be reunited with him. She now attends a weekly Bible study at her college where she has made close friends and can share the things that are most important in her heart. Here is what she wrote about reading the Bible.

The Bible Challenge is going really well. I haven't been able to read as much per day now that school has started, but I make sure that I always read at least a little bit every day. More importantly, though, it's become something that keeps faith on my mind pretty much all the time . . . Also, I can tell that it's something I want to continue. Not only am I sure that I'll finish it, but I'm also sure that once I do, I'll go back and study individual parts again. I am confident that daily reading will definitely remain a part of my schedule. Thank you for introducing me to this challenge; it's been a wonderful thing in my life. —ALLIE (AGE 17)

CHAPTER 13

Getting Practical: How to Help Adults Read the Bible

"How weighty to me are your thoughts, O God! How vast is the sum of them! I try to count them—they are more than the sand. . . ."—Psalm 139:17–18

"Were not our hearts burning within us while he was talking to us on the road, while he was opening the Scriptures to us?"—Luke 24:32

"The Scriptures teach us the best way of living, the noblest way of suffering, and the most comfortable way of dying."—Flavel

• ◆ •

The Bible is God's life-transforming Word. It will change and enrich your life. Here are some things that we encourage you to read and consider before you get started:

- Start The Bible Challenge at any time you wish.
- Read a portion of the Bible each day.
- Give yourself a year to read the entire Bible.
- Some individuals try to read the Bible in ninety days, but this short time frame can be daunting. The Bible has a profound message; take ample time to allow God's Word to penetrate your heart, mind, and soul deeply.
- If you need more than a year to read the whole book, move at the pace that works best for you.

Which Translation of the Bible Should I Read?

- We encourage participants to read *The New Oxford Annotated Version of the Bible*. It is an excellent, highly readable translation with helpful footnotes. *The New International Version of the Bible* and *The Common English Bible* are other fine and easily readable translations. There are many other translations. If you wish to read a different one, please feel free to do so. Bear in mind that using the *King James Version* to read the Bible for the first time can be difficult.
- Harness the power of technology. You can find eBook versions for the iPad, iPhone, Kindle, or Nook. The NIV Bible is readily available on CDs.
- Some Bible Challenge participants have chosen to use a 365-Day-Bible. Please note, however, this version usually omits some stories. Participants

do not benefit from reading some of the more challenging passages and teachings that are already omitted from the Common Lectionary, which prevents readers from entering deeper theological discussions involving questions of theodicy—the study of why God permits evil to exist—which are important to address.

- Most participants in The Bible Challenge read the entire Bible, which is what we recommend. If this task seems too daunting, then we encourage you to 1) read the New Testament or 2) read one of the Gospels or 3) read the book of Acts or 4) read the Psalter (the Book of Psalms), and tackle a larger challenge later.

- Some individuals enjoy reading *The Story*, a collection of seamless Bible stories published by Zondervan, which omits genealogies, dietary codes, and other less readable portions. Though it is very accessible for people not used to reading the Bible, it is not the full Bible, and it is not our first recommendation.

How Do You Recommend I Begin Reading the Bible?

- We strongly discourage individuals from reading the Bible from cover to cover starting with the book of Genesis and ending with Revelation, because most readers who try this fail to finish. There are many parts of the Hebrew Scriptures that readers find challenging and spiritually dry that discourage them from completing the Bible.

- We encourage you to read three chapters of the Old Testament, a psalm, and a chapter of the New Testament each day, which will help you read the entire Bible in a year. Reading a chapter of the New Testament and a psalm daily will sustain you through spiritually dryer parts of the Hebrew Scriptures.

- The Center for Biblical Studies website is *www.thecenterforbiblicalstudies. org*. We offer a scheduled read for those who want to follow a clear plan of Bible daily reading, which will help you conclude your reading in a year's time. Please see "The One Year Read" under the "Resource" section of the website. We also offer a "Read the Bible in a Year Lent to Lent Reading Plan," for individuals who wish to start on Ash Wednesday.

- Because the Bible is not a newspaper, it is best to read it with a reverent spirit. We advocate a devotional approach, rather than reading it as a purely intellectual or academic exercise. We encourage you to begin each session by putting yourself in the presence of God as you start to read.

- We like the ancient monastic practice of *lectio divina*, where you read the text, meditate on a portion of it, then offer a prayer to God and listen in silence for God to respond. We therefore encourage all readers to read the Bible prayerfully.

- We encourage you to read in the morning for twenty or thirty minutes, so that your prayerful reading will spiritually enliven the rest of your day. If you cannot read in the morning, read when you can later in the day when you can carve out a regular time.

- We encourage you to skim or skip over long genealogies, lengthy descriptions of the ephod or temple construction, animal sacrifice, or dietary codes found in the Hebrew Scriptures. Get the gist and move on so that you remain on task to finish reading the Bible.

- Many Americans make New Year's resolutions. The most common is to lose weight. The second most common resolution is to exercise more often. Within six days most Americans have forsaken their resolutions. Psychologists say that this occurs because persons making resolutions have no one to hold them accountable. It is vital to offer ongoing support and hold people accountable especially through the first few months of The Bible Challenge. Those who succeed in regular Bible reading for the first two months are likely to reach their goal. Tell a few family members and friends that you are participating in The Bible Challenge and ask them to help hold you accountable to your daily practice of reading the Bible.

Team Strength and Reaching Out for Support in Reading the Bible

- One way to hold yourself accountable to reading God's Word and to help you to read the Bible is to start a group within your church or community. By participating in The Bible Challenge together, you can support one another in your reading, ask questions about the Bible, discuss what you are reading, and share how God's Word is transforming your life.

- If you do not want to start your own group, we encourage you to find one in your church or local community or consider reading the Bible with a friend or group of friends. It is important to share what you are learning, ask questions about the Bible and share how reading God's Word is changing your life.

- At our church, we have called our support classes "Intelligent Talk about the Bible." Some churches use names like "The Good Book Club." These groups can offer support to novice Bible readers, especially during the first ninety days of reading when beginners are moving through the Hebrew Scriptures and struggling with stories of violence, wrathful actions attributed to God, women being treated poorly, and strange facts like persons living to be nine hundred and fifty years old. If a new reader can work through these difficult areas, success will be more likely.

- You may wish to put a notice in your parish newsletter that you are starting a Bible Challenge group and invite others to join you and to come together regularly to discuss your reading. Please see "How Churches can participate" on our website for helpful suggestions for starting a group in your church.

- If you do form a group to read the entire Bible together, we encourage you to hold a gathering or meal to celebrate your spiritual accomplishment. If you read the Bible on your own, find a way to celebrate when you finish. It's a major accomplishment worth commemorating.

Let the Center for Biblical Studies Support You

- As questions arise about what you are reading, we invite you to email them to The Center for Biblical Studies, and we will endeavor to respond promptly.

- We encourage you to have fun and to find spiritual peace and the joy that God desires for you in your daily reading. Our ultimate goal is to have you discover God's wisdom in your daily Bible reading and to create a lifelong spiritual practice of daily Bible reading. In this way God may speak to you in silence and solitude and guide you through each day of your life.

Life after the Bible Challenge

- If you have found reading the entire Bible and being part of The Bible Challenge to be a blessing in your life, then we strongly encourage you to share the blessing. Ask several friends or family members to participate in The Bible Challenge.

- Those who successfully read the entire Bible may wish to read it again using a different translation.

- Either way, we strongly encourage participants to make daily Bible reading an important spiritual practice for the rest of their lives. The Bible is a book worthy of a life's dedication to read and reread. It is a never-ending fount of wisdom that can bestow blessings upon us each day.

- There are those like President John Adams who made it a practice to read through the Bible each year during his adult life and felt greatly blessed by doing so. We highly advocate this practice.

- After reading the Bible through once, you will be more able to help encourage and support others in reading the entire Bible. We hope you will serve as an encourager and mentor for others.

May God richly bless you for committing to read the Bible and help you to honor your commitment as you faithfully read God's Word each day.

CHAPTER 14

Getting Practical: How to Help Your Church, Cathedral, or School Read the Bible

"I hold back my feet from every evil way, in order to keep your Word. I do not turn away from your ordinances, for you have taught me. How sweet are your words to my taste, sweeter than honey to my mouth!"—Psalm 119:101–3

"The more you read the Bible, the more you meditate on it, the more you will be astonished by it."—Charles Spurgeon

• — •

In order to encourage and support persons reading the Bible from cover to cover, the Center for Biblical Studies and I have found that following practices to be most helpful:

- A church can start The Bible Challenge at any time of the year.
- We have found that an ideal time to start The Bible Challenge is New Year's Day when many people make New Year's resolutions. You can encourage members of your church and friends beyond your parish to make a spiritual resolution and join you in reading the entire Bible during the year.
- Other good times to start include Lent, Pentecost, Kick-off Sunday in September, and Advent. Each year, the Center for Biblical Studies prepares a Lent to Lent Read the Bible in a Year Reading Plan, which can be found on our website at *www.thecenterforbiblicalstudies.org*
- Some churches sponsor a ninety-day challenge to read the entire Bible, but this short time frame can be daunting to slow readers or persons with very busy schedules. We also believe that it is more desirable to help people develop a life-long spiritual discipline through daily Scripture reading as opposed to a ninety-day spiritual event that is accomplished and concluded.

Providing Options

- We suggest inviting your entire parish to read the entire Bible with you in a year.
- In the second year as you re-launch The Bible Challenge, we recommend that you offer your parishioners options that include: 1) read the entire

Bible 2) read the New Testament 3) read one of the Gospels, or 4) read the Psalter. This way there is something that everyone can choose as a spiritual challenge. The Center for Biblical Studies offers a Read the New Testament, Psalms and Proverbs in a Year Reading Plan and the Fifty-Day Bible Challenge with the Gospel of Matthew on our website.

- Those who accept reading only a portion of the Bible in the first year may accept a larger challenge in the second year.

- Some parishes recommend using *The Story*, a collection of seamless Bible stories published by Zondervan, which omits genealogies, dietary codes, and other less readable passages. It is very accessible for people not used to reading the Bible. Others have used Eugene Peterson's contemporary rendering known as *The Message*. Both *The Story* and *The Message* are not true translations of the Bible, so we recommend not focusing on them initially. Rather we recommend introducing them as you re-launch The Bible Challenge for people who tried but struggled in reading the Bible in the previous year. They are fine options.

Harness the Power of Technology and Download the Bible for Free

- Encourage and allow participants to read the Bible using their iPads, iPhones, Kindles, or Nooks or to listen to the Bible on CDs. The NIV Bible is readily available on CDs.

- Participants can download the Bible to their electronic devices and have it with them at all times. *YouVersion.com* and *bible.com* offer numerous plans from read a Bible in a year to explorations of faith, love, and other themes. The site includes downloads of mobile apps and apps for a variety of devices and operating systems.

- *Oneyearbibleonline.com* offers a plan divided into daily readings, each containing a passage from the Old Testament, the New Testament, Psalms, and Proverbs. *Biblegateway.com* is a great searchable Bible with multiple options for finding just what you need. *Bibleresources.bible.com* is another site with helpful resources. *Amazon.com*, *Zondervan.com*, and *BN.com* offer an array of Bibles and downloads available for many smart phones and other devices, as well as NIV Audio Bible Dramatized and CDs.

Listen to the Bible

- There are many resources today that will allow Bible Challenge participants to listen to the Bible as they ride in the car, drive to school, walk their dog, travel, do arts and crafts or relax at home or in bed. For audio learners this is especially helpful.

- You can listen to the Bible in a variety of translations by using apps and programs from *Audio.com/Bible, listenersbible.com, BibleGateway.com, YouVersion. com, Pandora,* or *www.faithcomesthroughhearing.com. Faith Comes through Hearing* provides audio programs to listen to the Bible in almost seven hundred languages. You can listen to the entire New Testament in forty days by reading twenty-eight minutes a day.

Recommended Strategies for Reading

- We do not tell our participants how much of the Bible they are expected to read each week or month. Instead we offer a suggested reading plan and give suggestions on how to read the Bible in a fashion that is likely to help them read through the entire Bible.

- We strongly discourage participants from reading the Bible from cover to cover starting with Genesis and ending with Revelation, because most readers who do this fail to reach the end. There are many parts of the Hebrew Scriptures that readers find challenging and spiritually dry that discourage them from completing the Bible.

- We encourage participants in The Bible Challenge to read three chapters of the Old Testament, one psalm, and one chapter of the New Testament each day. This will help them read the entire Bible in a year. Adding passages from the New Testament and a psalm daily sustains readers through spiritually dryer parts of the Hebrew Scriptures.

- Our website offers a reading schedule for those who want to follow a clear plan of daily Bible reading that will help them conclude their reading in a year's time. Please see "The One Year Read" under the "Resource" section of the website at *www.thecenterforbiblicalstudies.org.*

- We advocate a devotional approach to reading the Bible as opposed to a purely intellectual or academic approach. We suggest that each reader put him- or herself in the presence of God before starting. We like the ancient monastic practice of *lectio divina*, where a reader reads the text, meditates on the reading, offers a prayer to God and listens in silence for God to respond. We encourage readers to pause during or after their reading to offer prayers to God.

- Participants may skim over long genealogies or dietary codes in order to ensure that they do not get bogged down in tedious sections of the Bible, but continue to read and reach their goal.

How to Promote the Bible Challenge in Your Church and Beyond

- We recommend placing an article in your church newsletter, using verbal and written announcements in Sunday worship, and sending a letter inviting your entire membership to participate in The Bible Challenge. You may even place an ad in the local newspaper, inviting members of the community to join you.

- We encourage each parish to invite people in the community who do not belong to the church to participate in The Bible Challenge. By doing so, the church will offer a vital spiritual outreach to others who may eventually join.

- Offer free Bibles to those who do not have one, if you can. It is a wonderful way to welcome people from outside of your church. The American Bible Society and other groups sell paperback Bibles at extremely reasonable rates.

- Ask your local newspaper to write an article about The Bible Challenge and the effect that it is having on your congregation. You may be pleasantly surprised by the positive reception and press coverage that you receive.

- Each month, invite one or more members to write a short article for your parish newsletter sharing their experiences of reading the Bible. It is powerful when lay persons share with others the joy and insights that they have received from daily Bible reading and how it has impacted their faith and brought them closer to God.

Reaching All Ages

- We recommend using age appropriate Bibles to allow children and parents to read Bible stories together.

- We recommend parents read *The Big Picture Story Bible* by Scripture Union with children ages 2–7, *The Spark Bible* (NRSV) or the *DK Bible* for older children.

- For more information visit the CBS website for "Resources for Children, Youth and Families."

- We encourage teenagers with a mature faith to join The Bible Challenge using the NIV Teen Study Bible. We also suggest inviting church youth groups to read and discuss one of the gospels every year and to read another book of the Bible such as the book of Acts.

- We suggest that those less certain of their faith read the New Testament first before attempting the entire Bible.

- We also suggest inviting church youth groups to read and discuss one of the gospels each year and one other book of the Bible as well.

Providing Ongoing Support

- We recommend offering a series of ongoing classes for participants to ask questions that come up during their reading. We call our classes "Intelligent Talk about the Bible." Others call theirs "The Good Book Club." We recommend that churches offer these on a weekly basis with daytime and evening options for the first twelve weeks of The Bible Challenge. These are the most difficult weeks when novice Bible readers, especially those reading the Old Testament, struggle with stories of violence, wrathful actions attributed to God, women being treated poorly, and strange facts such as persons living to be almost a thousand years old. If a novice reader can be led in working through these difficult areas, success will be likely.

- We recommend printing the names of everyone who participates in your church's Bible Challenge in your parish newsletter. This lets others know who and how many in your parish are participating, and it holds the participants accountable to their commitment. Participants can also seek each other out to discuss the Bible.

- We suggest using tools like Constant Contact to send out regular email messages to Bible Challenge participants to support and encourage them to reach their goal. Many readers said that this regular nudge inspired them and kept them from giving up.

- We recommend that clergy occasionally send individual e-mails to The Bible Challenge participants asking them how they are doing and encouraging them to continue. Replies from participants are often full of spiritual insights and questions. This communication is almost online spiritual direction as church members share insights and reactions to reading the Bible that they might not take time to share face to face with clergy members.

- Pray each Sunday for both members and non-members of your church who are participating in The Bible Challenge. Prayer is powerful, and it supports those participating in the challenge. In addition as people hear their names read, they realize that there is a faith community supporting them in reaching their spiritual goal. Many in our church were lagging in their reading when they heard prayers said for them in church; they returned home and reengaged in reading the Bible.

- Hold a celebratory banquet for those who participate in The Bible Challenge. Give a certificate to everyone who has been a faithful reader for a year and a special certificate to those who have read the entire Bible.

Re-Launch the Bible Challenge in Your Parish

- Ask those who have finished or have made significant inroads in reading the Bible to invite several friends or family members to join them in The Bible Challenge when you re-launch it the following year.

- Allow members of your church who have successfully read the entire Bible to preach or speak in an adult class to share how it has transformed their lives.

- Prepare follow-up classes for those who succeed in reading the entire Bible or those who have struggled and not been able to finish the task. Participants will have many questions and a deeper hunger to know more about the Bible.

- Encourage those who finish the Bible to become mentors for beginners when you re-launch The Bible Challenge or to lead new Bible studies or programs such as Education for Ministry, which is an excellent follow-up to The Bible Challenge.

CHAPTER 15

Getting Practical: How a Bishop Can Help His or Her Diocese Read the Bible in a Year

"For my thoughts are not your thoughts, nor are your ways, says the Lord. For as the heavens are higher than the earth, so are my ways and my thoughts than your thoughts. For as the rain and the snow come down from heaven, and do not return there until they have watered the earth, making it bring forth and sprout, giving seed to the sower and bread to the eater, so shall my word be that goes out from my mouth; it shall not return to me empty, but it shall accomplish that which I purpose, and succeed in the thing for which I sent it."—Isaiah 55:8–11

"I beg of you, my dear brother, to live among these books [Scriptures], to meditate upon them, to know nothing else, to seek nothing else."—St. Jerome

⋅◆⋅

One of the early Church Fathers wrote, "As the bishop goes, so goes the diocese." A bishop's stature and example can inspire thousands of people towards spiritual growth. Studies show that the most effective way to develop spiritual maturity as Christians is daily Scripture reading. Hearing the Bible read in church is like sitting in the passenger seat of a car. Being a passenger does not teach us how to drive a car or help us to learn the roads to our destination. We learn best when we are in the driver's seat.

The Center for Biblical Studies actively encourages each bishop to invite the clergy and laity of their diocese to join in reading the entire Bible in a year, with the ultimate goal of helping thousands of individuals to develop a life-long spiritual practice of daily Bible reading.

Studies reveal a person who reads the Bible for twenty-one days in a row has an 80 percent chance of developing a lifetime discipline of daily Bible reading and that reading Scripture four times or more a week has a positive measurable impact on moral behavior. In order to assist bishops, we recommend the following practices:

Timing

- Your diocese and you can start The Bible Challenge at any time of the year.
- We have found that some ideal times include starting on New Year's Day when many people make New Year's Resolutions. Encourage your clergy and laity to

join you in making a spiritual resolution as you read the entire Bible together during the calendar year. You can also start in Lent and use our Lent to Lent Read the Bible in a Year Plan as a Lenten discipline that continues throughout the year. Some bishops have begun The Bible Challenge at the beginning of the summer when many people experience a slower pace of life and have more time to read. Others have started in September and some have used Advent as a springboard to begin The Bible Challenge.

- Zondervan offers a ninety day challenge to read the entire Bible, but this short time frame can appear daunting to most readers or persons with busy schedules. Our preference is to follow a slower, more meditative reading of the Bible.

Which Translation of the Bible Should the Diocese Read?

- We encourage participants to read *The New Oxford Annotated Version of the Bible*. It is an excellent, highly readable translation with helpful study notes and maps. *The New International Version of the Bible* and *The Common English Bible* are other fine and easily readable translations. If you wish to read a different translation, please feel free to do so. Bear in mind that using the *King James Version* to read the Bible for the first time can be difficult.

- Some Bible Challenge participants have chosen to use a 365-Day-Bible. Please note, however, that these Bibles usually omit some sections and participants do not benefit from reading some of the more challenging Bible stories and teachings, which are already omitted from the Common *Lectio*nary. This prevents readers from entering deeper theological discussions involving questions of theodicy, which are important to address.

- We recommend that you offer free Bibles to those who do not have one.

Providing Options

- We suggest inviting your entire diocese to read the entire Bible with you in a year.
- In the second year as you re-launch The Bible Challenge, we recommend that you offer your parishioners a variety of options: 1) read the entire Bible 2) read the New Testament 3) read one of the Gospels or 4) read the Psalter. This way there is something that everyone can choose as a spiritual challenge. The Center for Biblical Studies offers a Read the New Testament, Psalms and Proverbs in a Year Reading Plan and the Fifty-Day Bible Challenge with the Gospel of Matthew on our website.
- Those who accept reading only a portion of the Bible in the first year may accept a larger challenge in the second year when you re-launch the challenge.

- Some parishes recommend using *The Story*—a collection of seamless Bible stories published by Zondervan that omits genealogies, dietary codes, and other less interesting parts. It is very accessible for people not used to reading the Bible. Others have used Eugene Peterson's contemporary rendering known as *The Message*. Both *The Story* and *The Message* are not true translations of the Bible, so we recommend not focusing on them initially. Rather the Center for Biblical Studies and I recommend introducing them as you re-launch The Bible Challenge for people who tried but struggled in reading the Bible in the previous year. They are fine options.

Harness the Power of Technology and Download the Bible for Free

- We recommend encouraging clergy and lay members of your diocese to consider downloading the Bible on their iPads, iPhones, Kindles, or Nooks or listening to it on CDs. The NIV Bible is readily available on CDs.
- Participants can download the Bible to their favorite electronic device and keep it with them at all times. *YouVersion.com* and *bible.com* offer numerous Bible reading plans from read a Bible in a year to plans exploring faith, love, or other themes. The site includes download links to mobile apps for smart phones, iPads, and Android devices. *Biblegateway.com*

Listen to the Bible

- There are many resources today that will allow Bible Challenge participants to listen to the Bible as they ride in the car, drive to school, walk their dog, travel, do arts and crafts, or relax at home or in bed. For audio learners this is especially helpful.
- You can listen to the Bible in a variety of translations by using apps and programs from *Audio.com/Bible*, *listenersbible.com*, *BibleGateway.com*, *YouVersion.com*, *Pandora* or *www.faithcomesthroughhearing.com*. *Faith Comes through Hearing* provides audio programs to listen to the Bible in nearly seven hundred languages. You can listen to the entire New Testament in forty days by listening twenty-eight minutes a day.

Reading Pace

- We encourage you to invite your clergy and laity to: 1) read three chapters of the Old Testament, 2) one psalm, and 3) one chapter of the New Testament each day. This will get you through the Bible in a year.

- This strategy leads to successful reading of the books of the Bible in sequence, and provides diversity to help those reading dryer parts of the Hebrew Scriptures.

Reaching All Ages

- We recommend using age appropriate Bibles to allow children and parents to read Bible stories together.
- We recommend parents read *The Big Picture Story Bible* by Scripture Union with children ages two to seven and *The Spark Bible* by NRSV or the *DK Bible* for older children.
- For more information visit the CBS website for "Resources for Children, Youth and Families." We encourage diocesan teenagers with a mature faith to join The Bible Challenge using the NIV Teen Study Bible.
- We encourage teenagers with a mature faith to join The Bible Challenge. We also suggest inviting church youth groups to read and discuss one of the gospels every year and to read another book of the Bible such as the book of Acts.
- We suggest that those less certain of their faith read the New Testament first before attempting the entire Bible.

Reaching Out

- We encourage bishops to reach out to friends and acquaintances in your diocese and beyond to join you in reading the Bible in a year, including seminarians from your diocese and all those seeking ordination.
- You are your diocese's number-one evangelist. We encourage you to lead by example and encourage your clergy to do the same in their parishes.
- Write about your success. Share the results. Let your diocese know how many active diocesan members and seekers are reading the Bible.
- Let them know if your college roommate or a close friend has accepted your invitation to read the Bible with you.

Communicating the Transforming Experience of Reading Scripture

- Share testimonials in your diocesan newsletter, parish visits, and diocesan convention about how The Bible Challenge is transforming you and others.
- Share with your diocese what you are discovering as you re-read the entire Bible.

- Discuss the portions of the Bible not found in the Daily Lectionary.

- Help those in your diocese comprehend the challenges of understanding portions of the Bible that associate God with violence and suffering.

- The Center for Biblical Studies website offers articles by Professor Walter Brueggemann about these issues that are good resources for diocesan study groups.

Recommended Strategies for Reading

- Give permission to those who participate in The Bible Challenge to skip or skim over genealogies and dietary codes, so they do not become mired down but complete their goal of reading the entire Bible.

- Since 2012 the Center for Biblical Studies website at *www.thecenterfor biblicalstudies.org* has offered a one-year Bible reading plan. It includes a meditation on each day's reading, a question and a prayer written by bishops, clergy, seminary deans, authors, and scholars.

- We advocate using a devotional approach as opposed to a purely intellectual or academic reading of the Bible. Each reader should put him- or herself in God's presence before reading.

- We like the ancient monastic practice of *lectio divina*, where readers read the text, meditate on it, offer a prayer to God, and listen in silence for God to respond—*lectio, meditatio, oratio,* and *contemplatio.* Encourage those who read the Bible with you to pause to pray during or after their reading.

- Our website *www.thecenterforbiblicalstudies.org* offers many resources to help the members of your diocese and you.

How to Promote the Bible Challenge in Your Church and Beyond

- We recommend writing all diocesan clergy and placing an article in your newsletter inviting the diocese to join you in reading the entire Bible in a year.

- Ask each rector to promote your invitation to join you in The Bible Challenge in their parish newsletter and Sunday announcements.

- Consider using newspaper ads to invite members of the community to join your diocese and you in The Bible Challenge.

- Ask your clergy to make a concerted effort to invite people in the community outside of their church to join The Bible Challenge.

Harnessing Free Publicity

- We encourage letting the media know that you and your diocese are participating in The Bible Challenge. It's newsworthy when Episcopalians read the Bible!

- Consider writing an article for the newspaper about your Bible Challenge. Since Anglicans are not known for being regular Bible readers, we have seen very strong favorable responses by the media to The Bible Challenge.

- Each month ask a member of the diocese to write an article for your newsletter sharing their experience of reading the Bible and how it is transforming his or her life.

Providing Ongoing Support

- It is vital to offer ongoing support, to hold people accountable, and to assist them especially during the first three months of The Bible Challenge. Those who meet with success in the first ninety days are likely to read the entire Bible.

- The most difficult weeks come at the start when novice Bible readers discover challenging stories that are never read in church.

- Churches can offer ongoing classes to support Bible Challenge participants in the first ninety days. Some churches call these groups "Intelligent Talk about the Bible" or "The Good Book Club."

Creating Accountability and Offering Assistance

- We recommend printing in your newsletter the names of everyone in your diocese who participates in The Bible Challenge. This lets others know who and how many are participating. It also celebrates their spiritual commitment and holds them accountable to their commitment.

- Participants will be aware of others participating in The Bible Challenge and can seek them out to discuss the Bible.

- We suggest collecting the names and e-mail addresses of those participating in The Bible Challenge so that you as their bishop can use Constant Contact or other means to send out regular messages of support and wisdom to participants.

- Many readers find this regular nudge inspires them to reach their goal. E-mail will allow you to offer special insights about the Bible. By sharing how reading the Bible strengthens your faith, you can inspire others.

- We recommend that bishops occasionally send personal e-mails of support to clergy whose parishes are participating in The Bible Challenge. This can create online spiritual conversations between bishops and clergy about the Bible and God, which they rarely share face to face.

- Consider establishing the domain on Facebook and Twitter for your diocese or state and The Bible Challenge to allow members of your diocese to follow and pose questions or share thoughts online.
- Encourage participating churches to pray each Sunday for the spiritual transformation of those participating in The Bible Challenge and mention by name several participants in the parish each Sunday.
- Preach about the importance of Bible reading when making parish visits.

Celebrating Your Diocesan Achievement

- At the end of a year, bishops are encouraged to hold a celebratory banquet for those who participated in The Bible Challenge.
- We recommend that you speak at the banquet or invite a guest speaker to talk about the spiritual gift of daily Bible reading.
- We encourage you to have clergy and laity offer brief testimonials about how reading the Bible has transformed their lives.
- Award a certificate to everyone who has been a faithful Bible reader for a year and a special award to those who have read the entire Bible.

Re-Launching the Bible Challenge in Your Diocese

- Have clergy and lay persons who have read the entire Bible offer testimonials at your convention and at other diocesan functions to share how reading the Bible has transformed their lives.
- Encourage participating churches to offer follow-up classes for those who read the entire Bible and those who have struggled and did not finish. Both groups will have more questions and hunger to learn about the Bible.
- Invite those who read the entire Bible to become parish mentors for those who participate in Year Two.
- Encourage those who read the entire Bible to join Education for Ministry (EfM), which is an excellent follow-up to The Bible Challenge.

Providing Options and Re-Launching the Bible Challenge in Year Two

- Re-launch The Bible Challenge each year in order to get more members of the diocese to read the entire Bible.
- In Year Two provide more options to participants such as:
  - Read the entire Bible with the bishop.

> - Read the New Testament with the bishop.
> - Read the Psalter in Lent with the bishop.
> - Read one gospel with the bishop.
> - Read the book of Acts with the bishop.

- Consider using the E100 produced by Scripture Union. This highlights one hundred Bible passages that convey the sweep of salvation history.
- Join your bishop in becoming part of a home Bible study.
- Read *The Message* by Eugene Peterson.
- Read *The Story* by Zondervan. It is designed for Bible novices.
- Invite those who have read the Bible with you in one translation to re-read it with you in Year Two using a different translation.
- Re-launching The Bible Challenge affirms that the goal for each reader is to become a life-long daily reader of the Bible.
- Focus on The Bible Challenge as a five-year-ministry elevating your diocese from a low to a high level of biblical literacy.

Building upon Your Success in Future Years

- Invite those who have read smaller portions of the Bible with you (the New Testament, Psalter or a Gospel) to take on a larger challenge the next year.
- Long after you have retired, the most important thing that you will have done for your diocese is to have shared God's Word, implanted it deep within the hearts of its members and inspired them to read the Bible each day for the rest of their lives.
- May God bless you in your ministry and in the vital work of sharing God's Word.

CHAPTER 16

Best Practices: Changing the Spiritual DNA of a Faith Community

"But [Jesus] said, 'Blessed rather are those who hear the Word of God and obey it!'"—Luke 11:28

"All Scripture is inspired by God and is useful for teaching, for reproof, for correction and for training in righteousness, so that everyone who belongs to God may be proficient, equipped for every good work."—II Timothy 3:16–17

"The Bible is the light of my understanding, the joy of my heart, the fullness of my hope, the clarifier of my affections, the mirror of my thoughts, the consoler of my sorrows, the guide of my soul through this gloomy labyrinth of time, the telescope sent from heaven to reveal to the eye of man the amazing glories of the far distant world."—Sir William Jones

• ◆ •

Around 2003, I borrowed a great idea from a colleague of mine who had been choosing a theme each year for his parish such as "Live Joyfully in the Lord" or "Serving Others in Christ" or "Have the Hope of Jesus in Your Heart." He would organize Sunday Forums and sermons, classes, and parish newsletter articles around the theme for the year. So our church and I began selecting an annual theme. It was successful, and we still do it. A theme a year does not necessarily change a congregation, however. When I was visiting England to share The Bible Challenge with bishops and church leaders across the United Kingdom, Bishop Michael Perham of Gloucester was very interested. Then he said, "The problem is that our dioceses over here are over-programmed. It's hard to fit anything new in. This year we are focusing on baptism, and next year we will be looking at the Eucharist. The following year we will be exploring prayer."

We Anglicans are good at emphases. A one year theme can add a lot of coherence to a year of programming and help us select speakers and prepare courses and sermons. Then it's off to something often completely different. Last year's theme is quickly forgotten. This year's theme is all the rage. The problem is the culture of a church cannot change in one year. If a church has had weak stewardship, poor worship attendance, little interest in Bible study, or a lack of focus on children and teenagers for a long time, it usually cannot make serious lasting change in a year. Better to think in terms of five years for real transformation.

Over fifteen years ago, I was attending a conference for rectors of large Episcopal churches on the East Coast. The group met at Trinity Church, Copley Square in Boston. A variety of speakers addressed the group. One of the speakers was the head of human resources for the Central Intelligence Agency. He was a parishioner at Christ Church, Alexandria, and the Rector Pierce Klempt thought that he had a message to share with us.

The man gave a thoughtful presentation about leadership and change. I had been the Rector of my church for a few years and was concerned the changes that I had implemented would not endure if I left. I saw the need to change the culture of the parish to become a more high-commitment environment that produced stronger ministry. When the question and answer time arrived, I raised my hand and asked, "How do you change the culture of a church so that when you leave the changes you have made continue and the church does not revert to the exact kind of church it was before you started?"

Our speaker said something that I shall never forget. "First of all, you never change a system. You merely elevate it. You take it from one level and lift it up somewhat higher."

That was a profound lesson for me. You do not change a system. You merely elevate it. Over the intervening years, I have come to believe he is right. In the Episcopal Church, our biblical literacy is incredibly low. That will not change in a year.

Thousands of people have participated in The Bible Challenge across the United States and around the world. Many participants have said that reading the Bible was the most important spiritual experience of their life. It helped them to see the grand sweep of God's activity in history and made them feel closer to God than ever before.

Many have said, "I loved The Bible Challenge, but I now have more questions than when I started." Our questions inspire us to keep reading and learning more. The Bible is a library of sixty-six books from which we can constantly learn as we strengthen our faith and develop a life-long daily spiritual discipline of reading. John Adams read through the entire Bible each year of his adult life, reading the same Bible over and over again. We can wear out a beloved old Bible and highlight verses that inspire, guide, and strengthen us.

Churches and dioceses can participate in The Bible Challenge and have an incredible experience. Some dioceses have had thousands of people participating in a year. Some churches have had more than half of their active adult membership take part in one year. Other churches have begun using The Teen Bible Challenge and The Parent Child Bible Challenge along with the Read the Bible in a Year reading plan for adults. The result is all generations in the church are being affected.

If the church does not continue to build upon this progress in subsequent years, however, The Bible Challenge will be just another program that the church did a few years back. It will become a distant memory, and the parish will not have changed substantially. The parish's spiritual makeup will not have changed greatly. In order to significantly alter the spiritual DNA, we recommend participating in The Bible Challenge for five years or more. During the first year, the Center for Biblical Studies and I recommend offering one option: challenge every adult member of your parish to read the entire Bible in a year. You may also want to offer the Parent Child Bible Challenge and The Teen Bible Challenge so children and teenagers can participate using age appropriate and interesting Bible materials.

During the second year, we encourage offering the parish the opportunity to read the entire Bible again. In the first year, you will get early initiators to try it. These are often people who will follow the Rector's lead in anything. If the Rector is behind it, they will do it. There are many other people who do not function like this. In fact, they think more in terms of "What's the Rector's new project now?" If they have heard from friends who participated in The Bible Challenge and have read their testimonies in the church newsletter or perhaps heard an individual preach or speak in a forum about their experience, they may be eager to give it a try. In many parishes, however, the likely response will be, "Oh, we did that last year. This year, we are focusing on something else. Sorry!"

In the second year, a lot of people who were not early adopters will try it. You may also get a lot of people willing to read completely through the Bible for a second time. In year two, we recommend also offering smaller opportunities such as reading through just the New Testament, Psalms, and Proverbs. We have a separate reading plan that calls for reading only one chapter of the Bible a day and one psalm. It is significantly more modest than reading three chapters of the Old Testament, one psalm and a chapter of the New Testament daily.

You may also suggest another option for people who are not big readers or who struggle in reading the Bible. This is the Fifty-Day Bible Challenge. Each year, the Center for Biblical Studies will be producing one or more Fifty-Day Bible Challenges, covering the gospel for the appointed Church Year, other books of the Bible, and topical themes as well.

Suggestions for Further Bible Reading

For those who wish to try new things to build upon their Bible learning, we offer these options:

1. **Consider reading the Bible in a different translation**—Some people read the Bible in a different translation each year. Each translation renders words and verses slightly differently, allowing the Bible to speak in fresh, new ways to us. You may wish to continue reading three chapters of the Old Testament,

a psalm, and a chapter of the New Testament each day or slow down and read only a chapter of the Old Testament, a psalm, and a chapter of the New Testament a day. The key is to read a little every day.

The following translations of the Bible have been authorized for use by the Episcopal Church (we particularly recommend the versions in bold):

> King James or Authorized Version (the historic Bible of The Episcopal Church, but challenging to read)
>
> English Revision (1881)
>
> American Revision (1901)
>
> Revised Standard Version (1952)
>
> Jerusalem Bible (1966)
>
> New English Bible with Apocrypha (1970)
>
> Good News Bible/Today's English Version (1976) (This is a paraphrase of the Bible.)
>
> New American Bible (1970)
>
> Revised Standard Version, an Ecumenical Version (1973)
>
> **New International Version** (1978)
>
> **New Jerusalem Bible** (1987)
>
> New Revised English Bible (1989)
>
> **New Revised Standard Version** (1990)
>
> **Common English Version** (2011)

2. **Read the Bible and read** *The Bible Challenge* **with it**—Our book *The Bible Challenge* coordinates with our Read the Bible in a Year reading plan and includes meditations, questions, and prayers to accompany each day's lessons, written by one hundred and three archbishops, bishops, cathedral and seminary deans, theologians, biblical scholars, and priests from around the world. The Bible Challenge book is printed by Forward Movement and is available at: *http://www.forwardmovement.org/Products/2114/the-bible-challenge-read-the-bible-in-a-year.aspx* or at Amazon or Barnes and Noble.

3. **Share your joy of reading the Bible with someone else**—If you have enjoyed and benefited from reading the Bible on a regular basis, share your experience with a friend or family member. Consider purchasing a Bible as a gift for them. Tell them about The Bible Challenge, or get their permission to sign them up. Consider re-reading the Bible with them and meeting regularly to share your thoughts and experiences. It will deepen your relationship with one another and with God and you will learn from one another.

4. Consider reading a Bible with a particular focus—Publishers are producing many exciting versions of the Bible that highlight passages of crucial interest to the reader. These include:

> *The People's Bible*—This New International Version of the Bible offers a visual guide to the Bible's most searched for verses by printing famous verses in larger, bold type. Visit *www.zondervan.com*

> *The Jewish Annotated New Testament*—This New Revised Standard Version of the New Testament has study notes by an international team of scholars written from a Jewish perspective. Visit *www.oup.com* or *www. amazon.com*

> *The Inclusive Bible*—This inclusive-language Bible offers a fresh, dynamic modern English translation, carefully crafted to let the power and poetry of the language shine forth. Visit *www.amazon.com*

> *The Financial Stewardship Bible*—This Common English Version of the Bible highlights over 2,000 verses about trust, provision, money, and dealing with possessions. Visit *www.americanbible.org*

> *The Poverty and Justice Bible*—This Bible highlights passages that speak about outreach, social justice, poverty, and caring for the poor and needy. Visit *www.povertyandjusticebible.org*

> *The Green Bible*—This New Revised Standard Version of the Bible helps us to see God's vision for creation and engage in the work of healing and sustaining the environment. Visit *www.harpercollins.com*

> *The Freedom Bible*—This Common English Version of the Bible includes over 3,500 highlighted verses that reveal the Bible's astonishing message of freedom. Visit *www.americanbible.org*

> *The Life Recovery Bible*—This New Living Translation of the Bible helps individuals struggling with addiction to the ultimate source of healing—God himself. Visit *www.liferecoverybible.com*

> *The C.S. Lewis Bible*—This New Revised Standard Version of the Bible intersperses quotations from C.S. Lewis, one of Christianity's most respected contemporary writers. Visit *www.harpercollins.com*

> *The Archeological Study Bible*—This New International Version of the Bible highlights the archeological, historical, and cultural background of the Bible as well as archeological excavations and discoveries that shed light on biblical stories. Visit *www.zondervan.com*

5. **Read the Bible using the ancient monastic practice of *lectio divina*—**For centuries, Christian monks have read the Bible in a slow, meditative fashion

savoring God's Word and letting it speak deeply to them. *Lectio divina* includes four movements: *lectio, meditatio, oratio,* and *contemplatio*—reading, meditating, praying, and contemplating the text. Select a book of the Bible to read. We recommend starting with a Gospel. Read no more than a chapter at a time, perhaps as little as a paragraph or two each time you read.

In step one, *lectio*, read the passage slowly. When something strikes you, pause and meditate upon the word, phrase or verse that has captured your attention. This is *meditatio*. Mull over the text like a cow chewing its cud. Then offer a brief prayer to God based on the text and how it has spoken to you. This is *oratio*. Finally, be quiet and listen for God to speak silently in your heart as you wait in solitude. This is *contemplatio*. This fourth step is perhaps the most important and difficult step to practice.

Visit our website at: *www.thecenterforbiblicalstudies.org* and check under *Resources*, then *Articles* to find a more detailed description of *lectio divina* or visit: *www.lectio-divina.org*. The goal of *lectio divina* is spiritual transformation rather than academic study. It opens God's Word to us in ways that are constantly refreshing and engaging.

6. **Scripture memorization**—Rick Warren, author of *The Purpose Driven Life*, says that Scripture memorization has been the most important spiritual tool in his life and ministry. When we memorize something, it becomes part of us. We can recall it, recite it, and use it to form our thoughts, guide our decisions, and articulate our beliefs. There is even an app called *BibleMinded* that helps you to memorize verses on your own or following one of several plans.

   We suggest reading a chapter of the Bible a day and highlighting one verse to memorize. Write it down on an index card. Spend a few minutes trying to memorize it. Take the index card with you and practice reciting the verse throughout the day. By the end of the day, you should have it memorized. Keep the index cards and review them once a week.

7. **Listen to the Bible**—There are many resources today that allow you to listen to the Bible as you commute to work, walk your dog, exercise, travel, or sit at home. This is wonderful for audio learners and those who can no longer read. You can listen to the Bible in many translations. Visit: *www. Audio.com/Bible, www.listenersbible.com, www.BibleGateway.com, www.daily audiobible.com, www.YouVersion.com,* and *www.faithcomesthroughhearing.com. Faith Comes through Hearing* provides excellent resources, including an MP3 player that allows you to hear the entire New Testament read aloud in forty days for twenty-eight mintues a day. The King James Version and the New International Version of the Bible can also be found on CD.

8. **Read and study the Synoptic Gospels**—The gospels of Matthew, Mark, and Luke follow a similar timeline. Students can read these three gospels laid out

on the same page in columns and compare how each of the evangelists told the same parable, story or teaching. This can be done alone or in a group.

We recommend using 1) *Gospel Parallels* edited by Joel B. Green and W. Gil Shin using the Common English Bible; 2) *Gospel Parallels* by Thomas Nelson Publishers, which uses the Revised Standard Version of the Bible; or 3) the *Records of the Life of Jesus* using the Revised Standard Version of the Bible compiled by Henry Burton Sharman, which can be purchased through Pendle Hill. Visit: *www.pendlehill.org.* We also recommend *Approaching the Gospels Together* by Mary C. Morrison, which is a book that offers a fresh approach to reading the gospels in small groups.

9. **Read the Apocrypha**—The Apocrypha is a group of ancient books found in some major translations of the Bible such as the New Revised Standard Version used by Protestants and Catholics. The Apocrypha are often found in a separate section between the Old and New Testaments or in an appendix after the New Testament. All of these books, with the exception of 2 Esdras, were contained in the Greek translation of the Old Testament known as the *Septuagint*, but were not part of the original Hebrew Old Testament. Some churches view them as Scripture. Others do not.

    The word "apocrypha" comes from a Greek word for "things that are hidden," for these writings were considered to contain mysterious and esoteric lore. Roman Catholic, Eastern Orthodox, Greek, and Russian churches consider these books authoritative, derive doctrine from them, and call them deuterocanonical. Protestants refer to them as apocryphal and do not derive doctrine from them. Anglicans read them for inspiration, but not for doctrinal use. We believe that these books are engaging, inspiring and worth reading.

10. **Consider reading *The Message* or *The Story***—*The Message* is a paraphrase of the Bible by Eugene Peterson that makes the biblical stories and verses come alive in fresh, new ways. Visit *www.messagebible.com*. *The Story*, published by Zondervan, is a seamless collection of Bible stories that reads like a novel. Transitional paragraphs connect the stories. Long dietary codes, genealogies, and repetitive stories of ancient kings have been eliminated. Visit *www. thestory.com*. *The Message* and *The Story* are helpful and engaging for people who have struggled to read the Bible.

11. **Read the Bible in a different language**—Brush off your Spanish, Latin, or French and read the Bible in a foreign language. It refreshes your language skills, but more importantly old familiar Bible stories come alive in new ways. We recommend *La Nouvelle Bible de Jerusalem* for French readers, the *Santa Biblia Dios Habla Hoy* by the American Bible Society for Spanish readers, and *La Vulgata* for Latin readers.

12. **Read a book of the Bible with a commentary**—Start by reading one of the gospels. Then move on to the book of Acts, some of the letters of Paul, and Old Testament books such as Genesis, Exodus, I and II Samuel, Isaiah, Jeremiah, and the Psalms. Read alone or in a group. Luke Timothy Johnson's *The Writings of the New Testament* is an excellent introduction with a chapter about each book in the New Testament.

    We recommend four commentary series: 1) *The People's Bible Commentary Series* is published in England by the Bible Reading Fellowship and features outstanding authors and scholars such as Professor Richard Burridge. Visit *www.brfonline.org.uk*; 2) *The New Daily Bible Study Series* published by Westminster John Knox Press and written by William Barclay is wonderful and easy to read and filled with down to earth illustrations. Visit *www.wjkbooks.com*; 3) *The For Everyone Bible Study Guides* published by the Society for Promoting Christian Knowledge in England and written by Tom Wright. Visit *www.amazon.com*; and 4) *The Old Testament New Daily Bible Study* published by Westminster John Knox Press and written by John L. Gibson. Visit *www.wjkbooks.com*.

13. **Read excellent secondary sources to assist you as you read the Bible**—Review The Bible in the Life of the Church study, *Deep Engagement Fresh Discovery*, available through the Anglican Communion website at: *www.anglicancommunion.org*. We also recommend the Morehouse Publishing series, *Conversations with Scripture*, prepared in cooperation with the Anglican Association of Biblical Scholars. Contributors include Marcus Borg, Cynthia Kittredge, and Stephen Cook. For those wanting to go a little deeper, we recommend Bruce Metzger's *Oxford Companion to the Bible*, a superb and very readable one-volume resource. Also visit our website at *www.thecenterforbiblicalstudies.org* and look under "Resources" to find a list of books about the Bible that we recommend.

14. **Learn how to read the Bible in its original languages**—Consider studying Biblical Hebrew with a local rabbi or learning Koine Greek so that you can comprehend new things by reading the Bible in its original language. There are also websites that can help make this possible. One illuminating resource is *interlinearbible.org*, which provides a transliterated version of the New Testament (in Greek) and Old Testament (in Hebrew), and links to the definition of each and every Greek and Hebrew word. *YouVersion.com* offers the Bible in scores of additional languages, in addition to numerous English versions. Translations in German, Korean, Swahili, and Swedish can be read in parallel with selected English translations.

15. **Go on a pilgrimage to the Holy Land**—The Holy Land is often referred to as "the Fifth Gospel." Nothing can compare to walking in the footsteps of

Jesus and the great figures of the Bible. Numerous groups provide wonderful pilgrimages to the Holy Land. We recommend Worldwide Pilgrimage. Visit *www.worldwidepilgrimage.com.*

Suggestions for Participating in a Biblically Centered Small Group

1. **Join or start a Bible study**—The Bible comes alive when we engage it with others. As we study the Scriptures together, we learn from others. Religion is not so much about having all the answers but asking the right questions. Ask your clergy and lay leaders about which Bible study might be best for you.

   You can start a Bible study in your home, school or church. Invite friends, family, and members of your church, book club, neighbors, and work colleagues to join you. Select a book of the Bible and study it carefully. We recommend starting with a Gospel or reading the gospel of Luke and then the book of Acts. Then consider reading Paul's Letter to the Romans or First and Second Corinthians. If you read the Old Testament, we recommend starting with Genesis and Exodus. These captivating books help to reveal the sweep of salvation, God's Covenant, and God's plan for humanity.

2. **Education for Ministry (EfM)**—This program, created by the University of the South at Sewanee, Tennessee, begins with an intensive one-year focus on the Old Testament followed by a second year-long study of the New Testament. In the third year participants focus on Church history. The fourth year is devoted to theology. EfM is an ideal next step for persons who have participated in The Bible Challenge and have many unanswered questions. Participants commit to this program one year at a time.

   EfM involves significant Bible reading, homework and group discussion. Each EfM group is led by a specially trained mentor. EfM is perhaps the top educational program offered by the Episcopal Church. It is well-organized and helps participants comprehend the great Bible themes, apply biblical learning to their daily lives, and reflect on their own spiritual journey. For many, EfM is a life changing experience. To learn more, contact your clergy or visit *www. sewanee.edu/EFM/* or *www.edowefm.org.*

3. **Participate in the Disciples of Christ in Community (DOCC)**—The DOCC Program seeks to strengthen individual churches by helping members better receive and give the love of Christ. Begun nearly forty years ago at Trinity Episcopal Church in New Orleans, DOCC has graduated over thirty-five thousand participants. Each week over a three or four month period, clergy or trained laypersons offer forty-minute lectures on the heart of the faith, grounding their talks in Scripture. Trained small-group leaders

help participants learn from one another as they apply the great themes of the Christian faith to their lives. Each small group strives to become "a beloved community." That sense of belovedness spreads to the entire church. Eighteen hours of training for presenters and small group leaders is required. To learn more, contact your parish clergy or the Rev. Canon William Barnwell at *wbarnwell@trinitynola.com* or visit *www.natonalcathedral.org/learn/docc.shtml* or *www.trinitynola.com/DOCC.*

4. **Participate in the Transforming Literature of the Bible (TLB)**—The thirty-six-week course strives to relate the great themes of Scripture to our own lives and stories. Once students have read the Bible in a year through *The Bible Challenge,* they may want to consider TLB. Course participants "plow deep" into transformative Bible passages and stories from Genesis, Mark, and Romans. In seminar style, participants reflect on the passages and make use of well-tested commentaries. Using suggested questions, they connect the passages to their own lives. Eight to ten hours of on-site training is required for both seminar leaders and participants. Experienced clergy and laypersons lead the training. To learn more, contact your clergy or the Rev. Canon William Barnwell at *wbarnwell@trinitynola.com.*

5. **Participate in a Kerygma Bible Study**—The Kerygma Program's resources provide stimulating resources to challenge minds and refresh spirits. Kerygma leaders are trained and receive a leader's guide that is designed to create opportunities to stimulate discussion and illuminate the Biblical material through small group encounters. For more information, visit *www.kerygma.com.*

If The Bible Challenge has been a good spiritual experience for you and has touched your heart and nourished your soul, we invite you to contribute to the Center for Biblical Studies to help us promote The Bible Challenge globally so that others may benefit from the daily reading of God's Word. Your gift can be made out to "The Center for Biblical Studies" and sent to St. Thomas' Episcopal Church, P.O. Box 247, Fort Washington, Pennsylvania, 19034.

CHAPTER 17

Lectio Divina: A Wonderful Way to Continue Reading the Bible

"As a deer longs for flowing streams, so my soul longs for you, O God. My soul thirsts for God, for the living God. When shall I come and behold the face of God?"—PSALM 42:1–2

"He said to me, O mortal, eat what is offered to you; eat this scroll, and go, speak to the house of Israel. So I opened my mouth, and he gave me the scroll to eat. He said to me, Mortal, eat this scroll that I give you and fill your stomach with it. Then I ate it; and in my mouth it was as sweet as honey."—EZEKIEL 3:1–3

"So I went to the angel and told him to give me the little scroll; and he said to me, 'Take it, eat it; it will be bitter to your stomach, but sweet as honey in your mouth.' So I took the little scroll from the hand of the angel and ate it; it was sweet as honey in my mouth, but when I had eaten it, my stomach was made bitter."—REVELATION 10:9–10

"Often, through the grace of the almighty Lord, certain passages in the sacred text are better understood when the divine Word is read privately. The soul, conscious of its faults and recognizing the truth of what it has heard, is struck by the dart of grief and pierced by the sword of compunction, so that it wishes to do nothing but weep and wash away its stains with floods of tears."—ST. AUGUSTINE OF HIPPO

• ◆ •

Throughout the post-Enlightenment twentieth century our approach to reading the Bible has been deeply analytical and most recently influenced by a way of interpreting the Bible known as the historical critical method. This systematic analysis of Scripture has yielded substantial results from a scholarly perspective and helped us to learn more about the Bible.

When taken on the whole, however, this method was a dry, scholarly, and rational way of reading the Bible. It spoke to the head, but rarely to the heart. The Bible was often approached as a historical document or merely as a piece of ancient literature. The Scriptures were not viewed as a means to test our hearts, motivate our wills, and form us more fully into the image of God. Rather, scholars and clergy approached the Bible like a body on an operating table. We were the trained professional surgeons. The text was given anesthesia. Then we cut into the body and carefully probed each tissue and fiber. Such a reading of the Bible was hardly devotional and left many people starved for spiritual nourishment.

167

While Bible studies and reading Bible commentaries or books about the Bible are helpful, nothing at all can compare with a bare reading of the Bible, letting God's Word speak profoundly to our hearts. This need not be an anti-intellectual reading. Rather it calls for a return to the ancient practice that monks and others have used for centuries that allows the Bible to speak in the most profound ways and to bestow on us its wisdom and teaching so that our lives can be transformed.

This method is called *lectio divina*, which is pronounced "lex-ee-oh di-vee-nuh." It is a Latin phrase that means "holy," "sacred," or "divine reading." Church Fathers and Mothers practiced this method of reading the Bible since the first century, and it can be argued that this approach yields the best fruit. It is something that we can easily teach in our churches to equip our members to practice on their own or in a group. "Vital hearing requires loving, calm, reflective, personal poring over the text," notes Mariano Magrassi in his book *Praying the Bible: an Introduction to Lectio divina*.

Kathleen Norris writes in her book *Bible Reading for Spiritual Growth*, "We feel the need for genuine spiritual refreshment as we wander through an environment all too often parched and dry. We long for an affirming relationship with God that will make a difference in how we experience daily life. We eagerly set out on the inviting journey of spiritual growth, seeking deeper relationship with God's very self." *Lectio divina* helps us to accomplish this.

Lectio Divina Suspends the Analytical Drive to Examine the Bible

Lectio is an ancient Christian practice that has been tested across the centuries. It allows Christians to encounter God directly through the Bible. It is a way of reading the Bible devotionally, rather than academically. It is specifically suited for those who, as the psalmist says, are athirst "for the living God." (Psalm 42:2) This way of reading the Bible sets aside the rational mind, which has been overly empowered since the Enlightenment. *Lectio* is not an analytical process, but rather a process of waiting for God to speak to us through Scripture.

I think of those old engravings by Albrecht Dürer and later by Rembrandt that show a man or woman sitting with the Bible open on his or her lap, hands folded, lost in thought as they reflect deeply upon something in the Scriptures. He or she is not so much studying the Bible as having a direct encounter with God: a dialogue with God through the Bible. After reading for a while, he or she has come upon something powerful in the text that caused him or her to pause and reflect and engage in prayer and have a heart-to-heart conversation and experience with God. This indeed is what *lectio* does, and it is constantly renewing to the soul. St. Jerome said, "The soul is fed each day with *lectio divina*."

Unlike the historical critical method of reading the Bible, *lectio* is not a cold, abstract, and speculative encounter with the biblical text, but a slow, persevering, and joyful engagement with the Truth itself. It is study and learning pursued with prayer and love. Louis Bouyer says *lectio*

> *is a personal reading of the Word of God during which we try to assimilate its substance; a reading in faith, in a spirit of prayer, believing in the real presence of God who speaks to us in the sacred text, while the monk himself strives to be present in a spirit of obedience and total surrender to the divine promises and demands.*

The Bible is not the only book to which this style of reading can be applied. I remember being taken on a tour of St. Joseph's Abbey, a Trappist monastery, in Spencer, Massachusetts many years ago. I knew every monk in the Benedictine tradition was required to devote at least an hour each day to sacred reading. I have always loved books, so I asked my guide what he was reading. He replied he was reading a volume by St. Bernard of Clairvaux.

"What book will you read after that?" I asked.

"Oh no," he said. "I am reading this book using *lectio divina*. I read about two pages a day. It will take me two years or more to finish it."

I was stunned. We are trained to read quickly. It takes training to unlearn the speed with which we have been accustomed to reading. When it comes to reading the Bible, speed is a vice not a virtue. For those who practice it, slow reading with *lectio* offers many benefits.

We live in an age where many people read for pleasure. When I ask someone I know what they are reading, they often reply, "Just some trash." In the ancient days, books were rare and expensive. You had to kill a flock of sheep to produce enough vellum to write a book and an individual or a team of scribes spent perhaps a thousand hours or more copying the text. Most individuals were illiterate. The vast majority of people never owned a book because it took years to copy and produce one volume. Only the wealthiest individuals or institutions like cathedrals and monasteries could afford to own them. Most people listened to them being read. *Lectio*, therefore, was a natural way to listen to Scripture and ponder its message. Monks learned to memorize and recite large portions of the Bible aloud. *Lectio* developed in this setting where monks ruminated for as much as an hour each day over a passage or page of the Bible. Large portions of Scripture were committed to memory.

Before beginning seminary, I visited a monastery in Leuven, Belgium several times while living in Paris. I stayed with the monks and worked outdoors with them. We raked leaves and cleaned the monastery grounds. We ate meals together, and I attended all of their worship services. Whenever they stood to recite the psalms, they never lifted the Psalter. Each of them had committed all one hundred and fifty psalms to memory. It was impressive to witness. In the course of a week, they recited the entire Psalter aloud, and over time they simply chanted it from memory. I can only imagine what it must be like to internalize all the psalms, to know them by heart, and to recite all of them each week. In time, they become part of who we are.

Saint Samargdus, a ninth century monk who lived near Verdun, France, wrote,

> For those who practice it, the experience of *lectio sacra* sharpens perception, enriches understanding, rouses from sloth, banishes idleness, orders life, corrects bad habits, produces salutary weeping and draws tears from contrite hearts . . . curbs idle speech and vanity, awakens longing for Christ and the heavenly homeland.

All of this rings true to my experience with *lectio*.

Lectio Divina Is a Way of Resting in God

Lectio is therefore an encounter with the living God. It is a form of prayer, not study. In *lectio* we become receivers of God's Word, not analysts treating the Bible as dead matter awaiting our careful dissection. To engage in *lectio* we must come to rest and set aside the burdens of our busy lives to listen and receive the gifts of wisdom and love that God longs to share with us. The gifts that we receive from *lectio* will vary on any given day. On one day we might receive the gift of seeing our need for increased kindness and gentleness with a member of our family or a colleague at work. On another day we might receive the gift of humility and realize that we have been acting haughtily and aloof to others.

Sometimes the gift that we receive is not for us. My spiritual mentor Fr. Basil Pennington used to say, "We receive a spiritual bouquet, which is intended by God to be shared with others. We are given a Word from our Lord to carry with us and give away to another person whom we shall encounter this day." *Lectio* calls for deep personal intimacy with God. It is getting to know and experience God up close rather than standing at a safe distance like a spectator watching a sporting event from the sideline. If we spend our entire life standing on the sideline then we never fully comprehend what it feels like to be on the field playing a sport. *Lectio* calls for us to participate more directly with a biblical text and fully engage God's Word.

The Bible tells us, "So God created humankind in his image, in the image of God he created them." (Genesis 1:27) *Lectio* was designed to help us encounter God in such a way that we might be transformed more fully into the image of God. By practicing *lectio* we become "ambassadors for Christ" as St. Paul says. We are equipped to be reconcilers for Christ wherever we go, trained and transformed into servant leaders. The mind of Christ is given to us. We are ready to be "doers of the Word, and not merely hearers who deceive themselves." (James 1:22)

Lectio Divina Can Be Done in Groups

Lectio can be done in private or it can be done in groups. If it is done in a group, the leader will read a passage of the Bible aloud and the other participants listen rather than read along. The leader should read no more than ten verses at a time. He or she should pause after reading the lesson, and give participants two or three minutes to contemplate what they have heard. Afterwards, the leader may facilitate a discussion by allowing each participant to speak for a minute or two about what he or she heard read aloud.

After everyone has had an opportunity to speak, the leader may read the entire lesson again or ask someone in the group to do it, especially if a person of a different gender can be selected. This time, the leader might encourage everyone participating to consider a word, phrase or verse that particularly stands out. Then the leader pauses again for two or three minutes to allow the Word of God to sink in and deeply penetrate into the souls of the listeners.

No one should feel compelled to speak. In fact, anyone who wishes to remain silent may simply indicate her or his desire to pass and let others speak in their place. It is important that neither the leader nor anyone in the group attempt to explain the text or interpret what another person has said. The goal is not analysis, but transformation and prayer. A participant may be encouraged to say, "I sense . . ." or "I hear . . ." or "I see. . . ." It is a personal statement made by someone who has listened to the Word of God being read aloud to her or him like a love letter written specifically by God to this individual.

The leader or another member of the group reads the passage for a third time. Before reading, the leader might ask each participant to think about what God is calling them to do in their lives as a result of the passage, or how the passage has personally touched their lives. This allows the participant to enter directly into the reading, rather than to stand on the sidelines, or sit like a moviegoer in a theater. When *lectio* is done well, the people doing it move from feeling like passive spectators to active participants in the Christian life.

Practicing *Lectio* on Your Own

I primarily practice *lectio* on my own, as do most people. This was the way the monks practiced it and continue to do so. *Lectio* is composed of four steps. Each step is described by a Latin word. The first step is *lectio*, which calls for merely reading the text, either silently or aloud to ourselves. In the ancient world, the text was always read aloud. In his autobiography *The Confessions*, St. Augustine of Hippo notes how shocked he was when he came upon St. Ambrose, the Bishop of Milan, silently reading to himself. Such a practice was rare in the ancient world. To pronounce the Word of God is to form the Word with our entire body, and there are some benefits to doing so. Each person must determine for him- or herself whether to read from the Bible silently or aloud. You can practice and see which way feels best for you and yields the finest results of reading and contemplation.

The second step is *meditatio*, which calls for meditating on the text. This is an entirely different approach from Bible study or rigorous analysis. Here we are not putting the Word of God under the microscope of our rational brain, but rather ruminating over the text like a cow chewing her cud. We may take a word, a phrase or an entire verse, especially if it is short, and mull it over again and again in our brains and in our hearts. Recently while on an airplane, I read chapter eleven of Paul's Letter to the Romans. It is not one of his most famous nor most inspiring chapters. But I found myself ruminating over verse eight where Paul quotes Scripture, saying, "God gave them a sluggish spirit." Perhaps because I was tired, it was late, my flight had been rerouted, and I had been placed on another airline this verse stood out for me. I kept silently reiterating it within myself, mulling it over, ruminating on it, wondering in what ways was I being sluggish in my spiritual life and in my life in general. No one around me knew what I was doing. I was prayerfully pondering the text in silence.

After college I traveled to France and worked for ten days in the grape harvest outside the city of Saumur in the Loire Valley. It was an incredible experience. My fellow workers and I would carry in large plastic containers with up to fifty pounds of grapes at a time. We emptied them into even larger containers sitting on a flat-bed wagon pulled by a farm tractor. They were then brought to the chateau where they were poured into large stone cellars. These grapes were later transported and poured into a large cylinder with contracting wooden ribs that squeezed them until their juice flowed out of the cylinder and ran down a stone rivulet into a large stainless steel container to ferment. I remember watching as they unloaded what was left inside the cylinder after the grapes had been crushed. It resembled horse manure: a brown, fibrous substance that was given to the French government as a 1 percent tax and used to make a strong liqueur.

Ruminating over the Bible metaphorically crushes the Word of God within us, internalizing it, squeezing out its nutrients, allowing it to be broken open in order that it might feed our hearts, minds, and souls. The spiritual nutrients are released as we chew over the same simple text again and again, instead of moving from chapter to chapter like a speed walker trying to get from one end of the Appalachian Trail to the other while racing past breathtaking scenery without seeing it.

The third stage of *lectio* is called *oratio*, from the Latin word for prayer. We get the word "oration" from it. Here we pause after our meditating on the Word and offer a prayer up to God based on what we have read, how we have been moved, or how we have been touched by God's Word. Perhaps we have read a text that makes us realize how busy and overburdened we have been, and so we offer a prayer asking

God to help us slow down and walk through life in a more relaxed manner. Perhaps while we ruminated over the text we recall being boastful and speaking in a selfish manner to someone, and we offer a prayer requesting God's forgiveness and asking God to help us increase our humility.

The final step is often the most difficult. It calls for being silent and listening to God, so God can get a word in edgewise. This fourth step is called *contemplatio,* and it is from this word that we get the English word "contemplation." Here we attentively listen. We sit quietly, as we should have throughout the entire exercise of *lectio,* perhaps on the floor with our legs crossed as if in meditation or at our desk or in a favorite chair at home, and we listen.

We listen for God to speak a Word to us based on the prayer we offered. This is the most difficult step because so many of us are trained to work hard, run hard, keep busy, and always strive to accomplish a task. Sitting still and doing nothing goes against the grain of how we live our lives. It is counterintuitive to believe that by being silent and still and waiting upon God, much will happen in our lives, yet this is just what *lectio* affirms. When we center down and enter a receptive mode in silence and solitude God can finally deliver a message that God has been waiting to share with us.

In his eighth-century work known as the *Ecclesiastical History of the English People,* the earliest history of the Church in England, the Venerable Bede, the great Benedictine author, monk, and historian, recalls how the illiterate poet Caedmon would memorize Scripture. He would be found by others "ruminating over it, like some clean animal chewing the cud." Caedmon would then transform the text into a melodious verse or hymn.

Archbishop Thomas Cranmer later picked up on this when he wrote his famous sermon about reading the Bible in which he said, "Let us ruminate, and, as it were, chew the cud, that we may have the sweet juice, spiritual effect, marrow, honey, kernel, taste, comfort and consolation" of the Holy Scripture. Cranmer's sermon was one of many model sermons that were distributed throughout the Church of England to every priest in order that they might be read aloud in every parish, instructing worshippers in the basic and vital components of the Christian faith.

This same spirit of "ruminating" over the text was captured in the famous collect or prayer that Archbishop Cranmer composed for The Book of Common Prayer, which reads:

> Blessed Lord, who hast caused all holy Scriptures to be written for our learning:
> Grant that we may in such wise hear them, read, mark, learn and inwardly digest
> them; that, by patience and comfort of thy holy Word, we may embrace and ever
> hold fast the blessed hope of everlasting life, which thou has given us in our Savior
> Jesus Christ; who liveth and reigneth with thee and the Holy Ghost, one God, for
> ever and ever, Amen.

When we practice *lectio* and learn the art of reading the Bible prayerfully, we marinate ourselves in the Scriptures. But we not only marinate ourselves, which suggests that the juices of God's divine Word bathe the exterior of our being, but the truth and wisdom of God's love penetrate deep within us. As we appropriate God's Word slowly, God's wisdom and love become part of us. We internalize God's truth. It convicts us, heals, forgives, replenishes, anoints, equips, strengthens, and comforts us. Our eyes are opened and our ears can hear. We are quieter and more centered. In doing and saying some things and refraining from doing and saying other things, we behave in ways that would have been impossible had we not spent time with God, whom we encounter most directly in the Scriptures.

Luke's Gospel alone tells the story of two of Jesus' disciples walking on the road to Emmaus after Jesus had been arrested, tried, and crucified. The two were utterly dejected. They hung their heads and walked as grieving people do, stunned and gutted of hope, downcast, and frightened. As they trudged along, a stranger came up beside them and asked them what they had been discussing as they walked along. One of them, Cleopas, asked, "Are you the only stranger in Jerusalem who does not know the things that have taken place there these days?" (Luke 24:18) They told him about how Jesus had spoken and acted mightily like a prophet and then was handed over to death and crucified. Then some of the women had gone to the tomb early that morning and found his body missing.

Jesus, who had come in the guise of a stranger, then opened the Scriptures to them and interpreted everything that the Bible had to say about the Messiah. After they invited him to dine with them and spend the night, Christ revealed himself in the breaking of the bread. Suddenly, their eyes were opened and they recognized that this stranger was actually Christ himself. Then he disappeared from their sight. Turning to each other, they said, "Were not our hearts burning within us while he was talking to us on the road, while he was opening the scriptures to us?" (Luke 24:32)

This is what occurs when we truly engage God's Word, not as students reading from an ancient book or historians examining records and reports from centuries ago. In *lectio* we have a real encounter with the living God mediated by the Word of God. You can actually sense God's presence and God's voice speaking as you read the Bible and ponder its significance for your life today. This is how God intended us to engage his Word.

CHAPTER 18

Resources for Going Deeper
in The Bible Challenge

Our goal at the Center for Biblical Studies is to help individuals develop a life-long spiritual discipline of daily Scripture reading that will transform their lives, impact the decisions that they make and help them feel deeply connected to God on a daily basis.

The best way to accomplish this is to read a portion of the Bible each day. We encourage those who finish The Bible Challenge to begin again and to re-read the Bible each year. Such reading, however, will generate questions in a thoughtful reader.

Therefore, we have created a considerable list of secondary sources to help you deepen your knowledge about various aspects of the Bible. As you continue to read God's Word each day, these books will help to enhance your understanding of Scripture.

Meditations, Questions, and Prayers to Accompany the Bible Challenge

The Bible Challenge: Read the Bible in a Year, edited by Marek P. Zabriskie, published by Forward Movement, Cincinnati, Ohio, 2012.

Basic Introduction to the Bible

An Introduction to the Bible by Robert Kugler and Patrick Hartin, published by William R. Eerdmans Publishing Company, Grand Rapids, Michigan, 2009.

Testing Scripture: A Scientist Explores the Bible by John Polkinghorne, Brazos Press, Grand Rapids, Michigan, 2010. Published in the United Kingdom by the Society for Promoting Christian Knowledge under the title of *Encountering Scripture*.

The Good Book: Reading the Bible with Mind and Heart by Peter J. Gomes, published by William Morrow and Company, Inc., New York, 1996.

Opening the Bible: The New Churches Teaching Series, Volume 2 by Roger Ferlo, published by Cowley Publications, Cambridge, Massachusetts, 1997.

What is the Bible? by John Barton, published by the Society for Promoting Christian Knowledge, London, 2009.

Don't Know Much about the Bible: Everything You Need to Know about the Good Book but Never Learned by Kenneth C. Davis, published by Eagle Brook Publishers, New York, 1998.

The Bible for Everyday Life by the Archbishop of Canterbury George Carey, William B. Eerdmans Publishing Company, Grand Rapids, Michigan, 1988.

A Walk through the Bible by Lesslie Newbigin, the Society for Promoting Christian Knowledge, London, 2011.

The Bible: A User's Guide by Nick Page, published by HarperCollins Publishers, London, 2002.

The Church's Teaching Series: The Bible for Today's Church by Robert A. Bennett and O.C. Edwards, published by The Seabury Press, New York, 1979.

The Bible Makes Sense by Walter Brueggemann, published by St. Anthony Messenger Press, Cincinnati, Ohio, 1989.

History of the Bible

Whose Bible is It?: A Short History of the Scriptures by Jaroslav Pelikan, published by Penguin Books, London, 2005.

How the Bible Came to Be: Exploring the Narrative and the Message by John W. Miller, Paulist Press, New York, 2004.

The Bible through the Ages published by the Readers Digest Association, Pleasantsville, New York, 1996.

Guides on Reading Holy Scripture

Scripture and the Authority of God: How to Read the Bible Today by N.T. Wright, published by Harper and Row, New York, 2005.

Transforming Scripture by Frank Wade, published by Church Publishing, New York, 2008.

Engaging the Word: The New Church's Teaching Series: Volume 3 by Michael Johnston, published by Cowley Publications, Cambridge, Massachusetts, 1998.

The Bible Makes Sense by Walter Brueggemann, published by Westminster John Knox Press, Louisville, Kentucky 2001.

A Beginner's Guide to Reading the Bible by Craig R. Koester, Augsburg Press, Minneapolis, 1991.

Read the Bible Again for the First Time: Taking the Bible Seriously but Not Literally by Marcus J. Borg, HarperCollins, New York, 2001.

Sensing God: Reading Scripture with All Our Senses by Roger Ferlo, published by Cowley Publications, Cambridge, Massachusetts, 2002.

Relating Biblical Teachings to Contemporary Issues

Ancient Laws and Contemporary Controversies: The Need for Inclusive Biblical Interpretation by Cheryl B. Anderson, Oxford University Press, Oxford, 2009.

Making Wise the Simple: The Torah in Christian Faith and Practice by Johanna W. H. Van Wijk-Bos, published by William B. Eerdmans Publishers, Grand Rapids, Michigan, 2005.

The Peoples' Companion to the Bible by Curtis Paul DeYoung, Fortress Press, Minneapolis, 2010.

Global Bible Commentary by Daniel Patte, published by Abingdon Press, Nashville, 2004.

Introductions to the Old Testament

An Introduction to the Old Testament: The Canon and Christian Imagination by Walter Brueggemann, Westminster John Knox Press, Louisville and London, 2003.

A Pathway of Interpretation: Old Testament for Pastors and Students by Walter Brueggemann, Cascade Books, Eugene, Oregon, 2008.

The Meaning of the Bible: What the Jewish Scriptures and Christian Old Testament Can Teach Us by Douglass A. Knight and Amy-Jill Levine, published by HaperOne, New York, 1989.

How to Read the Bible: a Guide to Scripture Then and Now by James L. Kugel, Free Press, New York, 2007.

Understanding the Old Testament by Bernard W. Anderson, published by Prentice-Hall, Inc., Englewood Cliffs, New Jersey, 1957.

The Bible as It Was by James L. Kugel, published by The Belknap Press of Harvard University Press, Cambridge, Massachusetts, 1997.

Introductions to the New Testament

A Beginner's Guide to the New Testament by William Barclay, published by Westminster John Knox Press, Louisville, Kentucky, 1995.

Reading the New Testament for the First Time by Ronald J. Allen, published by William B. Eerdmans Publishing Company, Grand Rapids, Michigan, 2012.

The Bible from Scratch: The New Testament for Beginners by Donald L. Griggs, Westminster John Knox Press, Louisville, Kentucky, 2003.

The New Testament: a Very Short Introduction by Luke Timothy Johnson, published by Oxford University Press, Oxford, 2010.

The Writings of the New Testament: An Interpretation by Luke T. Johnson, Fortress Press, Philadelphia, 1986.

The New Testament and the People of God by N.T. Wright, published by Fortress Press, Minneapolis, 1992.

An Introduction to the New Testament by Raymond E. Brown, published by Yale University Press, New Haven, Connecticut, 1997.

Reading the New Testament: An Introduction by Pheme Perkins, published by Paulist Press, New York, 1988.

New Testament History

New Testament History by F.F. Bruce, published by Doubleday (A Galilee Book), New York, 1969.

Reliability of Biblical Documents

The Old Testament Documents: Are They Reliable and Relevant? by Walter C. Kaiser, Jr., published by InterVarsity Press, Downers Grove, Illinois, 2001.

The New Testament Documents: Are They Reliable? by F.F. Bruce, published by InterVarsity Press, Downers Grove, Illinois, 1981.

Praying with Scripture and *Lectio Divina*

Sacred Reading: The Ancient Art of Lectio Divina by Michael Casey, published by Liguori/Triumph Publishers, Liguori, Missouri, 1996.

Praying the Words: An Introduction to Lectio Divina by Enzo Bianchi, published by Cistercian Publications, Kalamazoo, Michigan, 1998.

Praying the Bible: An Introduction to Lectio Divina by Mariano Magrassi, O.S.B., translated by Edward Hagman, O.F.M., published by the Liturgical Press, Collegeville, Minnesota, 1998.

Bible Reading for Spiritual Growth by Norvene Vest, published by HarperSanFrancisco, 1993.

Praying the Bible: A Parish Life Sourcebook by Elizabeth Canham, published by Cowley Publications, Cambridge, Massachusetts, 1987.

The Word is Very Near You by Martin L. Smith, published by Cowley Publications, Cambridge, Massachusetts, 1989.

Genesis

Talking about Genesis: A Resource Guide with introduction by Bill Moyers, Doubleday, New York, 1996.

Reading the Psalms

Praying the Psalms: Engaging Scripture and the Life of the Spirit by Walter Brueggemann, published by Cascade Books, Eugene, Oregon, 2007.

The Message of the Psalms: A Theological Commentary by Walter Brueggemann, Augsburg Publishing House, 1984.

Answering God: the Psalms as Tools for Prayer, by Eugene H. Peterson, published by Harper San Francisco, 1989.

Conversations with Scripture: The Psalms by L. William Countryman, published by Church Publishing, New York, New York.

Where Your Treasure Is: Psalms that Summon You from Self to Community by Eugene H. Peterson, published by William B. Eerdmans Publishing Company, Grand Rapids, Michigan, 1985.

The Psalms: SCM Studyguide by Stephen Dawes, published by SCM Press, London, 2010.

A Story of the Psalms: Conversation, Canon and Congregation by V. Steven Parrish, Liturgical Press, Collegeville, Minnesota, 2003.

A Liturgy of Grief: a Pastoral Commentary on Lamentations, by Leslie C. Allen, published by Baker Academic, Grand Rapids, Michigan, 2011.

Reflections on the Psalms by C.S. Lewis, Harvest HBJ Books, 1964.

Bringing the Psalms to Life: How to Understand and Use the Book of Psalms by Daniel F. Polish, Jewish Lights Publishing, Woodstock, Vermont, 2000.

The Psalms: Structure, Content and Message by Claus Westermann, published by Augsburg Publishing House, Minneapolis, 1980.

Prophecy in the Old Testament

The Prophetic Imagination by Walter Brueggemann, published by Fortress Press, Minneapolis, 2001.

Old Testament Prophets for Today by Carolyn J. Sharp, Westminster John Knox, Louisville, Kentucky, 2009.

The Prophets by Abraham J. Heschel, published by HarperCollins, New York, 1965.

A History of Prophecy in Israel: From the Settlement in the Land to the Hellenistic Period by Joseph Blenkinsopp, Westminster Press, Philadelphia, 1983.

Hopeful Imagination: Prophetic Voices in Exile by Walter Brueggemann, Fortress Press, Philadelphia, 1986.

Unbound by Time: Isaiah still Speaks by William Holladay, published by Cowley Publications, Cambridge, Massachusetts, 2002.

Old Testament Studies

Old Testament Wisdom: An Introduction by James L. Crenshaw, John Knox Press, Atlanta, 1973.

Jesus

Jesus: Then and Now by Richard A Burridge and Graham Gould, published by the Society for Promoting Christian Knowledge, London, 2004.

Simply Jesus: a New Vision of Who He was, What He Did, and Why He Matters by N.T. Wright, published by HarperOne Publishers, New York, 2011.

Who is Jesus?: History in the Prefect Tense by Leander E. Keck, published by Fortress Press, Minneapolis, 2001.

The Hard Sayings of Jesus by F.F. Bruce, published by Inter Varsity Press, Downers Grove, Illinois, 1983.

The Real Jesus: The Misguided Quest for the Historical Jesus and the Truth of the Traditional Gospels by Luke Timothy Johnson, published by HarperSanFrancisco, 1996.

Jesus Christ in Matthew, Mark and Luke: Proclamation Commentaries by Jack Dean Kingsbury, Fortress Press, Philadelphia, 1973.

The Meaning of Jesus: Two Visions by Marcus J. Borg and N.T. Wright, published by HarperSanFrancisco, 1999.

Jesus and Peter

Jesus and Peter: Growing in Friendship with God by Michael Perham, published by the Society for Promoting Christian Knowledge, London, 2012.

Jesus and the Bible

The Bible Jesus Read by Philip Yancey, published by Zondervan Publishing House, Grand Rapids, Michigan, 1998.

Reading the Gospels

Four Gospels, One Jesus: A Symbolic Reading by Richard A. Burridge, published by the Society for Promoting Christian Knowledge, London, 1994.

The Four Witnesses: the Rebel, the Rabbi, the Chronicler and the Mystic by Robin Griffith-Jones, published by HarperSanFrancisco, 2000.

Proclamation Commentaries: Mark by Paul J. Achtemeier, published by Fortress Press, Philadelphia, 1986.

The Gospel of Luke by William Barclay, Westminster John Knox Press, Louisville, Kentucky, 2001.

Proclamation Commentaries: Luke by Frederick W. Danker, published by Fortress Press, Philadelphia, 1987.

Conversations with Scripture: The Gospel of John by Cynthia Briggs Kittredge, Morehouse Publishing, New York, 2007.

The People's Bible Commentary: John by Richard Burridge, published by The Bible Reading Fellowship, Abingdon, England, 2008.

Reading the Synoptic Gospels (Matthew, Mark, and Luke) Side by Side

Common English Bible Gospel Parallels, edited by Joel B. Green and W. Gil Shin, Common English Bible, Nashville, Tennessee, 2012.

Gospel Parallels: a Synopsis of the First Three Gospels, edited by Burton H. Throckmorton, Jr., published by Thomas Nelson Publishers, Nashville, 1979.

Records of the Life of Jesus: Revised Standard Version, edited by Henry Burton Sharman, Guild for Psychological Studies Publishing House, San Francisco, 2009.

The Book of Acts

Conversations with Scripture: Acts of the Apostles by C.K. Robertson, published by Church Publishing, New York, New York, 2010.

The Book of Revelation

Conversations with Scripture: Revelation by Frederick W. Schmidt, published by Church Publishing, New York, New York, 2005.

Revelations: Visions, Prophecy, and Politics in the Book of Revelation by Elaine Pagels, Viking Press, New York, New York, 2012.

Understanding the Parables

The Parables of Jesus by William Barclay, Westminster John Knox Press, Louisville, Kentucky, 1970

Tell Me Your Story: the Parables of Jesus by Arthur E. Zannoni, published by the Archdiocese of Chicago Liturgical Training Publications, 2002.

Many Things in Parables: Jesus and His Modern Critics by Charles W. Hedrick, Westminster John Knox Press, Louisville, Kentucky, 2004.

Rediscovering the Parables by Joachim Jeremias, published by Charles Scribner's Sons, New York, 1966.

Parables of Grace by Robert Farrar Capon, William B. Eerdmans Publishing, Grand Rapids, Michigan, 1988.

Parables of Kingdom by Robert Farrar Capon, William B. Eerdmans Publishing, Grand Rapids, Michigan, 1985.

An Introduction to St. Paul

Paul: Least of the Apostles by Alan Decaux, published by Pauline Books and Media, Boston, Massachusetts, 2006.

Paul: A Very Short Introduction by E.P. Sanders, published by Oxford University Press, Oxford, England, 2001.

What St. Paul Really Said: Was Paul of Tarsus the Real Founder of Christianity? by N.T. Wright, William B. Eerdmans Publishing Company, Grand Rapids, Michigan, 1997.

Proclamation Commentaries: Paul and His Letters by Leander E. Keck, published by Fortress Press, Philadelphia, 1979.

Paul: Portrait of a Revolutionary by the former Archbishop of Canterbury Donald Coggan, Crossroad Publishing, New York, 1984.

The Mind of St. Paul by William Barclay, Harper San Francisco, 1958.

The Gospel According to Paul: The Creative Genius Who Brought Jesus to the World by Robin Griffith-Jones, published by HarperSanFrancisco, 2004.

Paul: A Critical Life by Jerome Murphy-O'Connor, O.P., published by Clarendon Press, Oxford, England, 1996.

The Cambridge Companion to Paul edited by James D. G. Dunn, Cambridge University Press, 2003.

Paul: Apostle of the Heart Set Free by F.F. Bruce, published by William B. Eerdmans Publishing Company, Grand Rapids, Michigan, 1977.

The Hard Sayings of Paul by Manfred T. Brauch, published by Intervarsity Press, Downers Grove, Illinois, 1989.

Saint Saul: a Skeleton Key to the Historical Jesus by Donald Harman Akenson, published by Oxford University Press, Oxford, England, 2000.

Rabbi Paul: An Intellectual Biography by Bruce Chilton, published by Doubleday Publishing Company, New York, 2004.

Paul: His Life and Teaching by John McRay, published by Baker Academic, Grand Rapids, Michigan, 2003.

The Theology of Paul the Apostle by James D.G. Dunn, published by William B. Eerdmans Publishing Company, Grand Rapids, Michigan, 1998.

Prayer in the New Testament

New Testament Prayer for Everyone by N.T. Wright, published by the Society for Promoting Christian Knowledge, London, 2012.

Into God's Presence: Prayer in the New Testament edited by Richard N. Longenecker, published by William B. Eerdmans, Grand Rapids, Michigan, 2001.

New Testament Studies

The Story of Romans: a Narrative Defense of God's Righteousness by A. Katherine Grief, published by Westminster John Knox Press, Louisville, Kentucky, 2002.

The Gospel and Epistles of John: A Concise Commentary by Raymond E. Brown, The Liturgical Press, Collegeville, Minnesota, 1986.

Bible Study and Reading Scripture with Others

Approaching the Gospels Together: A Leadership Guide for Group Gospels Study by Mary C. Morrison, published by Pendle Hill Publications, Wallingford, Pennsylvania, 1986.

Transforming Bible Study by Walter Wink, published by Abingdon Press, Nashville, 1990.

Conversations with Scripture and with Each Other by M. Thomas Shaw, SSJE, published by Rowman & Littlefield Publishers, Lanham, Maryland, 2008

Rick Warren's Bible Study Methods: Twelve Ways You Can Unlock God's Word by Rick Warren, published by Zondervan, Grand Rapids, Michigan, 2006.

Six Ways to Study the Bible: Textual, Literary, Exegetical, Historical, Theological, Devotional by Trent C. Butler, Chalice Press, St. Louis, Missouri, 2010.

The Development and Importance of the Bible

How the Bible Came to Be: Exploring the Narrative and Message by John W. Miller, Paulist Press, New York, 2004.

Captive to the Word of God: Engaging the Scriptures for Contemporary Theological Reflection by Miroslav Volf, published by William B. Eerdman Publishing Company, Grand Rapids, Michigan, 2010.

Understanding Violence in Scripture

Divine Presence Amid Violence by Walter Brueggemann, published by Cascade Books, Eugene, Oregon, 2009.

Moses

The Life of Moses: The Servant of God by F.B. Meyer, published by Emerald Books, Lynnwood, Washington, 1996.

Ruth

Abington Old Testament Commentaries: Ruth by Judy Fentress-Williams, published by Abingdon Press Nashville, 2012.

King David

David's Truth: in Israel's Imagination and Memory, by Walter Brueggemann, published by Fortress Press, Minneapolis, 2002.

David and His Theologian: Literary, Social and Theological Investigations of the Early Monarchy by Walter Brueggemann, Cascade Books, Eugene, Oregon, 2011.

Women in the Bible

Women in the Old Testament by Irene Nowell, O.S.B., published by The Liturgical Press, Collegeville, Minnesota, 2010.

Women's Bible Commentary edited by Carol A. Newsom, Sharon H. Ringe and Jacqueline E. Lapsley, published by Westminster John Knox Press, Louisville, Kentucky, 2012.

All the Women of the Bible by M.L. del Mastro, published by Castle Books, New York, 2004.

People of the Bible

Who's Who in the Bible by Joan Comay and Ronald Brownrigg, published by Wing Books, New York, 1971.

Who's Who in the Bible published by The Readers Digest Association, Inc., Plesantsville, New York, 1994.

The Bible and Ethics

The Moral Vision of the New Testament by Richard B. Hays, published by HarperSanFrancisco, 1996.

New Testament Ethics: The Legacies of Jesus and Paul by Frank J. Matera, Westminster John Knox Press, Louisville, Kentucky, 1996.

The New Church's Teaching Series: Ethics After Easter by Stephen Holmgren, published by Cowley Publications, Lanham, Maryland, 2000.

The Re-Enchantment of Morality: Wisdom for a Troubled World by Richard Harries, The Society for Promoting Christian Knowledge, 2008.

New Testament Foundations for Christian Ethics by Willi Marxsen, translated by O.C. Dean, Jr. published by Fortress Press, Minneapolis, 1989.

Early Judaism: The Ancient Culture and Writings

An Introduction to Early Judaism by James C. VanderKam, published by William B. Eerdmans Publishing Company, Grand Rapids, Michigan, 2001.

Archeology and the World of the Ancient Near East

The Oxford History of the Biblical World edited by Michael D. Coogan, published by Oxford University Press, Oxford, England, 1998.

Excavating Jesus: Beneath the Stones, Behind the Texts by John Dominic Crossan and Jonathan L. Reed, published by HarperSanFrancisco, 2001.

Bible Unearthed: Archaeology's New Vision of Ancient Israel and the Origin of Sacred Texts by Israel Finkelstein and Neil Asher Silberman, published by Touchstone Press, New York, 2001.

Archeological Study Bible: an Illustrated Walk through Biblical History and Culture published by the Zondervan Corporation, 2005.

The Temple: Its Ministry and Services by Alfred Edersheim, published by Hendrickson Publishers, 1994.

Ordinary Life, Culture, Customs, and Manners in the Ancient Near East

The Lives of Ordinary People in Ancient Israel: Where Archeology and the Bible Intersect by William G. Dever, published by William B. Eerdmans Publishing Company, Grand Rapids, Michigan, 2012.

Nelson's New Illustrated Bible Manners and Customs: How the People of the Bible Really Lived by Howard F. Vos, published by Thomas Nelson Publishers, Nashville, 1999.

The Essential Companion to Life in Bible Times by Moises Silva, published Zondervan, Grand Rapids, Michigan, 2011.

Daily Life in the Time of Jesus by Miriam Feinberg Vamosh, published by Abingdon Press, Nashville, 2001.

Manners and Customs in the Bible by Victor H. Matthews, published by Hendrickson Publishers, Peabody, Massachusetts, 1991.

The Bible and Art

How to Read Bible Stories and Myths in Art: Decoding the Old Masters from Giotto to Goya by Patrick de Rynck, Abrams Publishing, New York, 2008.

Anglicanism and the Bible

Anglicanism and the Bible: Anglican Study Series edited by Frederick Houk Borsch, Morehouse Barlow, Wilton, Connecticut, 1984.

Anglican Approaches to Scripture: From the Reformation to the Present by Rowan A. Greer, The Crossroad Publishing Company, New York, 2006.

The Bible's Authority in Today's Church edited by Frederick Houk Borsch, published by Trinity Press International, Harrisburg, Pennsylvania, 1993.

Reading the King James Bible

In 2011, we celebrated the four hundredth anniversary of the King James Bible. To gain a greater appreciation of what is often referred to as The Authorized Version of the Bible we commend:

In the Beginning: The Story of the King James Bible and How It Changed a Nation, a Language, and a Culture by Alister McGrath, published by Anchor Books, 2005.

Bible 1611–2011: the Story of the King James Version by Gordon Campbell, published by Oxford University Press, Oxford, England, 2010.

God's Secretaries: the Making of the King James Bible by Adam Nicolson, published by Harper Collins Publishers, New York, 2003.

The Book of Books: the Radical Impact of the King James Bible 1611–2011 by Melvyn Bragg, published by Hodder & Stoughton, London, 2011.

The Dead Sea Scrolls

The Dead Sea Scrolls: A Very Short Introduction by Timothy H. Lim, published by Oxford University Press, Oxford, England, 2006.

The Dead Sea Scrolls and the Bible by James C. VanderKam, published by William B. Eerdmans Publishing Company, Grand Rapids, Michigan, 2012.

The Archeology of Qumran and the Dead Sea Scrolls by Jodi Magness, published by William B. Eerdmans Publishing Company, Grand Rapids, Michigan, 2002.

The Dead Sea Scrolls: After Forty Years by Hershel Shanks, James C. Vanderkam, P. Kyle McCarter, Jr., and James A. Sanders, published by the Biblical Archeology Society, Washington, D.C., 1992.

The Complete World of the Dead Sea Scrolls by Philip R. Davies, George J. Brooke and Phillip R. Callaway, published by Thames and Hudson, New York, 2002.

The Gnostic Gospels

The Gnostic Gospels by Elaine Pagels, published by Vintage Books, New York, 1979.